JUST ANOTHER

SPIRITUAL BOOK

BO LOZOFF

HUMAN KINDNESS FOUNDATION
DURHAM, NORTH CAROLINA

ISBN: 978-0-9614444-5-7

Library of Congress Catalog Card # 90-084448

Printed in the U.S.A. by Sheridan Books

Editors: Sita Lozoff, Curry Morris, Bo Lozoff
Transcriptions: Judy Sookne
Cover design: Mark Heliger
Cover photo: Steven R. Miller
Index: Bob Shrager
artwork provided by prisoners as credited

sixth printing, 2006, Human Kindness Foundation (52,000 copies)

Copies of this book are sent free to prisoners and other indigents throughout the world. The Human Kindness Foundation is a non-profit organization which sponsors the Prison-Ashram Project and other programs promoting basic kindness and spiritual sanity. 100% of the proceeds from book sales and your donations go to support these programs. For more information, write:

Human Kindness Foundation
PO Box 61619
Durham, NC 27715

www.humankindness.org

Other Books By Bo Lozoff:

We're All Doing Time (Human Kindness Foundation, ©1985)
(published in Spanish as **Todos Estamos Encarcelados**, ©1989)
(published in French as **Nous Sommes Tous Dans Une Prison**, ©1995)
(published in Italian as **Siamo Tutti in Priogione**, ©1998)

Lineage and Other Stories (Human Kindness Foundation, ©1988)

Deep & Simple, a Spiritual Path for Modern Times (Human Kindness Foundation, ©1999)

THE FOLLOWING ITEMS ARE NOT AVAILABLE FREE TO PRISONERS:

It's a Meaningful Life, It Just Takes Practice (Viking/Penguin, ©2000)

The Wonderful Life of a Fly Who Couldn't Fly (Hampton Roads, ©2002) – Bo's first children's book, beautifully illustrated.

Dedication

This one's for Sita, my partner in the Great Charade, in which we all pretend we're not God, and pretend to strive and suffer and live and die. Dedicating a book to Sita is like saying "I dedicate this book to my skin, my blood, and my own face," because the lines of separation between us are subtle and harder all the time to decipher. And as for our son, Josh -- well, it would take a better writer than I to express our feelings about that fine young spiritual warrior.

Acknowledgements

This book is mainly a collection of talks, interviews and correspondence, which means there were people on the other end setting up the talks, asking interview questions, and writing me intimate letters of self-inquiry. So I'd like to thank them all for their role in my life as well as in these pages.

Sita, Curry, and Judy did an especially heroic job transcribing and editing over six hundred pages and whittling them down to the present book to save the reader from being bored to death by redundancies and repetitive dialogues.

I also honor the prison artists whose work is included here, and others also, who have sent us everything from tiny envelope art to huge paintings. We credited the enclosed artwork as best we could, but some of it was unsigned, some signed only with first names, and many were so old, the artists whose names we thought we'd never forget are now lost in the mists of our memories.

Most of all, I thank Neem Karoli Baba, my spiritual master who has been guiding me since childhood to see the singular truth and express it in the sanest and simplest terms. Though I never met him in the body, he continues to save me from myself by the power of his humility and love. He apparently will not let go until I finally surrender into being a simple,

fearless, loving person to a degree beyond my wildest imaginings; and to laugh a lot, too. If this book inspires you toward that state, I'm not to blame!

Table of Contents

JUST ANOTHER PREFACE

This book is a collection of talks, writings and correspondence spanning the past five years since publication of my first book, *We're All Doing Time*. Writing and teaching are an ironic proposition for me. A lot of my emphasis is for people to stop reading so many books and attending so many lectures and workshops. So it's humbling to produce yet another one.

If it's true that ultimately our answers and freedom must be found deep within us, then it stands to reason that a spiritual teaching should be the least distracting, least complicated influence possible; just enough to inspire us to turn inward. After reading a book or hearing a talk, the reader or listener should be more *in*dependent rather than waiting excitedly for the teacher's next book or talk.

So from my point of view, this book is about you. No other subject is possible for a spiritual book. It's about your whole life and your range of choices, from being a constant victim of external forces, to becoming a calm and clear hero who lives with grace and power and good humor.

Perhaps the best potential of *Just Another Spiritual Book* is to reveal how alike we are, from a ninety-year-old meditating great-grandmother to a twenty-five-year-old mass murderer; from a psychologist in training to a weary prostitute/junkie.

Like a roomful of mirrors with only one object in the middle, the hundreds of pages in this book reflect a single, simple truth: Life is The Great Mystery, not The Great Problem. Each of us can directly experience the Heart of the Mystery if we but learn to see clearly and act in truth. No one's life is easy, but living in truth is astoundingly different from what most of us consider "normal life;" astoundingly freer, more intense, powerful, magical.

It's also simple; not easy, but simple. As you'll notice throughout these pages, my inclination has always been to bring things back to our common ground. It doesn't take a rocket scientist to understand what spiritual life is about; it does take a hero to live it. I see us all as potential heroes, and I see no greater, more exciting goal in life than to work toward that state of being. I hope this book helps you do that.

Part One:

BEATING AROUND THE BURNING BUSH

Certainly there are spiritual mysteries to explore, and states of ecstasy or enlightenment beyond description. But as we mature it becomes clear that those special experiences are only meaningful when they arise from and return to a life of ordinary kindness.

IT ALWAYS GETS BACK TO KINDNESS

[from HKF newsletter, July 1987, announcing the renaming of
our organization as Human Kindness Foundation]

Aldous Huxley was interviewed toward the end of his life, and was asked "Dr. Huxley, perhaps more than anyone else in the world, you have studied all the great religions and spiritual traditions; can you summarize for us what you feel you have learned?" Huxley replied "I think just to be a bit kinder."

Sita and I heard that remark quite a few years ago, and as we've gotten older, it has sunk deeper and deeper into our hearts. For all our seeking and exploring, this simple, ageless wisdom remains the essence of a successful life on Earth, no matter what convoluted paths we may take to learn it.

There is no spiritual practice more profound than being kind to one's family, neighbors, the cashier at the grocery store, an unexpected visitor, the con in the next cell, the person who does the laundry or picks up the garbage or any other of the usually "invisible" people whose paths we cross in the course of a normal day.

Certainly there are spiritual mysteries to explore, and states of ecstasy or enlightenment beyond description. But as we mature it becomes clear that those special experiences are only meaningful when they arise from and return to a life of ordinary kindness. Whether we're sitting in silent meditation on top of a mountain, operating a drill press in a steel factory, or feeding the hungry in Ethiopia, a feeling of genuine kindness in our hearts is the practical expression of any spiritual path.

Kindness has taken a bad rap in many ways, being associated with weakness or meekness or labels like "goody-goody." But true kindness comes from strength, and is full of life. I'm not talking about formula kindness or phony gestures. I'm not saying we should walk around smiling constantly, saying "have a nice day" as if we were three-dimensional bumper stickers with no individual personalities.

I've visited spiritual communities and ashrams where people came up to me all day long saying with obnoxious sweetness, "Oh, how nice to see you; is there any way I can serve you; you're such a beautiful being." By the end of the day, I'm ready to pound somebody's face into the wall just to get a genuine reaction! Although the motives may be pure, a pasted-on smile and stale slogans come off as impersonal rather than personal; they tend to increase the gap between people rather than decrease it.

The real point is a matter of the heart, not the tongue. It's a matter of heartfelt respect for each and every experience of our lives, without presuming which are petty and which are significant; respect for each person, animal, machine, or anything else we find ourselves dealing with; To simply respect the mysteries of life enough to be present in each moment *without* formulas.

Any moment could be the last moment of our lives, so we want to be aware and open. Nothing spectacular, nothing particularly noticeable, but just truly present in a kindly fashion, wherever we are, whomever we're with.

The normal hustle and bustle of our lives brings forward a host of desires, anxieties and tensions which isolate us from the people around us, who are usually feeling all *their* desires, anxieties and tensions. Kindness is the opposite of isolation. It blooms from the power and happiness of inner success; from a quiet mind, an open heart, an honest nature which has learned and accepted the simple fact that every living creature wants to feel cared about, including ourselves.

In my own journey into this teaching about kindness, one of the biggest stumbling blocks was self-hatred (or if that sounds too strong, how about self-criticism?). I never imagined how much of it I had until I began to notice that I could shrug off a thousand sincere compliments, yet hold on to one insult or criticism for months or even years. That's pretty suspicious behavior. Sound familiar?

The more I opened to the idea that I was hard on myself, the more I saw it in action in a thousand big and little ways. It's as if there were two people in my body: One, a decent guy trying to make his life work, doing the best he could; the other, a stern, disapproving critic who seemed to be always pissed off at me at the drop of a hat, and who constantly expected me to be screwing up or at best a total fraud.

As I looked around, it seemed most of us are in the same boat: Never quite satisfying ourselves, never living up to our expectations and demands, never fully enjoying being the good people whom others perceive us to be. Often, the people most stuck in self-hatred are the ones who express self-confidence the loudest.

Who knows why we're so down on ourselves? Who cares? Does it really matter whether the cause lies in our dysfunctional families or disapproving parents, or goes all the way back to a built-in unworthiness in our whole species, stemming from original sin and separation from God? We could debate the causes endlessly while the precious moments of our lives tick away. It seems more practical to see it, work with it and move on.

I've found that the solution to self-hatred is neither irresponsible self-indulgence nor the defensive, narcissistic self-approval popular in many circles. Those attitudes are just reactions which mask the real problem and keep us too busy to understand. The real solution goes right back to Huxley's remark, but with the added understanding that being a bit kinder has to also apply to ourselves.

We can *use* all our hurts and joys, all the good and bad forces that molded us, to soften our hearts and embrace the world with kindness and respect. There's nothing in our lives we have to forget about or hide from. There's nothing we can't use to become kinder.

Our happiness can help to make us kinder because true happiness inspires generosity of spirit. Sadness can help to make us kinder because we can allow our sadness to remind us that every human being suffers sadness. Our strength can enable us to be kind if we understand that kindness doesn't diminish strength; it increases it. And even weakness, shame, and guilt can help us to be kind because, as with sadness, we can embrace those feelings in everyone and have more compassion.

The monk Sujata once wrote, "This living is so hard, how can we be anything but loving?" That's a powerful thought to work with; think about your own life, and think of all the people you know -- whether you love them or loathe them -- and let his comment keep running through your mind: This living *is* so hard, how can we be anything but loving?

So here we are back at the beginning. We look around, use some practices to keep our awareness as clear as possible, make our best guesses as we go through the course of every day -- all the same stuff we've been doing since the dawn of time.

And at the end of every so many years, when we've gone around in circles a thousand times and forgotten what it was we were after in the first place, when we've gotten sucked up and blown out from this movement or that teacher, this religion or that community, this drama or that scandal, somebody may write a little reminder like this or approach us at a retreat or on the yard or in the office and say "Hey, did you ever hear what Aldous Huxley said about kindness?"

And we nod our heads, laugh at ourselves, drop a hundred little burdens and complexities, and start all over again in the terrain of our simplest, moment-to-moment behavior. Whether toward ourselves, each other, other species or the environment, the best we've learned is just to be a bit kinder.

● ● ●

Gifts are great, the founding of temples is meritorious, meditations and religious exercises pacify the heart, comprehension of the truth leads to Nirvana -- but greater than all is loving-kindness. As the light of the moon is sixteen times stronger than the light of all the stars, so is loving-kindness sixteen times more efficacious in liberating the heart than all other religious accomplishments taken together. This state of heart is the best in the world. Let a man remain steadfast in it while he is awake, whether he is standing, walking, sitting, or lying down.

-- Buddha

These storms come. Grief, pain, loneliness, fear. And they rage, like Hurricane Hugo. Tossing about all the mobile homes in your mind. If you feel like you're a mobile home then it's hell. If you understand that you are actually the sky, it's rough, it's stormy, it's scary, but you were here before it came, and you'll be here after it leaves.
Clouds in a boundless sky.

CLOUDS IN A BOUNDLESS SKY

[excerpted from a talk given at St. Edward's University
in Austin, Texas, on July 13th, 1990.]

I don't really have a talk to give. Certainly not any sort of lecture about prison work, as though I were some kind of corrections professional. From my point of view, we gather together in groups like this because we're all seeking something very personal. What I discuss with prisoners is the same thing we can discuss with each other — the journey to enlightenment. It's not about "them," it's always about "us."

Some of you may be here in a clinical way, like, "Well, I'm not here about *my* life, I'm here because I'm interested in what this man does in prisons..." I want to be honest with you from the start: The only thing my life is about, in or out of prisons, is being as awake and aware as possible. I'm hooked on the Great Journey as described by holy women and holy men, saints and sages, of every major religion and philosophical tradition. To me it's all that really matters. Everything else — every condition of our lives, good or bad, wonderful or horrible, is merely the support system for that journey.

All I do in prisons is to deal with these issues. We talk about it, we do some timeless practices to clear the vision, to open the heart. We share some perspectives about what makes life so difficult. You've got your reasons why it may be difficult, and people in prison have their reasons why it may be difficult. But is there, or is there not, something indescribably, profoundly, inexplicably **wonderful** behind all the difficulties? That's the perennial question of the inner journey. Those of us who decide there is, are called people of faith. Those who decide there is nothing behind all the mess, are people who choose not to have faith.

In our hurried modern culture, many of us may never pause long enough to look into this business of whether we are people of faith or not. Most of the time in prison workshops, I may be the first person who has ever come along and reminded convicts that they are deep human beings who need to examine their basic spiritual/philosophical values.

So, I represent several bodies of wisdom and practice that have been handed down through the ages from every culture and country, by people just like us who have tried to resolve the big questions like, "What's it all about? What do I do? How is human life designed to work best? How is *my* life designed to work best? How do we relate to each other in a way that doesn't cause or perpetuate the insanity that we see going on all around us and the destruction of the planet, in a way that's not airy-fairy, hippy-trippy, New Age blather, but in a way that relates to what you and I are going through -- our crazy alcoholic sisters and neurotic mothers and fathers, our weirded out children, crimes we've committed, mortgages due, and how it relates to honest-to-God real life?"

So that's why I'm here. Now what I'd like to do is just ramble for a couple of minutes and then turn it over to you, to see where you want to go with it. And I invite you to take the same position I take tonight, which is that any of us could leave here and get run over by a truck and die, before we get home, and we could be the last people that we've spent the last hours of our lives with. So I am certainly not going to waste it by being phony, being diplomatic, holding back something that I had in my heart to say.

I invite you not to waste this opportunity either, because if you don't think that's true, you're not in touch with the real world. One of the great quotes that I love from the holy book, the *Mahabharata*, is

> *What is the greatest wonder of all? The greatest wonder of all is that, each day, Death takes lives beyond counting, and yet each day each of us says, 'Not me, not today.'*

It *is* us, and it *is* today. We're trapped in the elevator together, the building's burning, the baby's caught at the bottom of the well, life is precious and our time is all that we really have, so I invite you to make full use of it with me, no holds barred, and see what power of truth we can create together just by being straight with each other, just by exercising or expressing what you really came here for tonight, and if you don't know, looking inward and trying to find out.

What I'm here for tonight is that somewhere along the way, I tapped into the very simple realization that there is a Great Mystery going on here; that things are more than what they seem to be. Throughout the course of history, there have always been two things going on simultaneously. There have been the masses of people, societies, cultures, governments and civilizations, which have been operating from basically insane premises that don't work: power, greed, lust, money. We can easily see where it's come to; it just doesn't work well.

At the same time, all through history, there have been small groups of people meeting, sometimes under a big tree, sometimes in a little cave, sometimes by the seashore, sometimes in a dank prison basement, sometimes in the chapel of a university in Austin, Texas -- small groups of people coming together in the midst of all that insanity, saying, "Remember? There's a great truth somewhere, that has nothing to do with all that nonsense, remember? Remember the One? Remember the mystical center? Remember?"

Here we are doing it again. I saw this at some point and began pursuing it, and I discovered the essential difference between the qualities of life which have nothing to do with time, or what country you live in, what gender you are, how old you are, what you look like; nothing to do with anything that began in time or that will end in time. You could call it the Immortal, Eternal, Transcendent, Spiritual -- whatever you want to call it. And then you have all the things that *do* come and go with time: our identities, our personalities, our bodies, our breath, our lives, our cars, our jobs, even our ideas.

You begin to look at single lines from all the different bibles of the world, like from the western Bible, *Don't lay up your treasures where moth and rust doth corrupt, where thieves break in and steal.* Don't cling to things that do come and go with time, because you're going to lose them all. In a Hindu holy book, the way it's said is, *Of what can we be certain, except that whatever we have will soon be gone?*

Every bible, every holy book says it one way or another. Jesus said, *Don't believe in appearances.* And little tips, like *Seek ye first the kingdom of heaven, and all the rest will be added unto you.* At first you think, "Does that mean I have to spend 20 years in a monastery before I start living my life?"

Seek ye first doesn't mean sequentially; you could look at it as *background* and *foreground.* Ironically, the way most of us are raised, the foreground is our little lives, the ones that we are absolutely doomed to lose from the time we're born. I mean, just as soon as I get to run the 4-minute mile, my body is aging past my ability to do that. I am absolutely doomed to lose that, and the whole body as well. Yet we're raised with all of that as the foreground, and the background of our lives is, "By the way, be a nice spiritual person. Go to church, and something about God, something about 'love all mankind' -- yeah, yeah, yeah -- peace on earth, goodwill to everybody, yeah."

Look around at the insanity, the destruction of the planet, the strife between people, and it hits you, wait a minute, this is like changing channels on a TV with a hatchet. It may accomplish the job, but the TV gets butchered in the process. If we reverse the foreground and background, the foreground is: LIFE IS A SPIRITUAL ADVENTURE *FIRST*, a timeless spiritual quest for Oneness With God, Enlightenment, Awareness of the All, Self-realization, Actualization, whatever you want to call it. Life is *first* a spiritual journey, in which we are here to decipher something, to learn something, to grow and to love, to tap into the mysteries. The gender we are and the race we are and the ethnicity we are and our background, whether we're abused as children or grow up in a palace, or have a drug problem, or blah, blah, blah -- all of those conditions that come and go with time, are simply the story line, the script.

Then you look at one line in a Bible, like Jesus saying, *See, 1 shall make all things new*, and you go "WHOA!!! It's all new!! OK, I'm in prison. OK, I have a bad back. OK, I just had a hysterectomy. That's the script; that's the small stuff. That's where I receive my challenges; it's what forces me to express my courage; to find my faith."

All of the conditions of our lives are simply vehicles. And everybody's got them. There's not a person on this earth who doesn't have vehicles for learning these lessons.

You can imagine, reminding somebody who's doing 150 years in prison of this perspective can be pretty refreshing. Even 150 years is just a vehicle for learning what we need to learn. A cell is as much the center of the Kingdom of Heaven as a palace. I hate it when people say, "It's so good that you help prisoners to cope with being in prison." OOH! Cope?? I hate that word!

If we went to see an adventure movie, and there were just positive things going on, and Indiana Jones never did a stupid thing that almost got him killed, he never did a greedy, stupid thing, he never had a phobia or a fear like the rats and snakes and roaches; if it was just like he was walking around the university and someone says, "Dr. Jones, there's this artifact hidden in a cave," and he says, "Oh, great. We'll go get it," and they come back, "yes, we got it, everything went fine." [laughter] That isn't an adventure movie. We wouldn't pay four bucks or six bucks or whatever ridiculous amount it is these days, to see it. It wouldn't be worth it.

Yet in our own lives, it seems we're striving all the time to avoid struggle. We spend so much energy trying to avoid negativity and trying to create positivity, even if it's synthetic, we miss the point that each of us is Indiana Jones. Each of us is Ulysses, Odysseus, sailing home. At the moment we awaken to being here at all, we say, "Wow, what's life about? At that moment we are the heroes of this classic, timeless, spiritual adventure. We already know the movie's going to end, so the point is not to live forever, but it's to be heroic.

Each of us can be heroic in everything we do -- in a non-obnoxious way [laughter]. Good sense of humor, down to earth, understanding that it's not about avoiding this or grabbing that. It's not about what Ram Dass calls "manipulating the universe" all the time, and trying to redefine it: "Oh, it's a wonderful world." Because the world sucks, too. The most truthful thing we can say is, "It's QUITE a world. Yeah, it's quite a world!"

In every one of the cultures throughout history in which people have been looking at this, trying to make sense of this, trying to put things in the right background and foreground, trying to find the mystery, or how to at least live in balance, there has also been some technique, practice or method that in one way or another involved the most revolutionary act a human being can perform. The most revolutionary political act, the most revolutionary social act, and the most revolutionary moral, personal act, is simply learning how to sit still and shut up.

We call that meditation. Jesus calls it praying in a closet. Not out in the streets in the high seats of temples and making a big show of it. Going in the closet. Alone, in solitude.

Moses went on top of the mountain for forty days and nights. Jesus went out into the desert. Mohammed sat in a cave for years. The Buddha sat under the Bodhi tree for days on end without moving; all sorts of temptations, hallucinations, sights and sounds.

Instead of believing in somebody else's philosophy or theology, that process of *becoming still* seems somehow to have a great deal to do with reversing foreground and background, so that we become spiritual heroes who are walking the earth with the proper foreground. And by "proper," I don't mean morally, I simply mean the way life was designed to work.

So that's a lot of what I do, in my own life and also what I share in prisons and in places like this -- both the inspiration and the simple techniques of learning what in Buddhism is called the Noble Silence: silence of body; silence of speech; silence of mind.

What I share, and what I practice in my own life, is an age-old, simple balance between internal work on the mystery, on the stillness, taking responsibility for that -- I "be still" every day, for a certain amount of time -- and balancing that with *external* work of living as it has been revealed to me that life is designed to work better. Like lovingkindness. Like trying to leave each person and each place a little better for our having been here. Simple stuff.

It's interesting, of course, we find that as we learn more inner stillness, as the mind is quieter and as the heart is more open, we see a lot more clearly how to do that external work. When I was fully devoted to the political movement in the 60's, I carried a gun and shot at people. My mind was enraged all the time, and thank God that people like me didn't win and take over the government. It just wouldn't be much different than it is now -- except probably that more people would be wearing earrings. [laughter; Bo is wearing a long earring of Snoopy's friend Woodstock]

What I would love to do now is turn it over to you and see where we take that to fulfill why you're here; in as honest and open a fashion as you care to be.

Why do you consider meditation the most revolutionary act a human being can perform, and could you talk a little more about the balance between stillness and activism?

Meditation is simply about seeing reality and acknowledging it with bare honesty. Which means ultimately, as Krishnamurti put it, we stop relying on every form of external authority. That's very revolutionary.

When we're looking to make sense of our lives, or performing our everyday tasks, the degree to which we're able to see honestly who we are, what we need to do and how we relate to the world, is the degree to which our minds are noisy or quiet. Any method, whether it's meditation or anything else, which helps us to look more honestly, with a quiet enough mind, is revolutionary because it frees us from being controlled or manipulated.

By "quiet mind", I simply mean a mind open to the present moment of reality, basic reality; without bringing into each moment so many memories and behavior patterns and likes and dislikes, opinions, assumptions -- all of that baggage that forces us or tempts us to interpret things in a locked-in way, instead of just seeing what's actually happening. That's the kind of quieting that meditation helps us to do.

The reason I say it's such a revolutionary act is because it enables and requires us to take full responsibility for who we are and what we do. We don't just follow what the Bible says. We become that same vision which the Bible expresses. We see clearly, like when Jesus said things like, *Love thy neighbor as you love thyself.* That's not a moral preachment, it's not like *to be a good boy or be a good girl, love your neighbor as you love yourself.* He's saying, *If you could see what I see, if you could see how connected we are, if you could just see the truth, instead of being so afraid, instead of being so desiring, if you could just see the truth, you would love your neighbor exactly as you love yourself, because your neighbor is yourself.*

We all have the same desire to live, the same instinct to survive, we all want to feel connected, loved, safe, secure, and productive; we're all exactly the same in that way. And it's seeing clearly that creates the inner revolution from being people who are out for ourselves to being people who are standing in the middle of reality and responding in harmony, even when harmony means fighting or whatever. Responding in truth.

So, I consider it a revolutionary act for those reasons, that it makes each of us a fully alive human being who has no more excuses and follows truth in each moment, instead of anything more static than that.

In terms of the second part of your question, I certainly don't mean to imply that there's a 50-50 balance and all of us should be pretty much the same, spending X amount of time in meditation, X amount of time in social action, or whatever -- because the moments keep changing. Sita and I spent five years in an ashram, not relating to the outside world very much at all; learning self-discipline, and not to be so reactive, not to be so impulsive, not to be blind slaves to the mind, to the desire systems, etc.

There are times we need to intensify that inner work and times we need to intensify the outer work. The only way we can tell which is which, is if we have a clear and quiet enough mind. I could be working in prisons for twenty years and suddenly begin to feel I need to do more inner work. Without guilt, without confusion, without a presumption that my prison work is the greatest thing that's ever been created and I can't stop doing it, I might just find myself writing a newsletter saying "I'm going to be doing some inner work for a while and I'm not doing prison workshops." And the world keeps rolling on.

Yet at another time, I might go to thirty prisons in thirty days and people say, "Well, aren't you tired?" I don't know, who cares? This is what feels right to do. It's a constantly changing balance between inner and outer. It's not a *hassle* that it's changing, it's actually quite a freedom. Because we don't need to walk around with policies. We simply do our practices, our minds get a little quieter, and we gain a little more trust in the pulls and in our passions. We find a passion for writing and say, "I may need to be writing." One sure way to find out whether we're right or wrong is to just begin doing it and see how it feels.

For myself, I've coined a useful expression instead of the notion of enlightenment or spiritual liberation -- words which have been so clichéd, and are so vague. At the times that I'm completely free and awakened, being a fully alive human being, responding to truth and seeing things clearly, it's a state I call "spontaneous genius." A lot of stuff that we do at those times, or say or write, is really illuminated, it's magical, not because we "thought" right; but because we danced smoothly in tune with the Great Mystery.

Sometimes it gets astounding. I remember one time many years ago, when I first started teaching, I was sitting opposite somebody who came to me because he had problems and wanted to talk. We were sitting opposite each other, looking in each other's eyes. I quieted down and opened up into the moment. Suddenly I found myself leaning over and hitting him hard on the heart center, three times. I'd never done that before in my life. I'm not in any school of thought about healing, working with chakras, laying on of hands or anything like that -- nothing, I'm just, you know, regular guy, ex-hood, you know. I find myself leaning over, BOOM, BOOM, BOOM, and his heart chakra opens and he has this mystical experience, a born-again experience, the agony and ecstasy of the Christ.

After you do something like that, you find yourself with temptations like "Whew! Yeah; I'm hot shit." And you hang your shingle up, "Heart Center Opener." Or the opposite temptation, "Whoa, I don't even want to think about that. Forget it! Close it off, I don't know what happened, but forget about it." But all that happened is that two spontaneous forces sat together in truth, and a little old-fashioned spiritual magic happened. He was open from hurting, and I was open from willingness, so life became magical, a realm of almost any possibility.

Spontaneous genius is what gradually fills our lives as we simply see things as they are, and react in truth with faith. Like when our balance of seclusion or activism goes one way or another, not starting to be alarmed, not pulling back because we put all these conceptual eggs in one basket or anything. You may find your yourself signing up for a three-month silent meditation retreat, and as you're sending the form away, you say, "I'm signing up for a three-month retreat?!" But you allow yourself to do it, because it's not coming from an arbitrary, chaotic, whimsical mind, it's coming from a seat of intuition you've gradually been opening into, and you know you need to trust it more, even when it exceeds your limitations or boundaries or self-images.

So, that's how I can best relate to your question, is that the two answers are tied in to each other. I think that it is a practice of quieting the mind which helps us to see those continuing needs and balances.

You said something before that sounded like you always follow your intuitive pulls no matter where they lead. But If my husband came home and sequestered himself to do poetry or woodwork or something, we'd be in warfare. How could both of us do whatever we like? How do you keep that balance in a marriage?

In a marriage or in any friendship, in any partnership, one person's genuine gain or need is never at odds with a person they love. We are stuck together like glue. A lot of times, our desires or our fears can lead us to *believe* that we want something detrimental to the other. It may be that I have an *attachment* to my solitude, and you're feeling at odds with it, etc., and that you're the one who is seeing things more clearly. Or it may be that I have a genuine pull to have a period of woodwork or solitude, or whatever, and that *your* reaction is attachment, and that's going to have to be something that you look into about why it disturbs you.

Or it could be that we're both attached, or it could be that neither of us is. I think there is really a common-sense way to address all the needs of our lives. I don't feel that this intuitive faith I talk about is whimsical, like "Hey, I know we just committed to this mortgage, and I know we just committed to this project that helps those people over there, and I know this and that, but I'm sorry, I got this intuitive thing, gotta just go do woodwork, you're stuck with it."

In my experience I've never seen that be genuine. Yet following truth certainly can cause family discord. One person or another in the family may be attached, may have a limitation due to fear, or a craving due to desire, and one of the things we are here for is to work through those conflicts in love. Sita and I have been married twenty-four years, so we have some experience in this. We had a saying -- well, I guess we still do, but we haven't used it in a few years because we haven't needed to. When we would get in tremendous battles, one or the other of us would try to remember our saying to snap us back into reality, and what that was was, "Wait a minute. What's it all about, anyway?"

Between you and your husband, between me and Sita, what those battles are usually over is stuff that should be in the background, not the foreground. Like what we do with our time. Even if you think you're doing the most noble thing in the world, it is still just in time. There are anonymous men and women sitting in caves right now, somewhere in remote places in the world who are doing more for world peace than you or I are. We have to begin to see a bigger picture and understand that it is living in truth which brings the world to a state of harmony. It is not following our opinions and attitudes and conceptions about what we're *supposed* to do.

So, if we're in this battle and we say, "Whoa! What's it all about, anyway? It's supposed to be about love, it's supposed to be about the bigger picture," that always snapped us into seeing it in a different way, and realizing that "Well, maybe that *is* attachment on my part," or "Well, I still think I need to do this, but we just got so polarized -- I don't think that much that I need to do it, you just pushed me into feeling that way." And she thinks, "Well, I wasn't <u>that</u> much against it, I just got pissed off at the way you were pushing it on me.*"*

"What's it all about, anyway?" really helped us a lot. I had a teacher who used to say that a married couple is like a tag team to God. One or the other may be getting the crap trounced out of them, and that's when the other is the one who needs to pick 'em up. Sometimes you feel you're *both* on the mat. But you have to try to remember, "let's not throw out the essence for the details. Let's get back to the proper foreground and background. The foreground is, don't you and I want the exact same thing, which is our spiritual fulfillment, as long as we are together as two human beings, to live in truth? We can't get that by stepping on each other's necks."

You don't seem to represent any specific orthodoxy or philosophy, yet you speak with such authority about the spiritual journey. How did you become so self-reliant?

After some very powerful psychedelic experiences in the sixties, and seeing that we needed to get beyond psychedelics, Sita and I explored a lot of spiritual practices and methodologies -- various swamis, gurus, yogis, mystics, priests, rabbis, monks, nuns, and some phonies along the way; and finally it dawned on us that even if you find the very best, even if you spend all your money and time and finally hike up to a remote mountain in the Himalayas, and find the person that you were looking for all your life; after feeling the magic, witnessing the miracles, the very best that that person does for you is to say, "Sit still and shut up. Then you'll find everything you're looking for."

So, at a certain point we got the message. Instead of tripping off on every swami who came to town and every retreat we could find because somebody said, "Oh, this is a good one, that's a good one, and he gives "shaktipat" and she does auric healing....," we grew up, and we realized that you eventually must learn how to sit still and shut up. The time when you need to read a book, the time when you need to go to a talk or a workshop or a retreat, is when your inspiration is lagging, or when you're forgetting what it's about.

That hasn't happened for us in many years, so we don't automatically see all the "Ananda brothers" who come to town. I don't encourage people to come to my talks, either. My God, if you don't need to, don't come. In America, because we worship education so much, we tend to take an educational model into our spiritual development. You need an education to operate computers, to read and write and get along. But in spiritual development it's exactly the opposite. It's an emptying, it's not a learning, it's not an accumulating. It's to learn the *least* that you need to inspire you to become still and experience God for yourself. Not the most.

Not finding out how Kriyananda differs from Satchidananda from Kripalu Ananda and Amrit Desai and Bo Lozoff and Ram Dass and Louise Hay and -- who cares? Go to the fewest of those things that you can to get inspired. You find somebody who really touches you? That's it. Then just go home, and remember what that felt like. Remember what inspired you. Become it.

So, I'm in an ironic position doing these talks. That's why it's good you don't pay to get in [laughter]. Because I don't really believe in it very much. I feel like it's a last-ditch sort of thing. If my energy is clear enough to touch somebody, then that makes it worthwhile, so they get inspired to go home and be more interested in themselves than in me.

Sita and I meditate every day. We've gone through times when we've given that up because that becomes an attachment also. When we know that's the case is when we start feeling guilty about missing a meditation. But I do feel that in every culture there's a reason that some form or another of sitting straight and being quiet has been handed down and practiced, and I recommend it highly.

Fear seems to be a constant limitation to being able to live in the ways you describe. Would you talk about fear?

I learned something recently about fear. Some of you are probably familiar with Joseph Campbell's stuff on myths and Robert Bly's work. Well, the core of my life and my spiritual practice come from an ancient Hindu story called the *Ramayana*. That's the particular spiritual lineage that I find myself in. It's a story about demons and gods and goddesses and heroes, much like the Odyssey; tales in which our strengths and weaknesses are often seen in the form of creatures, demons, angels, etc.

In the Ramayana all the demons have boons that they were

given by the gods, for whatever reason, and also curses or limitations. It's the hero's job to see truth clearly enough to be able to see how to deal with each demon. If a demon, for example, has the power of immortality, then you don't waste your energy trying to slay it. You learn a strategy of incapacitating it instead. If a demon has the power of never being able to be slain by any weapon, then you decide what your weapons are and you put them down. It might be slain only by an openness, by total vulnerability.

So, recently, I don't know why, the nature of fear came to me, really pretty clearly, as a demon with boons and curses, and it's enjoyable for me to pass that on, because I think a lot of us deal with fear. One of the boons fear seems to have is the power to take almost any form -- the power of disguise, which a lot of demons in the *Ramayana* and the *Mahabharata* and other books have. The power of disguise. So we've got to see clearly past appearances.

Fear also seems to have two other boons. It has the boon of proximity and the boon of speed. What I mean by that is that fear has been given the power to get like a millionth of an inch away from our faces, and go BOOO! BOOOO! ARGGGHHHHH! [makes threatening and menacing noises], and it's been given the power to talk <u>really</u> fast, like, "Watch out, watchOUT, WATCHOUTWATCHOUT..."

But fear also has a couple of curses, a couple of limitations. The main one is that **it cannot actually touch us**. It can only get close, and pretend that it can touch us. It actually can never touch. And the other which is related to that, is that **it can't make us do a damn thing**. It doesn't have the power. It can only try to *scare* us into doing what it wants us to do.

So that's the demon known as fear. For example, you're a recovering alcoholic. You're in a situation where there's a lot of booze, and it's been a bad day, and you begin simultaneously feeling that desire to drink and also the fear that comes with it. And the demon fear starts using its powers. First of all, it gets RIGHT UP TO YOUR FACE. Then it starts using the power of speed and saying, "YOU'RE GOING TO DO IT DO IT, YOU'REGONNADOIT, GONNADOIT GONNADOIT!" And because we are *afraid* of being overwhelmed by fear, we find ourselves reaching for the damn drink to get it over with, because it has scared us into thinking that we're going to do it anyway, and we may as well stop lying to ourselves, and we can't take this, we're just not strong enough, etc.

But of course, *that's* the fear talking also, saying "YOU'RE NOT STRONG ENOUGH, NOTSTRONGENOUGH, NOT-STRONGENUFF, NOTSTRONGENUFF!! DO IT, DOIT, DOITDOITDOIT!" And it's getting closer and screaming faster, and we are afraid, because it's threatening, I <u>can</u> make you, I <u>can</u> touch you, and we're afraid that it can, it's working, and we find ourselves doing it.

Same as falling off a horse. I taught my son when he was small, "if you become part of the saddle, I've never yet seen a horse buck a saddle off." What happens when a horse starts bucking, is that fear begins to say, "You're gonna fall, your gonna fall, YOURGONNAFALL, YOURGONNAFALL, IT'S GONNA BE BAD, ITSGONNABEGAD, ITS GONNABEBAD, ITS-GONNABE <u>REAL</u> BAD!!!" At a certain point, you let go. You let go because you're afraid of how bad it's gonna be if you let go. And so, you let go so it'll be bad but before it gets <u>real</u> bad from trying to hold on too long. See how screwy it sounds? Yet that's fear's logic talking.

I have seen fear up close, I've seen terror up close. I took a lot of drugs, I've been meditating a lot of years, and I've gone through a lot of terrifying experiences, and it is clear to me that we must learn the strengths and weaknesses, the boons and curses of this demon, and act accordingly.

One of the ways to deal with fear in meditation is to let it come up, let it scream and rant and rave, and not budge. The thing about learning how to sit still, is that *everything* eventually comes up -- grief, fear, lust, loneliness, desire, hope -- everything eventually comes up because on the way to having a still mind are all these things that we keep pocketed around. You'll be sitting and start to get afraid -- afraid about your future, afraid about your life, whatever, and you just don't get up, you don't flinch, you remind yourself that fear does have the power of proximity and speed and disguise, but it does not have the power to touch, and it doesn't have the power to force you to do anything.

Fear comes up, "Wow, I'm really getting scared, I am, God fear is so awful, ooh, I'm scared." At a certain point, if you don't move, if you have the self-discipline to sit still and let it rant, you're not trying to push it away, you're not trying to minimize it. You see your fear of the fear, and you keep saying, "Well, that's OK, I want to feel it all. Come up, come on." Or like Jesus did in the desert with the devil, "Come on, come on. Give it a try. Come on. Give it your best shot." And fear will give you its best shot.

After a while, even about something you've been seriously afraid of for years, you're sitting still kind of going, [sarcastically] "Oh, wow, I'm really scared now. Oh yeah, whoo, you're gonna make me do that. Right." And you see, "My God, how have I been fooled for so many years into doing what fear wanted me to do because I was afraid of fear, when it really couldn't make me do anything at all?"

We begin realizing that courage is not the *absence* of fear. Courage is doing what we feel we need to do, or is right to do, *even in the presence* of fear. We are no longer trying to slay it. We are just letting it be what it is, which is this demon with powers and limitations, and we are being what we are and what we need to be. Try it.

By the way, as it turns out, when we do begin having that relationship with fear, and as the fear of fear is released, we experience a tremendous amount of increased power, personal power, from the available energy inside which fear has been occupying. The whole thing gets to be like a snowball, because everything we face like that -- compulsive behavior, addictive behavior, desires -- when we release the fear of it, the hold that it had on us, "my God, I feel bigger." Not because we have gained anything at all, not because we have found anything, not because we have discovered anything. The power has been here all the time, we've just had fear taking up so much of it, desire taking up so much of it, compulsive behavior taking up so much of it, etc.

As we allow them all to be what they are and we are what we are, what happens is that we become like the sky, which has no beginning or end. Where does the sky start and stop? Every one of our problems and struggles in life, which are purposeful, becomes like a cloud or storm system in a boundless sky. Clouds and storms do have beginnings and ends, the sky doesn't.

We sit, we walk, we act, we live, being the sky, and the peaceful days are great, and then suddenly a storm comes, whether that's addictive behavior, fear, a loved one dying, illness in the family, struggle, confusion about what to do with our lives. Storm starts coming, and instead of starting to push away and deny and try to sugar coat, which all comes from fear of negativity, fear of struggle, instead of doing that, we just say, "OK, here comes a storm. Let's see what it's made of, let's see what it does. I'm the sky. I'll be here after the storm is gone."

These storms come. Grief, pain, loneliness, fear. And they rage, like Hurricane Hugo. Tossing about all the mobile homes in your mind. If you feel like you're a mobile home then it's hell. If you understand that you are actually the sky, it's rough, it's stormy, it's scary, but you were here before it came, and you'll be here after it leaves. Clouds in a boundless sky. And you hear Jesus say, *See! I shall make all things new!* "My God, I was the sky all this time. I've been running from those storms all my life, when I was actually the sky!"

It feels good, it feels great, not to be controlled by fear.

So you're talking about not conquering our demons at all; you're saying they never had the power to affect us in the first place. I'm having a hard time keeping up with that idea. Could you explain it a little more?

The *Mahabharata* is another one of my favorite books -- the 16th chapter of which is the *Bhagavad-Gita*. Arjuna, the perfect spiritual warrior, is convinced by God, in the form of Krishna, to go into battle against his cousins and uncles and grandfathers; it's a horrible thought to Arjuna, but like the story of Abraham in the Bible, he obeys the will of God. Arjuna has a half-brother Yudhishthira, who is the son of Dharma, the God who knows what's right and what's wrong all the time, so Yudhisthira knows the right way to do everything.

Just as both armies square off and get ready to fight, Yudhishthira says, "Wait, we can't start fighting yet." He gets down from his horse, goes into the enemy camp and he walks up to one of the elders of the enemy army, and says, "Bhishma, I salute you. I honor you. May I have your permission to do battle against you?" Bhishma says basically, "Yes, and if you had not come to me, I would have had your ass in a sling. Thank you for respecting me; you have permission to do battle against me." Yudhisthira says, "And how may you be slain?" Bhishma replies, "I cannot be slain. Death cannot come to me until I ask for it."

Yudhishthira thanks him and then goes to another elder and he does this with three different elders. Each one gives him a different answer to "how can you be slain?" One of them says, "I cannot be slain so long as there is a weapon in my hand," and so forth. Little clues about their boons and limitations.

I realized a while back, that I come from a lot of anger. Big screaming family fights, intense grudges, etc. I may like it or not, but that's what I have to work with. Once again, it's resistance and denial that create the most important relationship with anger, same as with fear or anything else. We think that it just shouldn't be. We think that it shouldn't have happened. We think that we shouldn't have this in us, -- we're second guessing the movie, and saying "everything's kind of right, except I shouldn't be saddled with this."

Or it's like the *Bhagavad-Gita*. The whole conversation in the *Gita* has Arjuna saying, "I don't want to do battle against anything." And Krishna saying, "There are things that you have to do battle against, because it's right." Once again, I've experienced, merely by learning how to sit still, that if I feel anger -- I used to say "my anger" and now I'm trying to be a little more disciplined about just saying "anger" -- when I feel anger, if I can see it, salute it, say "Grandfather, I salute you, I honor what I've learned from you. Now how may I do battle against you, and how may you be slain?" Then the demon anger respects me for asking, and says whatever it may say, like, "I don't know if I can be slain or not, motherfucker."

And anger comes up, does its best in battle against me, I'll just feel it, and when everything in my heart is saying, "No! Close up! No! Don't!" I keep saying, "I want to open. I want to open. I want to keep opening. It's just a storm, and I am the sky. I can allow it to be exactly what it is without doing its bidding, without it ruling me. I am the sky. It's a storm."

Insanity is the same way. We've all got pockets of insanity, of irrational behavior. If our image of ourselves is small, and the cloud of anger, the cloud of addiction, the cloud of insanity is big, then when it comes along, we are engulfed. If we feel as big as the sky, and the cloud is exactly the same size it has always been, then we're big enough to allow it to move through us, instead of taking us with it. It makes all the difference in the world.

What I'm talking about is not in any way repressing, it's really just seeing more clearly how it is and how it works. It's the *opposite* of repressing. Repression is denial. We're not only not denying, we're saying "let's feel more closely what this thing is. Let's feel it all, and let's not budge, so that we can really feel it all. Let's pay complete attention to what it feels like to be enraged." And you just start thinking of what enrages you. Think of what the judge did to you. Think of what your sister's doing, your brother's doing, your mother's doing. Whatever it is that really gets you ticked off. Just feel it.

I had this spiritual teacher once many years ago, who used to purposely enrage us by saying or doing completely unfair, wrong, or immoral things; I mean, she was totally in the wrong. Then when we were finally worked up into fullblown fury, she would say "Okay, let it go." And you're standing there with all this justifiable anger, and she's just calm, looking straight into your eyes saying "Let it go!"

So you're going, **"But I'm right...!"** and she said, "Do you want to be right, or do you want to be free? Right now. Let it go or leave my teaching forever." And you say, "BUT!!" She painfully reminded us that the only time you can really give up anger is while you're in the middle of anger. It's easy to feel nice and peaceful and say, "Yes, I give up all my anger." But see, when we're angry, we always think we're right. That's what anger is about, you know, "AAAHHH, I'M RIGHT!!" And she would say, "You want to be right, or do you want to be free?"

You've been right so many times, it never got you anywhere. You know you really want to be free. You have to allow the anger to be exactly what it is without taking you with it. You can't kill it, you can't push it away. That's why she said, "let it go." It's like you find that anger is this cloud, and you're the one holding on. Just as fear can't touch you, neither can anger. None of these things can overwhelm the sky. They all have the same limitation. They can't touch you. They fool you into clinging to them; being afraid of them.

We just had to let go. We didn't push it away. We took a deep breath, we let go, and we watched anger just storm and swirl away, and just kind of move on to the next sucker down the block. It's amazing, sometimes when you sit in meditation, and you go through one of these big grief or anger or loneliness things or whatever, and it'll rage for a whole half-hour, and suddenly it's gone, and you haven't budged. It just pops like a huge bubble that got three miles wide but when it pops there's nothing left inside, and you realized that it had surface but no substance.

It's amazing, you're sitting there and a moment ago you had more lust than anybody's ever had before, every cell of your body wanted sexual satisfaction, and suddenly it's like, *gone*, you're still sitting there, and you haven't done anything. Then you sit another hour, and all this grief over your father's death comes up, and it rages and you feel so terrible -- but you haven't broken stride, you haven't broken down crying, you sit and you feel the whole thing, respectfully watching it, and suddenly it's gone too.

These experiences begin to give you that half inch of distance between the storms and the sky. Without becoming a zombie whatsoever; without becoming cold or ambivalent or callous or anything, you simply have more choice. Choice eventually translates to freedom. You realize, "All this time I have really been free. I've just thought that when you're free, you're not supposed to ever feel anger. When you're free, you're not supposed to ever feel fear. I always thought being free meant never having a bad day."

Suddenly it dawns on you, being free means that it can all be exactly as it is, and it doesn't control you. Wow! that's different. "You mean I can take down all those affirmations on the refrigerator, that redefine my world so that I never feel anything negative? I can allow negative to be negative, fear to be fear, anger to be anger, and it never touches <u>me</u>, it never forces <u>me</u>, it never controls <u>me</u>, because I'm the sky, and they are huge, threatening storms I have to respect -- I know the sky dims, I know everything changes, I know the wind blows, but I am the sky and they are storms, and I'm gonna be here when they're over?"

It's this incredible personal revelation of, *See, I shall make all things new.* Your hemorrhoids, the test you're studying for, the problems with your family, it's all got license to be what it is, including your part. You dive right into your life, you haggle over the price of bananas in the marketplace, you sweat to get your college degree, you hope your kid learns how to drive well before he gets wrecked, you do all of the stuff human life is made of, but none of it, the good or the bad, control the sky. You enjoy the beautiful cumulus clouds, and you endure the horrible storms.

Like Nisargidatta Maharaj, a holy man, said, "Pain can never be conquered. It's here to be endured." We don't usually want to hear that. "What do you mean, endured?" Endured like the sky endures a storm. Respectfully, realizing that things come and go. People come into our lives, they leave us, we're left sad and aching because of our feelings, and it's all OK. We can experience it all. That's the freedom, is knowing we can't be destroyed.

It's not being in a placid "New Age" attitude where all we do is smile and feel good. The freedom is, "My God, how Christ suffered on the cross!" And to be able to feel it. My God, how much it hurts, for my only son to no longer be a child. Oh, what a pain! Like wrenching my heart out without anesthetic -- he's gone. He lives 3,000 miles from us, and he's our baby. Oh, how beautiful to be able to feel so much pain and not be afraid of it. I mean, let's face it, the storms bring some beautiful lightning patterns. Awesome thunder.

That's the way in which we have to become as little children. A hurricane comes and all the adults are grim and serious, doing all the responsible things, and kids are saying, "Wow!" They're in awe of the intensity, of high drama, of natural danger, of life and of death. That's how we can be. For example, Sita and I have been married twenty-four years; the marriage everybody wants -- intimate, best friends, working together twenty-four hours a day, not driving each other crazy, profound connection -- well, think about how much it's gonna hurt when one of us dies before the other. Wow. [spoken hushed, with awe] Wow. It's going to be painful beyond belief. Wow.

As much as I hope we both live to a ripe old age, I'm excited at the intensity of experiencing that storm. It's going to absolutely *devastate* the survivor. Wow. "Wow" -- That's what kids say.

Except ye be converted and become as little children, ye shall not enter into the kingdom of heaven. Think about kids' reactions to things, both bad and good. It hurts? "Wow." Death of a loved one, "Wow," being humiliated hurts, "oh, wow," you hear that your teeth might get pulled when you get old, all your teeth pulled out, "wow." Children have a natural awe of all experience.

Some measure of suffering applies to everybody. People we love are going to die. We're going to be alone and frightened sometimes. Our health is going to fade. We're going to get old. We're going to look at our bald spots and our paunches, and we're going to say, "When did it happen?" The natural bitter-sweetness of life applies to everybody. But most suffering is what we create by our denial, by our resistance to anger, fear, illness, dying -- our resistance to endure or confront exactly what we were born to go experience.

Everything comes right on time, yet as soon as a storm comes into our sky, we say, "No, not now, not me!" Yet, that's what we were born to face, *exactly* at that moment. When we give up resistance and denial, I call it "full acceptance, no surrender." Acceptance and surrender are opposites. It's full acceptance of what reality brings, and no surrender of the "wow" that we are on a *spiritual* journey, and that all of this is Spirit.

We no longer say, "Uh, yeah, I know all that stuff about spirit, but this is serious! I mean, later for the meditation stuff, this is wrong." Full acceptance, no surrender.

It makes all the difference in the world, yet looks much the same from the outside; except there seem to be fewer storms as we don't mind storms. But boy, the ones that come, those natural ones, they're really big. God love 'em. Because that's what makes us into heroes -- letting our hearts break time and time again, learning to live with respectfulness and humility, like a child, in this magic garden of life, with all its beauties and wonders and thorns and snakes and hopes and terrors. Being free to experience it all is the simplest thing in the world. It's only our busy minds which keep making it complicated.

● ● ●

We are now on the wheel of life that turns and turns, we wander forever from one birth to another. Here we are kings, there we live out all our life on the tip of a blade of grass. What is this life flowing in our bodies like fire? What is it?
Life is like hot iron, ready to pour.
Choose the mold, and life will burn it.

-- Mahabharata, retold by William Buck

Life works, life is precisely designed, like your car or anything else. You don't start your car with a sledge hammer. You find the key. Life works with some simple, universal keys, and it doesn't work -- whether you're in the White House or in Folsom Prison -- if you don't express self-honesty, courage, kindness, humor, wonder -- the most basic human virtues.

SELF-HONESTY, COURAGE, KINDNESS, HUMOR, AND WONDER

Radio Interview On KLOS, Los Angeles 2/90
(host Frank Sontag in italics, Bo answering)

To start, there's so much to cover in the short time we have, first off let's talk about the Prison-Ashram Project: how long it's been around, how it came into being, what it's about.

Okay. How long it's been around is seventeen years. The short version of the story is that my wife and I were hippies in the sixties and political activists and anti-war activists, and then we completely burned out. We sailed off into the sunset, getting jobs on a sailboat in 1969, to leave the whole thing behind.

After about a year, the captain decided he'd like to make a little money smuggling 1400 pounds of pot from Jamaica to Miami on the boat. And for us it was like the old Dylan song, "Oh, no, no, no, we've been through that movie before!" We got off the boat before the pot was loaded, everybody was busted.

To make a long story short, my sister's husband was sentenced to 12 to 40 years for his part in that scheme. And everybody we knew -- the captain was sentenced to 6 to 20 -- basically everybody we knew was busted and in prison. Sita and I were back on land with nothing special to do.

After a couple of years, we found ourselves in an ashram, which is like a monastery only shorter term, a place to retreat from the world, learn spiritual discipline, turn inward. At the same time, we visited my brother-in-law in prison. So it's like that Reese's Peanut Butter Cup commercial -- prison, ashram, hmmmm -- the guy with the chocolate, the guy with the peanut butter running down the halls and crash, we got the Prison-Ashram Project.

The ashram was a farm. We were waking up early in the morning, wearing just a basic white uniform; a no-frills life, no movies or parties, etc. We were all eating group meals, working without pay. We went to visit my brother-in-law in federal prison, and by that time he'd moved his way out to the medium security farm instead of the big penitentiary.

He was waking up early in the morning, wearing a uniform, eating group meals, working on the farm with no pay, and we realized that the lifestyle was very similar; except that we'd given up all of our freedoms to do this because we were getting something profound out of it, and he was forced to be there.

So we began considering that if you give up the melodrama and bitterness about why you're there, and if you're tired of feeling like a convict, you can re-perceive your environment as an ashram. You can begin to explore why free people throughout history, who can experience all the pleasures that you wish you could experience, have given it all up to live a cloistered, regimented lifestyle. There must be a reason that monks and nuns and ashramites have done that for centuries.

And so, in a very low-key way, without feeling evangelistic about it, we determined that since I had family in prison, we would be willing to share our perspective with prisoners who were interested or intrigued by it. We never sat down and said "this is going to be our whole life," it just turned out that way.

How did you implement it? How was the prison system, were they receptive to the idea, how did it manifest?

Well, the first manifestation on my part was that at that time we were very touched by a book called *Be Here Now* by Ram Dass. So we smuggled my brother-in-law a copy of *Be Here Now* and a salami on one of our visits. He personally got off much more on the salami than *Be Here Now*, but the light bulb went on over our heads, that hey, this was something to do -- again, just for prisoners who were intrigued by that idea.

At the same time, we had met Ram Dass, the author of *Be Here Now,* and he said, coincidentally, "I've already sent free copies of *Be Here Now* to 1,500 prison libraries, and I'm beginning to get a lot of correspondence from prisoners. Would you like to take that over for me?" He started giving me money out of his pocket to pay for stamps.

Like I said, the Prison-Ashram Project really grew, it wasn't conceived and then implemented. I mean, we didn't know what we were doing. Our commitment is really just to doing it, it's like the Braille method, feeling our way along. And it's been that way for 17 years now.

It's this huge thing now -- my book, *We're All Doing Time*, is in several languages, and we get 50 or 60 letters a day from prisoners in 40 different countries. It's a big deal simply because that's the level of interest.

I'm rather taken aback. I didn't realize it was that big.

Oh, huge, huge, huge, Frank. Bigger than life (both laugh).

In one way, that's wonderful, and in another way that's kind of tragic. Again, the violence rate in this country seems to be perceived at an all-time high and the way in which the governments -- city, federal, state -- deal with the problem seems synthetic. They don't find out why people do what they do. They just want to build more prisons and lock them up and talk about this war on drugs.

And the way in which the personal freedoms of individuals are being inhibited at a greater rate, it seems like every week, at least in my understanding. What are your thoughts and feelings on crime in this country?

Well, let's face it, Americans love war, especially a righteous war. Our last war was dubious and divided the country terribly. We now have a war which has united rock stars, entertainers, sports figures, politicians, educators . . . . Jesse Helms to Jesse Jackson are all on the same side on the war against drugs.

When Jesse Helms and Jesse Jackson are on the same side of an issue, I start thinking about Canada. The war on drugs is almost an ironclad excuse for venting animosity and hostility toward somebody. Because, who's going to come forward except misfits like me and say "the war on drugs is a bad war"?

I'm glad my work is independent of this complex socio-cultural stuff -- even of the factors that put people in prison and that run prisons. If I had my way, if I had the authority, of course I would change the prison system entirely, I would change peoples' attitudes entirely. But that is the work of the prison reformers, and my work is really with individuals in a timeless way which doesn't hinge on anyone or anything else changing.

The name of my book *We're All Doing Time* suggests that whole perspective. I don't really have a particular interest in prisons. I'm a spiritual teacher. It's just that nobody else was offering non-religious spiritual teachings in the prison system.

Frank, if you wanted to learn meditation, you could go to a bookstore or a health food store and look on a bulletin board and see any number of classes offered, from Vipassana meditation to this kind of yoga, that kind of yoga; I just want to be that bulletin board for people in prison, because there are a lot of ancient traditions of value.

I'm a very practical person. People conceive of us -- my wife and myself -- as sweet, nice, naïve yoga teachers who go around and love everybody. That's not who we are at all. We're old hippies and radicals. I carried a gun for a year-and-a-half in the sixties, I shot at people, I've been attacked, I've been locked up. The spiritual journey is the most practical thing in the world. It has to do with getting in touch with reality.

I help prisoners turn inward to that ancient journey which is relevant whether they're in prison or not. At some point each one of us, whether it's on our deathbed or before, wants to find out the secret behind it all. We want to tune in to the Supreme Reality, whatever we want to call it. So I help people do that.

If I were actually in the prison reform business, I would be depressed and very pessimistic, because we're in an extremely repressive, backward, violent, ugly era of criminal justice. I want to be straight about that. I don't see it getting better yet, I see it continuing to get worse.

As you mentioned a few minutes ago, we're just building more prisons. Bush, as the general of this war on drugs, has taken almost all of the money away from treatment, away from education, away from rehabilitation, and put it into enforcement. So now, we're creating whole new categories of felons. A lot more teenagers, a lot more young people who were just fooling around with pot, are now going to be convicted felons doing time with bank robbers, rapists, muggers, killers.

The legacy of what we see going on today is going to be with us for decades before it gets any better. So it's a pretty bad time in that regard -- I'm glad that's not my field.

When one thinks of the word "criminal" it seems as if there's an automatic reaction amongst the masses, like "Oh, my gosh, there's someone different from me, or they're bad", or "let's lock them up and not ask why they become the criminals." In your understanding of life and your pursuit of what you're doing right now, do you find a direct correlation, for instance, with child rearing, abuse, fear, neglect, in some way working hand in hand when someone grows up into an adult and starts acting out in ways that they eventually end up in prison? There's a common tie there somehow.

Well, yes and no. I've been in maybe three or four hundred prisons in the last twenty years. I've known, oh, I'm sure, 100,000 prisoners, at least. It's very easy to see that the great majority of them have been abused children or neglected, abandoned, culturally deprived, economically deprived, or whatever.

But what is most critically lacking in the lives of the people we see in prison, whether they come from privileged or unprivileged backgrounds, is a sense of compassion, a sense of caring about somebody other than oneself. That is what cuts across the economic and social lines entirely. And nobody is looking at that. We're just looking at the material surroundings, we're looking at the environment, we're looking at job skills.

There are a lot of real jerks from every level of life, but the thing that they have in common is that they're narcissistic, they lead self-centered lives, they're trying to fulfill all of their desires. So the input that I have in prison is, "start being a caring person right where you are, even in prison. Begin to turn on to the fact that you're part of this human family, and begin caring about the person next to you. That's the beginning. That's the first step."

So you're saying the intertwined thread is, there's a sense of spiritual disconnection amongst them.

Completely.

What is your definition of spirituality? You just made reference to compassion and caring for fellow human beings.

Well, again, I'm a realist. I feel very clearly, from being on both sides of it in my life, that life works if you adhere to certain ways that life is created to work. And life doesn't work if you don't adhere to those ways.

Life works, for example, if you have some common universal virtues like self-honesty, courage, kindness, humor, wonder. Life can work, you can feel connected, like what native Americans called "walking inside the circle."

Conversely, there's a way of life I know very well, and most people listening know it too, either from their present or past, in which all of your energy is trying to push away the things that you're calling negative, and you're trying to cling to all of the things that you think are going to make things better; living in a way I call "as soon as."

Like, "How are you doing?" "Well, *as soon as* I get this raise, I'll be doing great, *as soon as* I get my car fixed I'll be doing fine, *as soon as* I clear this up with my wife, I'll be doing great, *as soon as* I get Jimmy off drugs . . ." And that's missing something.

There really is a spiritual truth, there is a mystical secret, a context for a life that works; it isn't arbitrary, as if it's up to all of us to decide our own ethics and morality because it's just a grab bag and you know, if you feel good exploiting people then you can do that.

Life works, life is precisely designed, like your car or anything else. You don't start your car with a sledge hammer. You find the key. Life works with some simple, universal keys, and it doesn't work -- whether you're in the White House or in Folsom Prison -- if you don't express self-honesty, courage, kindness, humor, wonder -- the most basic human virtues. It just doesn't work. Life is never going to work that way.

I explain that to people in prison. Many of them are at the low point of their lives, so they're open to hearing it. They say, "can it really be that simple?" And I say, "you're damn right it can be, because I know both sides of it, and I feel a power and a freedom that I thought was completely beyond me."

You know, I thought this freedom I feel was completely beyond life. I didn't have faith in life. Who would've guessed that the magic keys would lie in such simple virtues that are outside of whatever culture you live in, what century, what color you are, what gender you are, all the political issues of the time... I mean, can you picture any planet anywhere, any country, any century, where self-honesty, courage, kindness, humor and wonder would not be valued virtues; would not create a society which works out its problems in an honorable way?

A lot of people in prison are open to hearing that. They want to make their lives work. They're so tired of screwing up. I'm just giving them a chance to do that without shoving complex philosophies or theologies down their throats, without trying to explain why or how they should get out and live in a hypocritical and criminal culture, yet obey the law. I let all that take care of itself, because once they get those virtues together on their own, they can figure out the same way I do how to stay on the right side of the law. They'll figure it out for themselves.

Have you ever been afraid to do what you do?

Never. In fact, even my wife, who is a small, attractive woman -- and we've been doing this since our mid-twenties -- has never felt a moment of fear going into Attica, Joliet, Santa Fe Prison, before or after the riot. There's just -- well, we're not going there to sell anything, we're not going to convince anybody of anything, we're just going to hang out 'cause we're old hippies, and we want to tell people that the "good news" is better than they thought. And they appreciate that.

There's something they trust. Nobody's accusing us of being a tool of the administration or anything like that. Part of the year I have a big rock and roll band, I go around to some prisons in North Carolina and give concerts all day.

Something about rock and roll, huh?

It's a universal language.

Let me backtrack just a moment to the war on drugs. Everything is lopped together. It seems marijuana is the same in this day and age as crack cocaine. There are legalized drugs, prescription drugs, people are strung out on those, not even mentioning alcohol, nicotine, tobacco.

Do you have any personal preference...

Let's see, there was some Thai hash around '67 . . . . [laughter]

No, I mean as to the legalization of drugs? Do you think we should legalize drugs -- is that all of a sudden going to solve the problem?

I don't think anything is going to solve the problem of people wanting to escape a superficial, consumer-oriented lifestyle which is devoid of meaning. That's the underlying problem in our culture.

It's the only thing that scares me a little about what's

happened in the Eastern Bloc, is that right now, we're the big role model for what they want, because they see Levi's and they see MTV and they see McDonald's and they think, "yah!", so the rain-forests are going to perish even quicker now.

I don't think we're much of a role model for free enterprise or for democracy -- I mean, come on, Frank, we don't have democracy, we have people who can influence the media the most and people who can hire enough psychologists to learn how to sell messages to us in every subliminal way; those are the people who control votes and opinions. You put one Willie Horton on the air for a 15-second sound byte and it wins a presidential election.

So I don't feel like our democratic experiment and our free enterprise system is a great role model. Also I notice with interest that there are many native cultures, like South American Indian tribes, native Americans, Hindus and others, many native cultures in which some form of psychedelic has been used as a sacred substance for thousands of years, and there has never been drug abuse in those cultures.

Within the past twenty-five years, we began experiencing some drug problems and now just a few short years later, a joint is the same as crack cocaine is the same as heroin, and everybody's all on one side. It's this whole righteousness of the culture and a new drug fascism, you know -- "kids turn your parents in, and just say no if your Uncle Harold offers you a joint, he's trying to kill you." Yeah, I think there are some pretty insidious forces at work. Have you seen the movie "Flashback"?

No, I haven't, not yet.

Well, at the end of "Flashback", Dennis Hopper as the old hippie says, "The nineties are gonna make the sixties look like the fifties." And I turned to my wife and said, "you know that's a really nice thought, but frankly I think the truth is, the nineties are going to make the fifties look like the sixties."

Because we're *worse* than back in Ozzie and Harriet land. We're training youngsters now in *just say no* programs who are beginning to feel like Brownshirts, you know, like Hitler's Youth Brigade. The entire thing is a victory for people like Reagan and Bush who always felt there wasn't a single good thing to come out of consciousness expansion in the sixties. They're trying to make the sixties all an aberration. And there are a lot of people like you and me who know that is simply not true.

I wouldn't deny that there is a terrible drug problem in this culture. It's an imbalanced culture, a young culture. We think because we're so technically sophisticated that we're the wisest beings who ever lived. But we're an infant culture, we're only a couple hundred years old. This bizarre, unprecedented phenomenon of being a melting pot of nationalities and ethnicities from all over the world, we're really like in kindergarten but we think we're in graduate school.

So a few of us got hold of some powerful substances which are sacred in many cultures and which gave us tremendous insights into ourselves and the nature of life. And people like myself who, for example, LSD showed me that I had to go beyond LSD and leave it behind. I honor my psychedelic use in the sixties for what it did and I acknowledge as well that it can be a dangerous and hazardous path, like many other paths. Life is tricky, life is dangerous.

I don't do any drugs at all anymore, because for what I want, I need to have my mind as clear as possible and need to turn inward through meditation, and I'm making a lot of progress in that way. So, I also don't do prescription drugs. It isn't the culture to me which defines whether the substance is evil or good, it's my own mind. I don't want to do Demerol just because a doctor might prescribe it, because Demerol is still going to cloud my mind just like a joint would.

But there's a huge difference between psychedelics and narcotics, so far as whether anything good can ever come out of a psychedelic experience, and nowadays we're all being brainwashed. The war on drugs is a giant propaganda strategy to pretend that the sixties had no value, and I think that's a terrible step backward for our culture. Because the sixties were a major turning point in a lot of philosophical ways.

I happen to agree with you about the nineties, that there is this age of ignorance and reactionary-ism ushering in, like, since maybe the forties--

Yeah. Killer weed.

Kind of a tangent off that, there's still a sense in me that feels like the nineties are gonna be a decade of action, where people are waking up at an unprecedented rate, more and more people are seeking inner truths, they're seeing through the lies. Do you see optimism for the future as well?

I don't know, I hate to sound like a curmudgeon. I don't see great numbers of people turning inward to The One Source of a glimpse of reality. I mean, to me life is a *mystical* adventure, and that thing in us which some people try to address through drugs, which other people try to distract themselves from by overwork, that thing in us that's churning, that wants something, that's unsatisfied, that thing in us isn't going to be satisfied by any kind of great wholesome lifestyle or figuring out how to have peace in the Middle East or anything.

That thing in us is an inward pull to learn how to sit still, touch that divinity, touch that supreme reality, and then live in the world based on that being the center.

That's how I do my work. I don't see myself as some great prison reformer, I don't see myself as some great humanitarian or whatever; I see myself as somebody who keeps one toe in The One, in the transcendent, and the rest of me is just manifesting that clarity, that awareness, that fearlessness. I see more people turning inward like that, and I deal with a lot of them in prison, and it's almost ecstatic for me to see somebody in those surroundings doing that and really finding the ancient truth.

But at the same time, in terms of the overall culture, I have to admit I see us sliding a fair amount further down before we begin climbing back up. There are things being instituted now like the construction of new prisons, like the war on drugs, legislation just being passed, which is all going to have impact for years to come.

The money Bush has siphoned off from rehabilitation, education, housing and stuff like that, that impact is going to be felt long after his administration's over. So, it's interesting that the rest of the world seems to be waking up in a miraculous way, and *we* seem to be sliding back emotionally to the fifties, to the forties, to the thirties. We're retrenching to a John Wayne sort of spirit. And that's just fascinating.

Is violence ever an alternative? Is it ever a solution?

Violence happens. I'm not sophisticated enough to espouse philosophies that it's *always* this or *never* that. I'm steeped in several holy books, which make it clear that physical violence is one of the trickiest questions of human behavior.

Look at Gandhi's legacy. We have canonized Gandhi -- of course, that's what makes all our symbols safe, is to take real people and make them into symbols. Gandhi, Martin Luther King -- we're doing it with Mother Theresa while she's alive. We don't want to look too closely at the person, because it's more convenient to have a symbol.

If you look honestly at Gandhi's legacy, past all the bombast of how he personally inspires us by his example, India is really not less violent than before Gandhi. India is a terribly violent place. There is terrible religious and caste violence taking place that Gandhi was hoping to end all his life. It's not a simple question. I am awed by Gandhi's example, I'm impressed by Martin Luther King's example; at the same time, I see prisoners in situations in which it feels like violence is sometimes the only way -- like Malcolm X's comment that he doesn't even call self-defense violence; he calls it intelligence.

The martial arts, for example, are about violence as a constructive force, with no violence in the heart. The martial arts are predicated upon peace in the heart, and a genuine motive of lovingkindness, trying to bring a situation to harmony that is already out of harmony. So, if you see somebody raping your wife, that's a situation out of harmony, and to somehow sit down and just feel like, well, you have to turn the other cheek, you have to allow this to go on, etc., that's a very tricky question. I think maybe for some people that is indeed their route to Christ. I think for other people it would be cowardice.

In the same way, I think for some people, *stopping* such an attack with as little hatred and hostility as possible -- like in Aikido you're considered not a very good Aikidoist if you injure your opponent -- so stopping it with as little violence as possible is the right thing to do. I am certainly not about to set myself up as a judge of how prisoners should live in a culture which is entirely different from the culture that you and I live in out on the streets.

So what I do is simply inspire them to turn inward, because their best advice doesn't come from me, it comes from clearing their own minds and hearts. That's where all of the advice comes from. When Christ said "I am with you always," that's where He's talking about. I just turn them inward to quiet down and hear their own guidance. And then I trust what they do.

I'm going to ask you one more question and then we're going to open the phone lines. If one decides to be disciplined in the area of looking inside daily -- meditation, any type of relaxation technique -- personally speaking, what kind of changes have you experienced in your life? Does this stuff really work?

Of course. It wouldn't have turned out to be my whole adult life if it didn't work very profoundly. I have had some tremendous psychedelic experiences. Yet I have chosen to leave psychedelics behind because of the more profound experiences and promise of this route. I am essentially a mystic. And as I said before, having one toe in the transcendent enables me to live in a way that is so much more powerful than I had ever imagined, I walk around basically fearless.

I don't mean that in an arrogant way, I mean just not having all of the constant mental busy-ness, like, *is Frank going to like me, am I going to say the right things on the air, what if people are angry,* or *can I get him to say that I'm six feet tall?* My God, it's such a relief to just love you. It's such a relief not to be afraid wherever I walk, wherever I go, because I'm watching this whole thing from a different point of view. And that's what meditation helps you to do.

In a way, you could say meditation helps you to not take your life quite so personally. I have a good sense of humor and sense of perspective about what's going on. What's going on is a mystery, not a struggle. That's the sense of wonder that I mentioned as one of those five virtues. I live my life as an adventurer in a mystery, which is based around some kind of lovingkindness. That's the key to it. I can share that in a powerful way with people who are intrigued by it, and it seems to bring a tremendous difference to their lives.

As Ram Dass said, there is something special about being here now, being here in the moment.

Do you know of any other time that exists?

Bo, a thought just came to mind: movies, cinema, television, violence, revenge, retribution: does it kind of perpetuate the problem? Is it a reflection of what we really think and feel? Do we really like violence in this culture, in America? We're not going to talk about across the globe. The media, the cinema.

Well, it's books too. I think there's an interesting thing going on in our culture. I've noticed it because I've written books, and I see the publishing industry from the inside. And my son is an actor so I see a little bit of the entertainment industry as well.

It used to be that the central people involved in any of those media were gutsy people whose lives were passionately involved with that field -- whether it was film or newspapers or magazine publication or book publishing, the theater -- their lives were really involved with it and so sometimes they would take a chance on something that would be very offensive to the public, etc., but they would take a chance on it because of the quality in it, etc.

But now, in our consumer-oriented culture, the cart has come before the horse, so if we see that a movie like Friday the Thirteenth did big box office, that's all that's important. We see it's successful and so we just keep pumping that out, and that in part *defines* cultural tastes.

I'll give you an example in the publishing industry. The big chains, B. Dalton, Waldenbooks, etc., besides presenting literature, at this point also have stables of hack writers. They see what customers are buying and they say "OK, you write more of this, we'll publish it and sell it," because it's all about profit per square inch. The movies are about the same thing, about how much it's going to gross. Even art -- the only way it's evaluated now is how much it sells for, like Van Gogh's *Sunflowers* going for $43 million; nobody even mentions whether it stirs the soul, just how much was bid.

So in the sense that our media are now being created solely to fulfill the momentary tastes of gladiator audiences, yeah, if there's even a slight thirst for blood, then we're going to see a lot of blood in our movies until that desire is played out. And then suddenly it'll be all romantic pictures again. Not because we've changed ethically or because there's less violence in our culture, but simply because public taste is what's determining it.

Still of course, in every field to a certain degree, there are going to be creative people like Matt Groening, who created *Life In Hell* in print and *The Simpsons* on television -- I think he's a radical genius. His work ridicules the deepest roots of our superficiality in a gentle way, and somehow the very people he mocks have gone wild over it.

But for the most part, the big hits in books, movies, TV, etc., are just catering to what the public taste is, rather than in any way trying to expand the edges of that taste towards somebody's vision of it being better.

That's part of what artistic vision used to be about, was to challenge the public. If you think the public is a little too violent, well, challenge them by disturbing that and going out to the edge to try to get them into what you feel is a better place. That's what the artist wants to do. Now it's not about that, because it's not about art, it's about business. Business says "hey, don't be offensive to the public, don't try to challenge them, don't try to make them feel bad, let's just give them *Friday the Thirteenth Part 19.* Let's give them *Rambo 10.*"

So, to that degree, yeah, the media have certainly contributed to our climate of violence by pandering to it for bucks. I hear from kids who have committed crimes who are just copying things they've seen in movies.

But how did they *get* to the place where they're so cold-hearted as to even copy that? I think that's a separate problem. In part it's probably because they've been desensitized by seeing all the images on TV, but I think it still has to get down to personal responsibility. There's a lack of fulfillment in their lives.

As far as the prisoners you work with, once they get out in civilian life, I read an interesting story not too long ago about the majority of them saying "I don't want to go out in civilian life, it's nuts out there. At least here in the prison I know what's going on. I have my sense of home," if you will. Any success stories you want to share with us, people that have made it out here in civilian life through the work you've done, the knowledge you've shared.

Well, I've been doing this seventeen years, so there are too many tales to share. One of our favorite friends is a guy named Ray Neal, who was considered one of the most vicious convicts in the country at one time. He spent his entire adult life, eighteen years, in prisons. He was in Alcatraz when they closed it down, did time with the Birdman of Alcatraz, did time in Utah next to Gary Gilmore, robbed twenty-seven banks. He's been out now for almost 13 years, and he's a successful businessman in Texas, he's married, he loves his life, he's a good artist.

There are people like Ray who had simply never looked at their lives honestly and never, *ever*, considered turning within or knew what that was all about. I'm not some healer who goes and lays my hands on somebody and says, "Yayess, brothuh!" I just go around and remind people that there's this thing going on in them and I turn them inward to address it, and I tell them it's valid, that life isn't just about getting your GED and getting college skills and job skills and then going out on the job market to become a good American consumer; there's something a lot deeper going on, thank God!

Ray Neal and thousands of others like him, who had completely given up on living outside of prison, are finding, "Wow, life can be a whole different thing."

One of the reasons many of them are *in* prison was their rejection of a society that they saw as hypocritical, shallow and vain, and for the most part our culture *is* that way. I just helped them see that crime is *also* hypocritical, shallow, and vain. The culture changes when people change. So, change yourself. Just learn how to sit still and shut up, and you'll begin finding some answers. It's really that simple. I think it was John the Baptist who said, "Before kingdoms change, men must change."

Let's take some phone calls. Mona, good morning! You're on the Impact program here on KLOS.

Bo, I've read your book Lineage, and in that book you describe a situation in which prisoners are kept on buses, chained up and traveling around all day. And, it seemed like a horrible way to live your existence. I mean, it would seem like it's a violation of human rights. And I was wondering if you could describe that a little bit more, and shouldn't somebody like Amnesty International be trying to fight for these men? Why are these men kept on buses traveling around?

Well, Amnesty International deals only with people they consider political prisoners, so they tend not to get involved in issues that affect prisoners from a lot of different crimes.

What you're describing is mostly in the federal prison system, because there are such great distances between federal institutions all over the country. It's the American gulag. When a prisoner is being transferred on a bus from one federal institution to another, during that transfer time he has no rights. All of the rights that apply to him in a prison about exercise space and access to a lawyer and family visits and rehabilitation programs don't apply because he's in transfer.

The way the government abuses that, as I expressed in my story, is that when an official in the federal system has a grudge against a prisoner for being an activist, for filing too many grievances, etc., they give him "bus time." I've known people who were kept on buses for over two and three years, with no rights, no programs, no visits, no phone calls, nothing.

They're in a legal limbo and officially, bureaucratically, well, they're just being "transferred" and you don't have any right to know where they are until they get there. They keep some of those prisoners "riding the circuit" so that they can't land in a prison and enjoy their rights or organize more people or complain about the system. And yes, it does go on. The story was fiction but that was based on true incidents.

-- *Shocking.*

Anything else, Mona?

-- *Yes; In what you practice in terms of meditation, are you teaching them sort of like detachment, is that what you're asking them to do? To become observers of themselves and sort of detach from everyday living?*

I'm just helping them take the first classic step of turning inward to address what being human is all about. You can call that detachment, but only from the point of view that our usual state of mind is "normal" and the inward state is "abnormal."

From where I see it, there's nothing we're being detached from. We're trying to experience a very natural state we have been denying and blocking for many years. We're trying to heal ourselves of this myopic state that we find ourselves in of thinking that all we are is what we see in the mirror.

Mona, thank you for your call. We're a couple moments away from one o'clock. This is KLOS Los Angeles. Brian, good morning, you're on the Impact program.

Good morning. My question for Bo is, do you propose we eradicate the prison system?

No. There are abolitionists who feel that all prisons are the problem and need to be torn down. But I know a lot of very dangerous people who, if I had the authority to open up the doors tomorrow, I couldn't in good conscience just turn the key and let them out.

But I'll be frank with you, I think we're talking about <u>at most</u> five to ten percent of the prison population who need to be incarcerated. And the way in which even those five or ten percent need to be incarcerated is in an environment where they can experience kindness, which they have not experienced much in their lives; where they can experience hope and opportunity rather an ordeal in which we punish them like dogs and then let them out and say, "Now, you'd better not screw up again."

So, a two-part answer: I think about five to ten percent of the people who are currently in prison need to be removed from the possibility of harming others. The rest could all be far better helped in a non-prison environment. I'm not being naïve about what it takes or how dangerous people can be, I'm being a realist. You can't just hurt, hurt, and hurt and then let somebody out and assume they're going to be a better human being.

If we're going to let somebody out and we want to be safer in their presence, we have to hope that while they were inside we helped them find something that had been lacking from their lives and helped inspire and encourage them to have more compassion to be a more caring human being.

Anything else, Brian?

-- OK. Why, Bo, are your five virtues that you mentioned any different from those that have existed since ancient Greece?

The five virtues I mentioned have existed from the moment a human being set foot on Earth. They're not different at all -- I'm not coming up with something new. My wife and I have experienced many spiritual, religious, and philosophic traditions over the past twenty-five years, and all I'm doing is consolidating them instead of making them so antagonistic toward each other.

I'm saying what they're really all about is some basic human virtues. You could rename them other things, but I'm just covering bases by saying self-honesty, courage, kindness, humor and wonder. People embodying those virtues wouldn't be killing each other over the name of God, they wouldn't be at war with each other over petty things, they wouldn't say, "I want to use all the world's resources, I don't want you to have any."

So, they're *exactly* the same virtues that realistic people have tried to embody since ancient Greece and far before. But <u>really</u> embody. I mean <u>really</u> embody. A *profound* self-honesty, not a psychological, twentieth-century self-honesty, like, "yes, I'm angry and I have a right to be;" I'm not talking about gobbledy-gook. I'm talking about profound stuff.

But why those five? Could you elaborate a little?

Well, until we're honest with ourselves we don't know what the hell's going on. That's the first requirement: Are we willing to take an honest look at our lives, at our strengths and weaknesses, hopes and disappointments, etc.?

Once we're living with a reasonable amount of self-honesty, courage naturally becomes the next challenge because self-honesty shows us things we need to change, and it usually takes courage to move beyond our old habits and limitations. A common example of this self-honesty/courage step in our culture is when somebody admits they're an alcoholic and reaches out for help.

After awhile of self-honest awareness and courageous action, we start to gain some self-respect, we start feeling a little more charitable toward ourselves because we're doing what we believe in. We like ourselves more. Our hearts soften a little. That's the beginning of the third virtue, kindness. Because we can never be genuinely kind to others until we feel kindness toward ourselves. Until then, it's kindness from the head, not from the heart.

What often happens next is: We're living with self-honesty, courage, and kindness, and we pride ourselves on doing everything so "right," we fall into "Well, aren't I special?" A little self-right-eousness creeps in. Soon we fall flat on our faces from that holier-than-thou attitude, and that's when we have the opportunity to pick up the fourth virtue, the sense of humor. In some respects, if I had to choose just one of the five, I'd feel safest with a sense of humor. We pick ourselves up, dust ourselves off, have a good laugh about human nature, and get on with our journeys.

Finally, you could be living with self-honesty, courage, kindness and humor, and be merely a well-balanced, happy, psychologically together human being. It's the fifth virtue, a sense of wonder, which keeps our journey in touch with the BIG truth which all the spiritual traditions are about. By sense of wonder, I simply mean that we never get in the position of thinking "Yeah, I know what it's all about now." Because we don't.

The wonder is what keeps us wide open to reality, because we recognize that we never know what the major events in our lives are going to be, or what's going to happen next, or whom we're going to meet, etc. All we really know is that we seem to be here right now, and the bedrock of human experience seems to have something to do with love. And you know what? That's all we need to know. We deal with that, and it makes for a great, exciting life of endless possibilities and adventures.

Brian, I thank you for your phone call. Marty, good morning, you're on the Impact program with my guest, Bo Lozoff.

-- Good morning. Bo, it's a pleasure to speak to you. I've yet to find someone such as yourself who is both a mystic and a realist. I have a couple things to point out about what you'd said about your drug experiences. I think I've had a similar experience. It's good to hear somebody mention that drugs are, can be, have been used for spiritual purposes, and yeah, it looks like there's a problem in our culture with the abuse of drugs as an escape. Yet I'd hate to see them denied from people for the purposes of the eye-opening that can come from LSD.

Well, at the same time, as I said earlier, I don't feel psychedelics are necessary for that eye-opener, but I feel we're missing the point anyway. The ingestion of a psychedelic, whether that's LSD or peyote or mescaline or hash or pot, for the purposes of spiritual expansion of consciousness, is never going to be a widespread problem in any culture, because that's a very private and serious journey. What we're experiencing as a drug epidemic is, as you said, escapism, and I think we have to look honestly at that: My God, why are so many people unhappy with their lives? Why are so many people trying to escape?

Our nation is not addressing that at all. All we're doing is locking up more people. We're saying, "Ah! the fault is the pushers, let's kill them all."

— Certainly doesn't solve the problem. It seems that the creation of drugs as being illegal creates a problem of drugs. And in making drugs illegal, it's created such a high-profit business that people who are pushing drugs are able to have such money at their fingertips for advertising that you have word-of-mouth advertising and it never would have existed with it being legal. I'm not advocating drugs, and in fact, I don't want to see people doing them. I think that as a spiritual eye-opener, yeah, but like you said, there's a point where you learn to do it on your own.

When I talk in drug rehab groups, a lot of times the staff people wind up hating my guts, but the inmates or clients relate to it perfectly, and I think I'm a very good influence against their using drugs. But the position I take is, "Number one, I want to *congratulate* you on your <u>motive</u> for taking drugs, if it was to experience something deeper than a superficial, boring, consumer consciousness. Congratulations on that."

"Number two, obviously, drugs didn't exactly do what you hoped. But the good news is that there are *natural* ways to reach something deeper; very simple ways. And so here we go."

I also tell them, "When you were stoned or drunk, if you've ever felt a moment of universal peace, of ecstasy, of oneness with all creation, never let anybody convince you that was evil or an hallucination or anything like that. You have touched a mystical reality, and that's great."

And then, I show them some ancient methods of learning how to sit still, in which we can touch that transcendent reality again. And that in fact, it's one of the purposes of life. Those people trust what I have to say, because I'm not coming in and saying, "You were misled by the Devil, you're evil, drugs got a hold on you and they wouldn't let go!" I honor and acknowledge what they did and why most of them did it. We work on refining the methodology, because drugs are not a very good way of doing that.

Let's take a couple more calls and then we'll wrap it up. I've got a couple other quick questions to ask you as well, Bo. Let's talk to Whitney. Good morning, you're on the Impact program.

Bo, why can't we make prisons more like schools? I don't under-stand why there's so many people in situations or get themselves in situations like they do, and I think also what everybody in our government should look at is maybe why are people doing these things? And the program you had on I think it was a week ago, with Dr. Joshua Weissberg, he mentioned that 82 percent of all people on death row were abused as young children. And Bo had mentioned something about that earlier as far as these people's upbringings. And I just think everyone should look at that a lot closer, especially our government.

You know, we live in an interesting culture. Your question was why can't we make prisons more like schools, and my immediate response is, well that's OK, we've made schools more like prisons.

[laughter] *That's exactly what I was thinking.*

We're just not mature enough yet, Whitney. We're an infant culture and we think we're in graduate school, but we're in kindergarten. There's nothing wrong with being in kindergarten if you know that's where you are and you don't try to drive a car. Our culture is in its infancy, yet we think we're the be-all and end-all of how to handle everything. We're terribly infantile in those ways. We don't know how to treat people who break the rules.

Well, that's a good point. I think also what you said as far as life or what you do every day is mysterious and an adventure. If people thought about that more, maybe they'd take things easier. I don't take things the easiest sometimes, and my wife would tell you that also. But I think that what you said is, it comes from a lovingkindness. And maybe it's more like human kindness. That's what the whole world should think about. World peace would be wonderful but it's — I don't know if it's inevitable or not.

Well, it can only begin to come about if Whitney and Bo and Frank, and everybody who is concerned with these questions begins to find peace in themselves and begins to become more mature than kindergarten. Then slowly, gradually, we become a society that's not completely in kindergarten. We have to become wise ourselves. That's why I'm a reminder of that internal part of the journey instead of always working externally on social change.

Whitney, I thank you for your call. Bo, thanks for coming down tonight. It was a pleasure to interview you and and spend some time. And, this is the portion of the show where you get a chance for a closing comment, if you have anything you'd like to say in passing.

I don't really have anything to say in closing except I hope, with the sheer volume of words that have transpired, that I didn't make an extremely simple message more complicated than it needs to be. All I really do is share an inspiration to turn inward, not in an obsessive, fanatic, or dogmatic way, but just to dip one toe of our consciousness into the transcendent, because even that tiny dip is enough to make all the external conditions of our lives appear in an entirely new light.

There's a certain fearlessness and power with which we walk the earth at that point, which is reminiscent of the promises of beings like Jesus and Buddha and Ram and Krishna, etc., of what a human being and what a human life can feel like. The message I often tell myself is just to keep learning to sit still and shut up.

It's not about reading a lot of books, it's not about being well-versed in sophisticated philosophies or theologies. Because they all lead to the same thing: "When are you going to learn to sit quietly, turn inward and address this mystery going on?"

Get one toe in the mystery and <u>then</u> go look at the problems of humanity. Do your part from a clear mind and an open heart, and you'll see magic take place all over. It's a very magical world; it's not depressing when you're coming from that place. You're just a part of this mysterious process going on. So that's really the simplicity of it, that's all that I share with people in prison, too.

Well, I thank you for your kind words, tonight. Goodnight.

● ● ●

Life is so generous a giver, but we, judging its gifts by their covering, cast them away as ugly, or heavy or hard. Remove the covering and you will find beneath it a living splendor, woven of love, by wisdom, with power. Welcome it, grasp it, and you touch the angel's hand that brings it to you. Everything we call a trial, a sorrow, or a duty, believe me, that angel's hand is there; the gift is there, and the wonder of an overshadowing presence.

-- Fra Giovanni, 1513 A.D.

Could there be this much pain in the spiritual journey? You mean it's not just a matter of feeling a little better every day? You cry, "I don't think I can bear that pain!" And you hear the voice of God inside you saying, "That's why it's called unbearable pain, schmuck!"

FEARLESS ADVENTURE VERSUS ENDLESS STRUGGLE

[from HKF newsletter, Spring 1989. From a talk at Church of Religious Science in Salt Lake City, 10/88. The full talk is available on a 90-minute "Talks And Discussions" tape from Human Kindness Foundation.]

If we accept two essential facts which are incontrovertible -- facts which know no turning -- then the doorway to a kind of spiritual liberation is opened, which takes full advantage of the Great Adventure, the Great Mystery.

Not the kind of spiritual life which is just about being "nice," and about trying to insulate ourselves from negative experiences by having affirmations posted all over our refrigerators. But a kind of spiritual freedom which Christ displayed on the cross, which Buddha displayed under the Bodhi tree; a kind of spiritual freedom which is far beyond our wildest imaginings when we think of living a good life. Those two essential facts are,

> 1) Our mortal selves -- our bodies and egos -- are going to die. We're all going to die. Some of us are going to die as children and some of us are going to die as very old people, and a lot of us are going to die in-between, but we're all going to die. So we don't have anything to lose in that regard. If you eat good food, you're going to die. Eat junk food, you're going to die. That's one incontrovertible fact.

> 2) The other is -- and this may offend some of you -- we're all saved. Already. We don't have to do a damn thing for God's sake. We don't have to earn our salvation, we don't have to earn our immortality, we don't have to earn brownie points for Heaven; We are all saved. Christ did that for us. Buddha did that for us. Many beings have done that for us. We are saved.

Those two simple facts -- we're all going to die, and we're all saved -- open up a certain doorway, that for a lot of us takes away all of the reasoning which has led us onto the spiritual path. Because the vast majority of us are on a religious or spiritual path because we want to in some way or other deny our death. We want to insulate ourselves from sickness, disease, old age, essential loneliness. We want to surround ourselves with positive statements and positive people and pretend that maybe all that other stuff's not going to happen, or it's at least a long way off. That's a motive of <u>fear</u> as a basis for religion or spirituality.

So if we accept the first fact, "we're all going to die," a lot of the motive for religious life begins to be eroded. And if we accept the other one, "we're all already saved," then it's like 99% of our other motivation goes down the tubes.

"Why do I have to get up early on Sunday?" "If I'm saved, why can't I be as much of a lecher, as much of a glutton, as much of a greedy slob or pig, and unkind to my neighbors, as I want to be?" And guess what? You *can* be! And you're still as saved as I am. You're still as saved as Mother Theresa.

The Divine Mother does not love you any less if you're a greedy, gluttonous, unkind pig and you die that way.

So why do any of it? Why read the books? Why wake up early on a Sunday? Why meditate? The only valid reason -- if we accept that we're all going to die and we're all already saved -- is that each of us, in our deepest hearts, houses an unbearable pain of feeling separate from God. God does not care if we unearth that pain, if we open to it and conquer that illusion, like Christ conquered it on the cross. We do it because <u>we</u> can't bear the pain of feeling separate from God. Notice I'm not saying "*being* separate from God." I'm saying "*feeling* separate from God."

We explore the spiritual life because something in us is churning like a nuclear reactor, and no matter what we do or how successful we are, no matter how many treatments we do or how many affirmations we have on our refrigerators, no matter how kind our friends are, or the great degree of longevity that runs in our genes; in our aloneness, in the quiet of the night, there's something nagging. Something's missing. That's the Buddha's First Noble Truth: Something's missing.

It's never going to be fully satiated in a church service. It's never going to be satiated by speaking gently or doing good works. What each of us is on the journey of doing at some time or other, is what Christ and Buddha, and countless other beings whose names we may know or not know, have done -- which is to <u>open</u>.

Instead of trying to become like happy horses in a pasture,

finding just the best grasses and the safest places, hoping death doesn't see us if we're under the shade of a certain tree, hoping loneliness, pain, grief somehow spare us if we're doing the right things and we're prancing around in the right areas of the meadow; instead of being like that, which comes from having no idea how _BIG_ we are, we can open up to that "bigness," which we tend to feel a lot more comfortable worshipping than becoming.

We can worship it for many, many lifetimes, but at some point we *are* going to become it, because it's going to bother us -- that unbearable pain of feeling separate from God. The unbearable pain of not being fully enlightened. The unbearable pain of pushing away what we call "negative," and clinging so fearfully to what we call "positive." The unbearable pain of keeping up all of this activity based on an illusion -- that we're small, that we're separate. That pain becomes too much for us. Then we say, "Okay God, I want the real thing, I want the Big Enchilada. And I know it's going to hurt."

I had a surprise experience this morning, just a normal day -- I mean, this doesn't happen to me every day, but it was just on a normal morning. I woke up, began getting ready to come here, and I picked up my guitar and I sang a song to God; I sang a song to the Divine Mother. And at the end of the song, a couple of faces from yesterday's prison workshops began appearing in my mind. Especially one young woman, a beautiful young woman, last night at the women's prison who talked with me afterward about feeling guilt from having murdered somebody.

So I was doing my normal kind of prayer this morning -- which loosely translated is, "God, please help!" (laughter) -- that's my normal waking prayer -- and I began to feel this young woman's pain. Then the face of a guy from the men's prison joined hers, and I began to feel his pain, for having killed his best friend. And, in my personal practice, what it's about is opening rather than closing; that's the key image. Because when we feel pain in some way, when we feel what we call negativity, the instinctive reaction is, "shut it out." It's "Okay, let's tighten up all our affirmations, let's tighten up all our positive thoughts, because we don't want to get into this."

But the genuine spiritual path has never been for people who demand a comfortable way. So when I began to feel that pain this morning, I said to myself, "Don't close down!" And I kept opening, widening my embrace like the Divine Mother widens her embrace.

You come to the Divine Mother and say, "Oh yeah, well how's this for evil: I raped my three-year-old daughter, forced her to drink tabasco sauce, and then cut her limbs off and put her in a trunk!" The Divine Mother doesn't close up and say, "Oh no!!" The Divine Mother goes, "I gotta get BIGGER to hold that one."

That's the meaning of "resist not evil;" it's knowing, "I'm big enough. I'm big enough to feel it. I'm big enough to allow it to be *exactly* what it is, without sugarcoating it or distorting it, without 'transforming' it in some fictitious new-age way in my mind."

My God, it hurts to be that big. Could there be this much pain in the spiritual journey? You mean it's not just a matter of feeling a little better every day? You cry, "I don't think I can bear that pain!" And you hear the voice of God inside you beginning to chuckle, saying "That's why it's called *unbearable* pain, schmuck!"

Do you think Christ could bear it? He cried out like a man. He cried out the unbearability of that pain. Then three days later, He said, "Here I am. We did it. We did it. It is accomplished."

So I found myself this morning in my hotel room, opening, opening... One part of my mind was saying "Oh no, John's picking me up in fifteen minutes and I'm starting to have a mystical experience." These things are so inconvenient! [laughter] And I started crying like a baby. I cried like I haven't cried in years. I was just sitting in the University Park Hotel, crying my eyes out, and then got to a point where I couldn't even -- I wasn't even able to sob, I was just sort of gagging because the pain was getting so bad.

By that point it wasn't just the woman's pain and the man's pain from the prison yesterday; it was my own pain, it was your pain, it was the pain of all of us suffering this delusion of separateness from God. It was the pain of feeling our separation, it was the pain of being cast out of the Garden of Eden. And I recognize by this point in my journey, the only way to be what I really need to be; the only way to be a gift for you, to make it worthwhile for you to wake up early this morning, the only way, as hard as it is -- as *unbearable* as it is -- is to keep opening; to go through it all, instead of pretending the pain is something other than what it is.

The punch line turns out to be, that while "agony" and "ecstasy" are two separate words, they're not two separate experiences. Because when the pain goes past bearability, when it becomes literally *unbearable* pain, you're in the ecstasy of the Christ as well; which is also what happened this morning. You realize, even at that depth of pain, there's something within that -- it's hard to find words for -- which is ecstatic because it's so *pure,* it's so full, it's so intense.

It's like something inside of you is saying, *You feel this pain because you have so much Love. There is so much Love, it breaks your heart into pieces to see yourself and all of these people on this planet in so much pain! It breaks your heart because you have so much Love.*

I just wanted to share that experience with you since it happened here in Salt Lake City. This spiritual path is about becoming free enough that, like the Divine Mother's embrace, *everything* fits within it. That's how I can go into prisons without being burned out. That's how I can meet with people who have done unspeakable things.

Your "envelope" becomes wide enough so that person sitting with you, looking in your eyes, doesn't feel like you're sitting there feeling separate, like "I have compassion for you, but you did something I could never do, and I don't understand how you could do that to somebody." Instead, somebody looks in your eyes and, "My God, I don't know how, but he *does* understand, and he's not judging me." And they can feel comfortable.

It's a wonderful experience to accept those two essential truths -- one that we're all going to die, and very quickly, by the way. If you don't think it's quickly, ask somebody on his death bed whether it seems too soon. And the other, that we're already saved. Because from those two truths, we can cultivate a fearlessness, realizing... Well, like a wonderful line from the *Mahabharata,* the Hindu holy book which the *Bhagavad Gita* comes from, where this very virtuous and righteous king, this great spiritual king named Yudhisthira, is challenged by an evil king to throw crooked dice, and the whole kingdom is at stake, and this great king is going to be banished, with his brothers, into the forests for thirteen years if he loses.

He already knows it's a crooked game, it's a rigged game. But it's not virtuous of him to deny the challenge. Somebody says to him, "Why are you doing this?" And he says, "Kingdom or forest, what's the difference? Over the next thirteen years, I'm going to experience happiness and misery, tragedy and beauty, good times and bad times, whether I roll the dice or not."

We are all at the tables in Vegas with unlimited chips, because we're all going to die and we're all saved already. There's nothing to lose and there's nothing to shoot for. There's this direct experience within us that is unsatisfied feeling separate from God. It's not somebody convincing you that you have to become this or that, that you have to develop this or that, to be a good girl, to be a good boy. There's a direct experience in us that is unsatisfied. We don't have to earn anything. Grace is free.

That can give us a wonderful fearlessness, the understanding that we can all go through life like King Yudhisthira, and our hands don't even have to be shaking on the dice.

Zen master Suzuki Roshi said, "Life is like stepping on a boat which is about to set sail and sink." [laughter] That's a *liberating* feeling! Because now, we can do anything with our lives that we feel directed to do, to open up further; to get at this pain of separateness; to open up to our power, our BIGNESS, our incredible Godliness. We can do it without <u>fear</u>, because there is nothing at stake.

When we walk into a church or a spiritual path like a gambler with his mortgage in his back pocket, and our hands trembling on the dice, and there's so much at stake, because we're unhappy, and we feel like our lives are passing us by and we really want to become better people before we die because we're afraid of what's going to happen to us then -- when there's all that fear, you know that's the person who always loses at the table.

But if we walk through life understanding that <u>everybody</u>, from sleaze to divine, is already saved, and we're all going to die; and we chart our course based on the wholeness that we want to feel <u>directly</u> -- not for any conceptual reason at all -- directly, because not feeling whole, not feeling free, not feeling fearless, is unsatisfactory to us. Then we become what is called, in many cultures, a "Spiritual Warrior," who is not clinging so hard to the positive and happy experiences and not pushing away so hard the sickness and misery.

Then, when we do a healing, for example -- well, it's a natural instinct that if you're sick you want to get better. We don't do it because we feel that sickness is negative, that sickness is bad, sickness is uncool spiritually, whatever. You know, like many of us are blaming ourselves for cancer these days. Everybody's going to die. Sickness is all right. But it's natural to want to feel better.

So *without* fear, *without* those conceptual models of embarrassment for being sick, we use whatever skills we have, which include a lot of power in our minds. We use them as well as we can, but not because we're so attached to getting well, not because that's so important -- after all, we know that at some point we're not going to get well -- but because this is what we're here to do: To live passionately and fully, as spiritual warriors, using all the tools we have, but without fear, and without denial, and with that full embrace of the Divine Mother.

That's about all I can say in twenty minutes. Thank you.

• • •

Dear Bo and Sita,

Today read your spring newsletter, "Fearless Adventure..." and it hit the spot. The spot being a pain, a voidful feeling deep within. And this when I'd just come from Mass! I tried an Amy Grant tape, no luck; how about Wanda Jackson...nothing. "Something" made me search your newsletter, which "I hadn't had the time" to read yet... then came the tears and the knowledge of what was paining me. I did unearth a bit of my pain (of which I was totally unaware -- I'm a great one for positive thinking, gratitude, affirmations, etc., etc.).

I could not bear the pain of feeling separate from God. Somehow I had a vague feeling this morning that I needed to feel closer to Jesus but "I" couldn't make it happen. And then reading Bo's words told me I was okay and on the right path (however shaky and feeble).

I'm a recovering alcoholic (9 years sober), Alanon, codependency group, Cursillista, returning-to-the-flock Catholic, etc... and believe me, this is giving me a new life. But in the past year or so (after years of fear) I've had the courage to face the fact that my two sons are in prison; had the courage to read We're All Doing Time, *the courage to become involved in one son's recovery and* therapy in prison. And the courage to say "no" to the other son (hardest of all because of my guilt and his manipulations) but still love him and pray for him. This was one of the back-burner things which was troubling me this morning.

The other was a decision of whether to accept an invitation to serve in the Peace Corps in Africa for two years. This is the dream of a lifetime, and took a year to get through paperwork, but now I know that I could not run away from my family again. My service is going to have to be right here, and that's okay.

Thank you both for opening a door -- not only for "prisoners", but for those of us prisoners outside the walls who must bear the burdens along with our sons, daughters, help carry their crosses and lighten their loads, and assume our responsibility along with the rest of society. "There but for the Grace of God."

You know, when Bo talked about "I gotta get BIGGER to hold that one" -- I am realizing that thru your book and words I am indeed getting BIGGER. I attend lifer's events (my sons are not lifers) and chat with the men at picnics, etc., and can feel compassion -- not the former fear and repulsion. I can love my sons and not their deeds. And who can judge my deeds versus theirs? I know I am capable of murder, and can lie, steal, cheat, cause pain to others...

You know, though, that you have blown away many of the concepts which I've been incorporating into my life these days -- "let's keep it positive, baby!," etc... But what you have given me to put in its place -- the prospect of becoming a "Spiritual Warrior" -- Yahoo! I am learning ways now to become more deeply, honestly involved in the lives of my family, friends, and community. Thank you.

I Love you both, J

[J died a few months after writing this letter. She had successfully "cleaned up" her life and relationships just as she wished.]

● ● ●

Dear Bo,

I have a question about your Spring '89 newsletter titled "Fearless Adventure Versus Endless Struggle." At the close of the talk you say "This is what we're here to do. To live passionately and fully...without fear, denial..." etc.

My question is, where does that conclusion come from? Is it an Ultimate Truth revealed through personal experience? If so, how do you know that it is true for each of us? Maybe it is a choice, a personal commitment on how you want to live. Maybe that is not at all what others are "here to do." Maybe many people are well aware that they do not live passionately and fully, that they are limited by fears, denial, feelings of loneliness, separation, etc., but that's okay with them; the pain of it is bearable and preferable to the effort, etc., they believe to be involved in overcoming fears, limitation, etc.

Isn't a belief that you are here to live passionately and fully the same as being "attached to getting well," and therefore not so important? What's wrong with a little fear and denial? Isn't pushing those away an avoidance, too?

Love Always, H (a psychologist)

Dear H,

I do *know* that we're here to live passionately and fully without fear and denial, etc. That's not a belief or opinion, it's awareness. Somebody standing in water doesn't believe he's wet; he's wet, and he knows that anyone else who stepped in the water would be wet, too, whether they denied it or not.

I guess that's a main difference between spirituality and psychology. Psychology tends to shy away from the idea that any truths are absolute, in favor of the idea that each of us might have a different truth. That's catchy, but it's not always true. There are universal truths which are true. Period. We can be aware or unaware of them, biased toward or against them, but they're true nonetheless.

A spiritual teacher imparts these truths with the power of personal experience. Anybody can talk the talk; and many people can write the right words. But as a teacher I must speak what I know, and as a reader or listener you have the task of feeling the power or lack of power behind it. That's how it works.

By the way, toward the end of your letter you say "what's wrong with a little fear and denial?" You misunderstood me. Nothing at all is wrong with fear and denial, just like nothing is wrong with piss or shit. They're part of the natural process of living, and we're designed to eliminate them regularly in order to be healthy and whole.

Nothing is wrong with the whole process; I'm just encouraging people not to walk around constipated. That's not the same as attachment or avoidance. I don't encourage anyone to avoid anything. I hope I've made my end a little clearer.

Love, Bo

● ● ●

Dear Bo and Sita,

Thank you for your excellent newsletter dated spring 1989. It is impossible to read your materials and remain untouched by your sincerity and commitment. In a world that seems consumed at times with greed and self-serving avarice, yours is a message of hope and an important inroad against the damaging effects of cynicism and apathy.

Because I'm an atheist, I cannot always appreciate your statements as would a tried-and-true believer, but there is still a basic goodness about what you say that resonates with my human spirit. And the fact that you are DOING something about the so-called "refuse" of society, the men and women who are incarcerated in the hell-holes we choose not to think about in America, is more than commendable. My hope is that you get many, many encouraging letters to buoy you up in this all-too-often thankless path you have chosen.

Without being argumentative, I must take issue with your statement at the beginning of your spring 1989 newsletter, in which you state that there are two FACTS which are incontrovertible, the first pertaining to the inevitability of our individual deaths, and the second statement that we are all saved.

That the first fact is true needs no discussion. All men and women who have ever lived have also died. There are no exceptions, and the FACT that no exceptions exist makes this assertion absolutely true. Your second proposition, however, is an opinion, not a fact. It cannot be proven, by evidence or logic, that anyone needs to be "saved" from anything, and as such this statement is not within the realm of fact. The fact that a concern about immortality has been in evidence in all human cultures is noteworthy. The fact that most people fear death can be demonstrated easily.

It is also a fact that just because millions of people believe (or don't believe) something neither makes that "something" true or untrue. Only careful inquiry can separate fact from opinion, and often this requires more training and objectivity than the average person possesses. That's why we rely on the entire body of scientific knowledge and the constant testing of all our assumptions before we confidently state that we have the "facts" (and even then we keep the door open for new discoveries).

Enough of my soapboxing. Whether this means anything to you or not, I may never know (unless you respond to this letter). My only hope is that you exercise great care in presenting facts -- as opposed to beliefs or opinions. We may have lot of opinions about the facts, especially as they are made apparent within our cultural reality, but their one glorious feature is that facts will be true for everyone around the world, at all times, and it makes no difference whether you believe them or not. That is the "salvation" of pure truth -- and its ultimate neutrality and amoral reality.

May your work prosper!

J

Dear J,

Thanks for all the kind sentiments about me and my work. Just wanted to respond briefly to your position about facts, beliefs and opinions. You say the "one glorious feature is that facts will be true for everyone around the world, at all times, and it makes no difference whether you believe them or not." Is that a fact?

If you and a deaf person are standing together and a loud noise erupts, is that noise a fact? The only way it would "be true for everyone" in that case is if the deaf person accepts on faith that the fact of a loud noise occurred. If you were standing with a blind person and asserted the "facts" of a blue sky, green leaves, etc., once again that "fact" would rely on his or her faith in your perception.

My perception that we're all "saved" is as clear to me as your perception of a loud noise or a blue sky. You can choose not to accept it on faith, but then, so could the deaf person deny the noise and the blind person deny the colors. So that's the predicament we're in. I could be diplomatic and say "well, it's really just my opinion," but I'd be lying. I've experienced many very real mystical phenomena and revelations of truth, and such experiences are part of my system of "facts" just as yours are yours. My perceptions certainly aren't unique; mystics and holy people through the ages have described precisely the same truths.

I share your respect for science and repeatability. The scientific method is fine for approaching many phenomena on a particular level of reality, but for you to assume that it defines every type of phenomenon on every level of reality, makes you a very religious person indeed -- your religion being science. Your religious credo is that "pure truth" exists with "ultimate neutrality and amoral reality." That's quite a statement of faith, J, certainly as much as any belief in God or Divine Providence.

But enough. I don't enjoy quibbling over words or ideas, because as you noted, our common goodness is what's important anyway (by the way, is that a fact?). If I were addressing a convention of atheists, I probably wouldn't have used the same words ("we're all saved") as I did in that church service. Yet I would have expressed much the same thing, and the atheists would have responded just as well as the Christians did. Words and even ideas aren't really what I'm expressing. I'm just trying for the goodness in me to make love with the goodness in you, and it usually works out regardless of the phraseology.

Again, thanks for your kindness and your support.

Love, Bo

● ● ●

" I saw a stone one day that could fly.
It flew because it felt no weight, while I,
I wait, and wait, and wait for such a state.
So stone-like I sit, stone-like I move,
stone-like I may even die.
But what? What's this? What bliss to realize:
' Whatever can fly, let fly.
Whatever can die, let die.'
Now smiling, I feel myself rise."

You see, one Human Being to me --
even a Bum on the street --
is worth more than all
the holy books in the world.
That's just the kind of
Guy I Am.

AN IMPATIENT LETTER TO ALL OF US FROM GOD

[from HKF newsletter, Christmas 1989]

Watch out, I think we're really starting to get on His nerves
-- Bo

DATE: *Eternity*

<u>FROM:</u> *GOD*
<u>TO:</u> *My Children on Earth*
<u>RE:</u> *Idiotic religious rivalries*

My Dear Children *(and believe me, that's all of you)*,

I consider myself a pretty patient Guy. I mean, look at the Grand Canyon. It took millions of years to get it right. And how about evolution? Boy, nothing is slower than designing that whole Darwinian thing to take place, cell by cell and gene by gene. I've even been patient through your fashions, civilizations, wars and schemes, and the countless ways you take Me for granted until you get yourselves into big trouble again and again.

But on this occasion of My Son's birthday, I want to let you know about some things that are starting to tick me off.

First of all, your religious rivalries are driving Me up a wall. Enough already! Let's get one thing straight: These are *your* religions, not Mine. I'm the Whole Enchilada; I'm beyond them all. Every one of your religions claims there's only one of Me (which, by the way, is absolutely true). But in the very next breath, each religion claims it's My favorite one. And each claims its bible was written personally by me, and that all the other bibles are man-made. Oh, Me. How do I even begin to put a stop to such complicated nonsense?

Okay, listen up now: I'm your Father *and* Mother, and I don't play favorites among My Children. Also, I hate to break it to you, but I don't write. My longhand is awful, and I've always been more of a "doer" anyway. So *all* your books, including the bibles, were written by men and women. They were inspired, remarkable people, but they also made mistakes here and there. I made sure of that, so that you would never trust a written word more than your own living Heart.

69

You see, one Human Being to me -- even a Bum on the street -- is worth more than all the holy books in the world. That's just the kind of Guy I Am. My Spirit is not an historical thing, It's alive right here, right now, as fresh as your next breath.

Holy books and religious rites are sacred and powerful, but not more so than the least of You. They were only meant to steer you in the right direction, not to keep you arguing with each other, and certainly not to keep you from trusting your own personal connection with Me.

Which brings Me to My next point about your nonsense: You act like I need you and your religions to stick up for Me or "win souls" for My Sake. Please, don't do Me any favors. I can stand quite well on my own, thank you. I don't need you to defend Me, and I don't need constant credit. I just want you to be good to each other.

And another thing: I don't get all worked up over money or politics, so stop dragging My name into your dramas. For example, I swear to Me that I never threatened Oral Roberts. I never rode in any of Rajneesh's Rolls Royces. I never told Pat Robertson to run for president, and I've never *ever* had a conversation with Jim Bakker, Jerry Falwell, or Jimmy Swaggart! Of course, come Judgement Day, I certainly intend to...

The thing is, I want you to stop thinking of religion as some sort of loyalty pledge to Me. The true purpose of your religions is so that *you* can become more aware of *Me*, not the other way around. Believe Me, I know you already. I know what's in each of your hearts, and I love you with no strings attached. Lighten up and enjoy Me. That's what religion is best for.

What you seem to forget is how mysterious I Am. You look at the petty little differences in your scriptures and say, "Well, if *this* is the Truth, then *that* can't be!" But instead of trying to figure out My Paradoxes and Unfathomable Nature -- which, by the way, you <u>never</u> will -- why not open your hearts to the simple common threads in every religion?

You know what I'm talking about: Love and respect everyone. Be kind. Even when life is scary or confusing, take courage and be of good cheer, for I Am always with you. Learn how to be quiet, so you can hear My Still, Small Voice (I don't like to shout). Leave the world a better place by living your life with dignity and gracefulness, for you are My Own Child. Hold back nothing from life, for the parts of you that can die will surely die, and the parts that can't, won't. So don't worry, be happy (I stole that last line from Bobby McFerrin, but who do you think gave it to him in the first place?)

Simple stuff. Why do you keep making it so complicated? It's like you're always looking for an excuse to be upset. And I'm very tired of being your main excuse. Do you think I care whether you call me Yahweh, Jehovah, Allah, Wakantonka, Brahma, Father, Mother, or even The Void or Nirvana? Do you think I care which of My Special Children you feel closest to -- Jesus, Mary, Buddha, Krishna, Mohammed or any of the others? You can call Me and My Special Ones any name you choose, if only you would go about My business of loving one another as I love you. How can you keep neglecting something so simple?

I'm not telling you to abandon your religions. Enjoy your religions, honor them, learn from them, just as you should enjoy, honor, and learn from your parents. But do you walk around telling everyone that your parents are better than theirs? Your religion, like your parents, may always have the most special place in your heart; I don't mind that at all. And I don't want you to combine all the Great Traditions into One Big Mess. Each religion is unique for a reason. Each has a unique style so that people can find the best path for themselves.

But My Special Children -- the ones your religions revolve around -- all live in the same place (My Heart) and they get along perfectly, I assure you. The clergy must stop creating a myth of sibling rivalry where there is none.

My Blessed Children of Earth, the world has grown too small for your pervasive religious bigotries and confusion. The whole planet is connected by air travel, satellite dishes, telephones, fax machines, rock concerts, diseases, and mutual needs and concerns. Get with the program! If you really want to help Me celebrate the birthday of My Son Jesus, then commit yourselves to figuring out how to feed your hungry, clothe your naked, protect your abused, and shelter your poor. And just as importantly, make your own everyday life a shining example of kindness and good humor. I've given you all the resources you need, if only you abandon your fear of each other and begin living, loving, and laughing together.

Finally, My Children everywhere, remember whose birth is honored on December 25th, and the fearlessness with which He chose to live and die. As I love Him, so do I love each one of you. I'm not really ticked off, I just wanted to grab your attention because I hate to see you suffer. But I gave you Free Will, so what can I do now other than to try to influence you through reason, persuasion, and a little old-fashioned guilt and manipulation? After all, I *Am* the original Jewish Mother. I just want you to be happy, and I'll sit in The Dark. I really Am, indeed, I swear, with you always. Always. Trust In Me.

Your One and Only, *GOD*

• • •

Dear Bo and Sita,

I sure wish you guys were Christians! I love your sense of humor, outgoing compassion and love for the prisoners, and the fact that you refuse to do "aggressive" fundraising!

I'm a convert to Christ from many years of "New-Ageism" -- a journey which included much meditation and study of Hinduism, Buddhism and Sufism (in that order, more or less). How well do I remember the days of grooving on Ram Dass! His books, like Grist for the Mill *and* Miracle of Love, *were practically scripture to me at one point. And I'm grateful for the insights I got in those days, most especially the understanding that material things don't matter much; that the unseen world is* at least *as real as the world our senses perceive; that God is love, and He is all that really matters after all; and a concept of the spiritual heart in each person which needs to be purified.*

However, I now wish I'd become a Christian long before I did...It took being shaken up by a dangerous practice of kundalini yoga (which took me into realms of the occult I wished I'd never entered!); and the gradual awareness that the supposedly high teachers in the Tibetan, Hindu and Sufic traditions that I'd come in contact with (some of them very *highly and widely revered) were not only ordinary (more or less) mortals but actually lacked basic integrity in many cases although they were psychic magicians.*

Now I know that love for Jesus and the way of the cross brings peace, cleansing, and is the antidote to man's pride and the endless illusions and misery that pride fosters (maya, if you will). And I'm concerned, Bo and Sita, that many of your prisoners may end up in the realm of the occult, without the lifeline that turning to God in Jesus Christ provides. So, sadly, I feel I can't support you in your teaching.

I do believe in the love you hold in your hearts for the prisoners, and the compassion. May God bless you for it!

Love in Christ Jesus, Grace

Dear Grace,

That's quite a letter you wrote! But the thing that's amazing, Grace (sorry, couldn't resist it) is that somehow you don't understand that I'm a very good Christian and love Christ as you do. You're welcome to stay on our mailing list or be taken off, as you requested, but who gave you the authority to determine who is Christian and who isn't? It certainly wasn't Jesus, because He's alive in my heart, and finds no fault with my work or my writings.

The most ironic thing is that you speak from a fundamentalist perspective made popular by people like Jim Bakker, Jimmy Swaggart, Jerry Falwell and so forth, yet then you talk about the "new age" and "eastern" teachers you met who lacked integrity. My God, isn't it clear by now that teachers in every tradition can be pure or impure??

As for your occult and kundalini experiences which shook you up, I must point out that there is *no* realm of experience beyond the reach of Christ. I have had such experiences, with Christ firmly leading me through all fear and weirdness. Those realms aren't "unholy" or out of bounds; they apparently were just ill-timed for you, or perhaps simply too shocking to your system.

Believe me, if you continue to love Christ, you'll be led through those very same realms before it's all over. Did you think that Christianity would be a safe or easy way? It's about losing oneself entirely, about conquering all fear and even death itself -- just like every other spiritual tradition.

The crucial thing you seem not to have grasped through your long search is that every tradition leads to one state of being; there is none other than the One. It's fine for you to relate to that One through Jesus, but you miss it by a mile when you draw a magic circle around yourself and say that no one else sees the "Right One."

I mean, take an honest look again at your letter. Can't you see how ridiculous it sounds to tell us that we're wonderful people with a lot of love, and "I sure wish you guys were Christians!?" What do you think Christ was trying to tell us when He said that many will come in His name, but the real Christians were the ones "doing My Father's work?" Wake up, Grace. Sita and I are just doing exactly what He asked us all to do -- loving one another as He loves us.

In His Love, Bo

● ● ●

Dear Bo, Sita, and all God's family,

I have been trying to embrace both Christianity and also, hatha yoga. I have been trying to figure out how they are similar and how they can be yoked together to accomplish the end results. How do you work the Eastern in without knocking the life out of the other?

If Jesus Christ is our means of salvation and has taken our karma upon himself, why must we work out our karma through all these spiritual practices, when the sole purpose of the practices is to be liberated and set free? If we do this are we not rejecting the salvation of the Lord Jesus by means of the cross and the blood which covers all our sins (karma), and sets us free? Why dwell so much on this body anyway if it is only going to decay in the end?

I am not saying one is right and the other wrong. I would love to embrace both, if I knew how to do this and not be denying the finished works of our Lord Jesus Christ.

Also, if there is no devil as depicted in the Bible, then who took Jesus upon a high pinnacle and showed him all the kingdoms of this world? I'm sorry if I sound like a rattle-brain, but God has dropped this in my heart and will not rest until I find out the answers.

God bless you all, J

Dear J,

You said in your letter that God has dropped this confusion in your "heart," but what I read in your letter is just confusion of a busy mind. Your heart knows that there is absolutely no conflict between the blessed saviour Jesus and any other path which helps you to feel more whole and in control of your life.

It's true that Jesus attained salvation for all of us. We're all already saved. But there's a difference between being saved, and being free enough to enjoy it. Many people who have been "born again" become very depressed when they see that their lives don't automatically change as they had expected. We *are* saved, but we also need to work in order to rid ourselves of all the thought patterns and habits which prevent us from experiencing it.

There's only one religion: God. A Hindu who rejects Christ hasn't found it. A Christian who rejects Buddha or Krishna, hasn't found it. It's almost insulting to the limitless powers of the Divine to try to solve arguments over historical words and facts as if we can tie up all the loose ends like a television plot. Our spiritual journey is so much greater and more wondrous than this constant competitiveness between religions!

Your real journey is an opening into the wordless, not to solve contradictions like "Is there a Satan or isn't there?" With your tremendous spiritual drive, you could rise above that level of development forever -- right now -- if you choose to do so. Just let it all go, and turn inward into the quietness where you've always known the Truth, and where Jesus isn't an historical figure, but rather a living, powerful presence hanging out with you just like He promised when He said "I am with you always."

If you use every moment of your life trying to be open to the Holy Spirit, using *any* methods you wish, all of Jesus's promises to you will be fulfilled.

Love, Bo

● ● ●

If we could just love one another as much as we say we love Him, I suspect there wouldn't be so much trouble in the world, would there?

-- Eva LaGallienne, in the film "Resurrection"

The "New Age" culture has become the largest, wealthiest pool of consumer suckers in history.
We're P.T. Barnum's wildest fantasies come true: consumers who not only believe everything somebody might claim about their teaching or their product, but who don't even blame anybody when things go wrong!

WHAT IN THE NAME OF GOD?

(condensed from <u>The Sun</u> magazine, #99, Jan. 1984)

No New is Good New

Creeping steadily toward my forties, I find myself in a peculiar position. On one hand, I'm part and parcel of the "New Age": I'm director of the Prison-Ashram Project, have studied with swamis, teachers, and masters, have taught meditation and yoga for a decade, performed many years of disciplines and diets, lived in ashrams, communes, forests and school buses, gone crazy and gone sane, worn long hair, short hair, no hair ... get the picture?

I certainly sound like a "New Age" person, don't I? And this isn't the part where I amuse you with my re-entry into society as a successful stockbroker; no, I'm still out here in the bush, threading my way through the Mysteries. If anything, I appreciate more than ever the richness of the mystical, the indescribable. It's at the center of everything I do.

On the other hand, I find a few things bugging me as the years roll by. For one thing, the term "New Age" sounds ridiculous and arrogant, as if we're the first people to reach for wholeness, or the hippest people to ever walk the Earth. It embarrasses me. We're not "on the verge" of anything; there's nothing new going on. We're all just doing what we can, like earnest men and women have done throughout history.

Maybe a few years ago the words "New Age" seemed useful to help people get together and to encourage understandings which were fragile or embryonic, but now the very same words only separate and condescend. We don't need a rallying banner to set us apart from anyone else; we can't afford it, if what we're after is *real* wholeness. By calling something "new," we not only belittle the spiritual awareness of people in the past, but we also splinter ourselves in present-day society rather than advance the whole.

Worse still, any such banner tends to lump together a lot of people and activities that don't belong together; it becomes a convenient label for profiteers, megalomaniacs and mad-dogmatics who have discovered how to use space-age communications and computers to manipulate people toward their own ends. In the name of wholeness, such "New Age" hustlers have led us into more painful, fragmented partialness time and time again, which brings me to my second gripe.

Gullible's Travels

Hands down, the clearest ethic of the "New Age" has been to appreciate the diversity of all paths to the One, which of course, sounds one-derful. It's the stuff of non-judging, openness, tolerance, harmony; right on. But how long have we been distrusting our God-given gut feelings in the guise of "not judging?" The "New Age" culture has become the largest, wealthiest pool of consumer suckers in history. We're P.T. Barnum's wildest fantasies come true: consumers who not only believe everything somebody might claim about their teaching or their product, but who don't even *blame* anybody when things go wrong! ("*Well, it was terrible for me, but I'm sure it's just perfect for some people.*") After all, who are we to judge, right?

Wrong! We've been throwing out the baby with the bathwater. To avoid being judgmental, we have set aside our vital skills of discrimination. We have allowed a high-powered marketplace of teachers, schools, and products to thrive without ever being challenged or critiqued. The pure and impure have succeeded equally well because we have copped out on our responsibility to evaluate or distinguish between them. Even book and movie reviews in the new-age publications are generally in glowing, "uplifting" terms. Doesn't a book ever stink? Isn't that worth mentioning?

Openness to others is wonderful, but it's only *half*-openness. We also need to be open to our own honest feelings. Why do we forget that our hunches and instincts come from God, too? Our own consciences -- that deepest sense of right and wrong -- may be our closest touch-point to God. Sure it's subtle, very tricky, to weed out our true gut feelings from our busy judgmental thoughts, but it's a required course.

Ramakrishna, a great saint, taught that it's just as necessary to use keen discrimination as it is to give up judging. Discrimination *is* wisdom; we can't get anywhere without it. And we certainly can't wait until we're enlightened before we share our opinions with each other.

One time many years ago I lay awake all night in a motel

room with paper-thin walls, listening to the amorous passions of a famous swami having noisy sex with one of his followers. The swami was supposedly celibate, preached chastity, and made many public statements about the purity of his own lifestyle. As bizarre as this sounds, I was so true to my new-age ethic that I convinced myself for three years that maybe he was teaching her a profound *pranayam* (breathing technique), although every fiber of my being really knew what was going on.

Three years later the young lady left him, in despair and anguish over the hypocrisy in which she allowed herself to become a pawn. How unworthy, how separate from God, I must have felt, to have denied my own senses so fully!

Quack Quack

There's an old saying: "If it looks like a duck, walks like a duck, and smells like a duck, then maybe it's a duck." At some point we have to begin calling things as we see them, realizing that of course we'll turn out to be mistaken sometimes, but that's okay as long as we don't pretend to be infallible. Jesus encouraged us to be trusting, but he also said to be as clever as foxes. Meher Baba said that following a false teacher is like letting a madman sit on your throat with a razor. The Buddha told us not to accept teachings based on what other people say, or on what the teacher claims or promises, or on the enthusiasm of others, but rather solely on the basis of our own gut feelings, our own personal experiences.

I'm not talking about being cynical or closed-minded. But we've got to appreciate that the "New Age" is not immune to corruption, faddism, fundamentalism, empire-building, and delusion.

In any age, a variety of appealing fads take place alongside genuine spiritual evolution. The decision to surrender to a teaching or teacher is not one to be taken lightly. I'm not suggesting that we only look for things that feel "good" or which we can understand; not at all. Feeling "right" is very different from feeling "good."

Often the very best teachings are those which rip us apart, force us into our pain and weaknesses, and push us past our rigid models of how holy people should look or act, or what our spiritual journey should be like. But as Mike Harper, an inmate at

Georgia State Prison, wrote recently:

> *My mind is open, my Spirit seeking light, but not so gullible as to embrace any and every philosophy stumbled across. Not every light you see is the coming of dawn; it may be just some bum firing up his stogie.*

Which Came First, the Duck or the Egg?

It's an interesting little bit of social anthropology to reflect on how some of the current spiritual empires may have come about.

Almost a million seekers have bought and treasured Ram Dass' monumental book, *Be Here Now,* since it was published in 1969. To legions of us who had struggled through the psychedelic era and were a half-step away from abandoning our last shred of faith in anything greater, *Be Here Now* was a lightning bolt of wisdom and grace. Its purity, relevance, and spiritual power provided a lot of the momentum for our "New Age" subculture.

Much of that power came from Ram Dass' account of finding his Guru, Neem Karoli Baba (known simply as "Maharaj-ji," a common title of respect in India). Through the pages of his book, we witnessed the transformation of Richard Alpert, Ph.D., into Ram Dass -- a *bhakta*, or lover of God. We shared the most painful experiences of his ego, of the limitations of his mind, and we came away with renewed hope for our own transformations.

But it was inevitable that we would also pick up some *new* limiting models, like the enticing scenario of sitting at the feet of an enlightened being, a genuine Christ. How wonderful it would be to have such a saint chide us, tease us, force us beyond and beyond, all the while heaping divine love upon us as we had never experienced before. How lucky Ram Dass was!

But Neem Karoli himself wouldn't cooperate. As soon as a few hundred Westerners tracked him down as a result of *Be Here Now*, Neem Karoli Baba died. Such interesting timing, too, since some Indians say that he had been in that same body for about three hundred years. He left the stage just when the scene around him became worldwide, and he firmly instructed Ram Dass not to have any ashrams or disciples. Ram Dass was able to lecture and love and write and teach, but he was to leave each person more independent, not more bound.

What happened next? Swamis and yogis came to the West as

they had for years, but now what they found were hordes of us who were deeply yearning to experience what Ram Dass had felt at the feet of a real-live Guru, a living Christ.

The word *swami* is a Hindu religious title analogous to a priest; it describes a man who has renounced normal worldly life in order to minister to people's spiritual needs. The word *yogi* is much more vague; it can be self-applied by anyone who feels he or she (*yogini* for a female) lives fully within the practice of any form of yoga.

Neither *swami* nor *yogi* imply enlightenment, no more than *priest* or *minister*. These are quite different from the sacred word *Guru*, which should be used solely to describe a true saint, a liberated master.

But the swamis and yogis wore long robes and looked like God, and were very nice. Some of them had a lot of power and wisdom, some were very eloquent. So we nearly raped them into being Gurus in our own re-enactments of *Be Here Now* (maybe *Be There Then*?). We insisted on calling them "Guru" and treating them as saints, and many of them didn't protest.

So we got our robes and beads and instructions and enjoyed living out our fantasies, but there is a serious price to pay when we go around inviting spiritual teachers to be Christs. Jesus left the stage early on, as soon as he had gotten his message across. Neem Karoli Baba often denied his powers and yelled at people who told others of his miracles.

Ramana Maharshi, another modern saint, said that the only purpose for a Guru is to awaken faith in a few disciples; when that's done the Guru can leave his body. At the time of his own death, a disciple cried, "Oh Master, don't leave us!" Ramana Maharshi looked surprised and replied, "Where could I go?"

Those Gurus were very different than the teachers we have ensconced in luxury villas, private airplanes, limousines and bodyguards, and complex multinational corporations. It hurts to think how many of us have settled for quasi-gurus, and keep blaming ourselves for the fact that they haven't advanced us as we had hoped.

Jao! Jao!

If we read *Be Here Now* carefully, we may notice that as idyllic as Ram Dass' Guru-story sounds, he spent much more time stumbling about on his own than at the feet of Maharaj-ji. Maharaj-ji's most oft-used word was *Jao!*, which means "Go away!"

Like Jesus and Ramana Maharshi and countless other saints, Neem Karoli seemed to be trying to get a point across: "Go away; go get happy and sad, wise and confused; go get corrupted and ashamed and repentant and angry; go mix and mingle, live anywhere, do anything; Love everyone; I am with you always."

Hasn't it always been the same message? It leaves room for us to grow and learn, to become hermits and stockbrokers and potheads and teachers and police and parents and the whole range of human possibilities. And at those times when we despair, when we sit brokenhearted and empty of all but the thinnest sliver of faith, we can reach inward to the Guru and discover the tender quiet guidance which we usually go to great pains to ignore.

Christ, Neem Karoli, Meher Baba, Buddha, Ramana Maharshi, Ananda Mayee Ma, Mother Mary and many others are available to all of us just as much as to the people who may have sat at their feet. Meeting such a being in the body may or may not happen to any of us; only God knows. But imitating such a meeting -- and expressing absolute surrender to one who is *not* truly free -- corrupts that person as well as ourselves.

Think about the various organizations boasting "Gurus." Can any of them *afford* to say "Jao!"? With mortgages, staff salaries, retreat centers and ambitious plans for expansion which require millions of dollars to support, can they encourage self-reliance? Can they be objective about sending us out into the open world?

I Live in Every Heart

True Gurus awaken our own indestructible connection to God -- a connection which can hold up in the streets of Calcutta or a beautiful countryside ashram, in a Manhattan penthouse or at the hands of a Salvadoran death squad. Like mother birds, they kick us out of the nests so we can discover that there's no "cold, cruel world" out there. In every language they have told us, "I live in every heart." It's a wonderful day when we finally get the message.

• • •

There wouldn't be such a thing as counterfeit gold
if there were no real gold somewhere.

-- Sufi Proverb

We don't do spiritual work to get closer to God; there's no distance in the first place. We do spiritual work to become more aware, so we can enjoy the depths of this closeness.

NO SECOND THING...

[from Human Kindness Foundation newsletter, Fall 1987]

> *There is Spirit alone in this Universe. There is no*
> *second thing in existence.* -- Krishna

I did some workshops -- both in and out of prison -- in Alberta, Canada, recently. I make it a practice not to think ahead about what I'm going to say. That way, the talks express whatever it is that's most alive for me at the time.

In Alberta, what came to life was Krishna's statement above -- that everything, every part of our lives, everything beautiful and ugly, every nuisance, fear, joy, and struggle, is Spirit. There are no other items on the menu.

In a dream, what is everything made of? Just dream-stuff, mind-stuff. The people, the props, the places, how could any part of our dream be made from anything other than our own essence? It's just our minds creating and expressing themselves in those many forms. That's exactly what Krishna is talking about, but from the view of God as the dreamer.

A mother in Edmonton asked how she could devote herself to her spiritual life amid all the demands her kids made on her time. But her kids and their demands *are* Spirit; that *is* her spiritual life. A musician in Calgary wondered how to better balance her worldly life and spiritual life. Balance what? Who separated them in the first place?

A yoga teacher was concerned about his beer-guzzling couch-potato friends who aren't living spiritually. But their lives are just as spiritual as ours; what else could they be? Popcorn and beer are made of spirit too!

Don't get me wrong; I'm not saying it doesn't matter what we do. Not at all. Though everything is spirit, there are natural laws to this spirit, and we can do easy time or hard time depending on our own actions. Both the seeker and the couch-potato are pure Spirit, and their lives are both spiritual, but the seeker is aware of this and therefore is trying to live more in harmony with how the whole thing works. The couch-potato is pretty much on automatic pilot, which is not very satisfying in the long run.

Living a lazy life, avoiding challenges and inspiration, satisfying only our crudest whims and hungers, is like owning a priceless work of art and using it as a dartboard. Still, each person must be given the dignity to make such decisions for himself. The couch-potato isn't any further away from God than you or I. How far away can God be when everything is spirit?

There's so much power to this teaching! It can lighten us up tremendously. We can stop judging ourselves and others so harshly. We can stop struggling as if we're always coming from behind. We can give up all those suffocating fears which make us think we'd become lost souls if we were to allow ourselves to laugh or relax for a few minutes.

Best of all, we can let go of the false notion that our spiritual work is some sort of obligation on our parts, and instead see more clearly that it's a joy of the highest order. In other words, we don't do all this work to get closer to God; there's no distance in the first place. We do spiritual work to become more aware, so we can enjoy the depths of this closeness.

With the quiet awareness we can develop through practices like meditation, the truth of this can sink all the way in: **Everything is spirit.** What a difference it makes! Not so much to the details of things that happen to us, but rather the entire "us" to whom those things happen.

For example, a few minutes ago Sita read me a letter from a new 19-year-old prison friend who wrote, "My whole life just seemed to fall apart in one week...I lost my mother, stepfather, an ear, a very pretty girlfriend, and my freedom."

Our hearts tear open for him, not just for the circumstances themselves, but even more for the hopelessness he's feeling. If his deepest attitude could know that this is all Spirit, that there is no other thing going on, then the pain softens even in the middle of all the crises. It doesn't wipe it all away like a fairy tale, but it does mean that these aren't accidents, or random curses from an unloving universe, nor cruel punishments from a judgemental God.

A timeless spiritual journey is taking place, taking him through terrible pain and frightening challenges, through confusion and hope and despair, often teaching him the painful results of his own poor decisions -- but a perfect journey nonetheless, one which is slowly leading him to total enlightenment.

This is the coming together of God the Father and the Divine Mother. The Father throws spears at us, and the Mother reminds us, "Don't duck, don't run, don't hide, stand straight and they'll pass right through you, my child." It's all a dream, a cosmic adventure, which has something to do with developing fearlessness, compassion, and respect for every experience.

This all-embracing receptivity of the Divine Mother is so hard for us to deal with. The Mother opens Her arms in an infinite embrace. We think She won't embrace our bad thoughts, our sick deeds, our guilt and laziness and selfishness and fantasies and cruelties; but the Mother's hug just gets larger and larger. It embraces it all. All the love, and all the killing and senselessness; every rotten thing we've ever done; the hug just keeps widening.

We throw something at Her like "Aha, what about Hitler?!; what about Ethiopia?", and the hug just widens a little more to consume Hitler, to consume all the starvation and misery, all our shame and fear, in Her Love. It shuts out nothing. There is Spirit alone; Nothing lies outside the Mother's embrace.

And that embrace is within each of our hearts. That's the power which frightens us so much.

This idea of taking courage and embracing life shouldn't be confused with the pop-spirituality being marketed today. There seems to be a tremendous attachment to positiveness -- affirmations, prosperity, good health, world peace -- which is very sweet and well-motivated, but very attached. It's like standing on one leg; we're too easily knocked over by a strong wind.

It has never been true that external behavior or achievements are what the game is all about. I get all these spritual promo's in the mail that say things like "Ten Ways a Spiritual Person Should Act," or "Affirmations for Perfect Health and Prosperity," "Visualize World Peace."

But be honest with yourself: Deep in your bones, doesn't it always feel artificial, even a little creepy, to be around a group of people who are so immersed in one of those positive-thinking, affirmation-projecting, big-brother-is-loving-you trips? Honestly, now. You look around and see a group of wonderful human beings who were created with unique passions, personalities, likes and dislikes, and yet they're all smiling alike, talking alike, trying to think alike. That's such a waste!

Maybe it's not as destructive as throwing darts at the priceless painting, but it's sort of like hanging it on the wall at ankle-height. It hurts to see so many thousands of people falling into a yuppie-ish "spiritual growth industry" which is like a giant sausage factory that turns our spiritual spark into conformity. That's just not what the profound spiritual mysteries are really about.

Some people who read this are going to want my head on a platter for including "world peace" in my examples. After all, what idiot could be against world peace? It's not that I'm against it. I just see it differently. First of all, it seems to me that the only lasting world peace would be a by-product, not a goal. It's what occurs when every individual in the world has found personal peace. Political peace couldn't last otherwise, because new, unpeaceful people would sooner or later come to power and screw things up.

Secondly, I don't feel a sense of drama or urgency about the possible destruction of our planet, because it's been clear for a long time that the planet, beautiful as it is, can only be temporary. Whether the sun destroys us in three billion years or nuclear weapons do the job in three days, either way we have to understand that even the planet is just a circumstance, subject to change. It doesn't take priority over the inner work, the work of tapping into that which is beyond all change and form.

I don't mean to sound as if I'm suggesting people shouldn't work for peace, or that all affirmations or positive-thinking are foolish. I work for peace. I do self-healing. I enjoy feeling positive. It's the most natural thing in the world to try to stay in good health and try to keep the planet alive, the environment clean, and all the other good things we believe in.

But we can do these things with or without *attachment*. And attachment, no matter how noble, will ultimately add to our suffering rather than relieve it. Attachment prevents us from seeing the truth. Attachment makes us forget that our true nature is beyond all change and that every outcome of our efforts, win lose or draw, is equally spiritual.

That's the wonderful punch line of the joke. That's the whole

Bhagavad Gita, Koran, Old Testament and New Testament right there: *Do your best, work as hard as you can for the good of all, but remember that the results are My department. Don't get too lost in the dream.*

A dear friend who died of cancer a few years ago was a devotee of a yogi who teaches that all disease is "dis-ease", which means if she could only figure out what she was "doing wrong," the cancer would go away. She was so pure, yet for years she felt a sense of shame for having cancer. I hate that teaching. It makes people blame themselves for being sick and even for dying.

It also ignores the fact that many great saints have died from diseases like cancer or diabetes, including Ramakrishna, Suzuki Roshi, Ramana Maharshi, and Neem Karoli Baba. Any one of them could have healed themselves.

Part of the problem is that we tend to confuse the wrapping with the goods. Let's say Susie Jones walks out in the woods one day and sits under a tree eating artichokes. Let's say, for whatever cosmic reasons going back millions of years, she gets totally enlightened that day, and when she comes back home everybody can see that she's got a light around her the size of Chicago.

Within a week there would be thousands of us sitting under trees eating artichokes. And once a year on that day there would be artichoke celebrations and all sorts of rituals. Little kids would be wearing t-shirts saying "My parents sat under Susie Jones' tree and all I got was this lousy t-shirt." That particular species of tree would become holy. We'd wind up killing people on the other side of the world who aren't interested in hearing about Susie Jones. Teachers would spring up all over the place charging $300 per weekend to help us look and act more like Susie.

But Susie's enlightenment may not have had anything to do with the tree or the artichokes or what she was wearing or her personality. The best way we can come to the same point is not by imitating or worshipping her, but by continuing to find ourselves. Like the Buddha said, "Don't follow in my footsteps; instead, seek what I sought."

And what the enlightened ones have sought is a state of truth, not a smile-face personality or a formula for behavior. In Calgary recently, I said something negative about the Harmonic Convergence hysteria, and a guy raised his hand and said "I don't mean to be confrontive, but...", and proceeded to argue with what I had said.

The difference of opinion was fine, but what tickled me was "I don't mean to be confrontive." The truth was, he *did* mean to be confrontive. He didn't like what I said, and he wanted me to know that. And that's perfectly okay! How can we learn about ourselves if we avoid all conflict? We don't have to pull out knives or beat each other, but neither do we need to pretend that we're not arguing when we are. Who ever said that's the "spiritual way?"

We can keep our minds clear enough to argue, even passionately, without forgetting to respect each other; without forgetting that we are all spirit, and our honest differences are spirit too.

Trying to live a positive life is one thing, but lying to ourselves is another. We've become so afraid of negativity that we twist ourselves up in mental/verbal knots rather than face it openly with a sense of adventure. During a workshop some years ago, a lady interrupted me and said, "Excuse me, Bo, but you just used the word 'problem'. In our ashram we don't use that word; we say 'growth opportunity' instead."

Yecchh! How would you like to live in that ashram? The thing is, when we really know that every problem is an opportunity, then we don't need to switch words. This journey is not about being afraid of words, it's about opening so wide that our definitions take on a deeper understanding. Like when Jesus said, "See, I shall make all things new!"

So with our deepest understandings, we can once again say things simply, like "Bobby died" instead of "Bobby shed his earthly body but his eternal soul is still with us." Isn't that a relief?

Every person's path is unique; we are all pioneers. Our freedom comes from turning inward honestly enough to see the truth, and then taking the courage to live our lives in line with what we see.

The point is simply that life is a mysterious and wondrous spiritual journey in all its forms from the hideous to the sublime. And I freely admit, that includes all the popular teachings about affirmations and prosperity and positive-thinking that I've just trashed. But the journey also includes my criticisms and humor toward those teachings, and your reactions one way or another.

It includes whether we get paroled, whether we drive a Yugo or a Rolls, whether Johnny gets better or dies of cancer, whether we make a million bucks or die in the streets. It's a big journey, and it doesn't run out of room.

And in all honesty, life is a much greater adventure this way, because we leave ourselves wide open on both feet rather than standing on one and spending all our effort just trying to stay up. It's a much richer experience when we don't all have the same personality and we see that no matter what we may learn from others, we have to make most of our decisions on our own.

Let's not settle for a whitewashed plastic copy of our enlightenment when we can go for broke toward the real thing. What is there to be afraid of? Win, lose or draw, *There is Spirit alone in this universe; there is no second thing in existence.*

● ● ●

Bo and Sita,

I liked what you said, Bo, in the newsletter about positive thinking groups and "working" for world peace. It's always good to hear someone else speak your own thoughts.

But I was surprised at your comments about not being responsible for our own situation as in the case of the woman with cancer, who had been told it was "dis-ease" and felt guilty. Just because we may have created the illness or condition in this or a prior lifetime, there's no reason to feel guilty. We only create what we need, whether it's a karmic debt, a catharsis of some sort, or just an opportunity to understand and minister. If I'm not responsible for my circumstances, I want to complain!

Thanks for sharing your thoughts, K

Dear K,

I think the main differences between you and me on this issue of responsibility and creating or not-creating illness, would be semantic rather than substantive. I surely agree that we create it all, if you want to look at the largest picture which goes back many lifetimes and so forth. But why stop there either? One more level out, and there's only ONE of us anyway, and no words at all.

It seems to me that once we trust our deepest understandings, we can feel free to use ordinary language, with respect for its limitations and benefits. When I say my friend didn't create her cancer, I mean in this lifetime, at any level of choice, she didn't bring this on; and so needn't burden herself with the misguided distortions of pop-spirituality, e.g., if she could only see where she went wrong, she could heal herself.

From where I sit, the most basic misconception of all is the one no one mentions: What's wrong with cancer in the first place? The viewpoint which evaluates spirituality from a basis of good health is already off track. So in my opinion the whole debate is guaranteed to go straight downhill from that flawed beginning.

Shiva looks out at us with His bottomless soft eyes like honey, with a loving smile and even laughter as we go through the illusion of cancer, diabetes, Altzheimer's and so forth. Everyone dies of something, and it doesn't matter what form that takes. As you pointed out, it takes the form we can most benefit by. That's why I say, the differences between you and me are more semantic than anything else.

The reasons for my comments in the newsletter, though, aren't semantic. Many people are immersed in delusions perpetuated by yuppie-ized treatments of the ancient truths. We're all spiritual kindergartners, and yet we have fellow infants like Werner Erhard and many others who truly think they're all grown up and understand what it is Christ knew on the cross or Buddha knew after sitting motionless for 27 days.

So I argue against that with the most ordinary terms I can use, from one kindergartner to another. I understand what you say about larger pictures, but that's not so relevant to what I'm trying to point out; it's too confusing and doesn't yield enough benefit to get into it.

It's like Don Juan's *controlled folly.* We can't do what we came here to do if we keep reminding ourselves that we created every moment of it. In a sense, we came here to *forget* that, so we can develop the courage and so forth that comes from dealing with ordinary consciousness.

Let me know if there are still wrinkles in this; It's nice to have something to say to you besides "Thanks" for your wonderfully loyal support for so many years.

Your friend, Bo

Dear Bo,

That was an unexpected treat to get such thoughtful feedback from you, for I know you're continuously busy with prison correspondence. The only "wrinkle" for me was in your statement: "We can't do what we came here to do if we keep reminding ourselves that we created every moment of it. In a sense we came here to forget that, so we can develop the courage and so forth that comes from dealing with ordinary consciousness."

I don't see how knowing that we are operating within universal law could keep us from developing courage. Knowing that I am experiencing what I need to find my way back doesn't keep me from dealing with pain, frustration or distress -- but it does make it easier to accept, even embrace, and to see the humor you so wisely point to.

Ram Dass said we must be able to have compassion without being sucked into the fire -- be of two minds so to speak. Until that time I was unable to face suffering without recoiling. I would have sharp pain in my testicles even when I saw a cripple on the street. (What does that tell you about the state of my chakras?)

Although I still may feel the hurt, I can accept the suffering within the knowledge that your suffering and mine are all accomplishing the same thing as we teach ourselves the rules of the game -- that it's OK. But it's important that we <u>know</u> it's OK. Otherwise, we end up blaming somebody or something for our predicament and miss the whole point.

Reading this over, I see that what was so clear in my head is only muddled on paper, but it's too late to start over, because I want to get the check in the mail tonight -- so I'll just quit.

Love, K

Dear K,

Just a quickie, because 1) I'm leaving town for two weeks, and 2) now I'm surer than ever our differences are more semantic than substantive.

There's knowing and then there's *knowing*. Yes, it's the truest thing in the world that knowing the bigger truth not only helps, but is *necessary* in order to feel true compassion, patience, etc.

But the "knowing" I object to is more of a self-conscious kind, very popular right now, which involves constantly reminding our-selves or reaffirming basic platitudes and so forth. You know what I mean. To me, most of that comes from fear, not wisdom.

Look at it this way: When children act in a play, they not only know they're acting a part, but they also giggle about it while they're doing it, or turn toward the audience and smile or wave to their parents. As a result, the play might be very sweet but the acting stinks. The best adult actors certainly know they're playing a part, but they're secure enough not to have to "know" it con-stantly in that more superficial way. They can surrender so deeply into their characters that their performance touches our very souls.

When I visit most ashrams or meet many "new-age" people, they're very sweet, but the acting stinks. They feel the need to constantly remind themselves or me or both that there's a larger unity between us, that our problems are just karma, etc. I prefer living as a human being, able to say "Shit, a flat tire!," without being reminded that the flat tire must have a good purpose for my spiritual growth. *Of course* I know that! But it brings me out of character to have to reassure myself of it all through the day.

And yes, I do think playing our characters is essentially what we came here to do. Our souls are already free and enlightened. It's *only* the characters we're playing who need to develop courage, self-honesty, kindness and sense of humor. We're in a divine play. We don't have to be afraid of losing those deeper understandings. Fear is always the greater attachment. So, I know that you know, and you know that I know. All I'm saying is, we can trust it more implicitly, both in ourselves and with each other. The roof won't fall in.

If you get upset over your losses in the stock market, I won't mistake your character's line for your real soul. I know you too well. My response would be, "Yeah, that really sucks;" not "Oh K, it's all for the best." And we both know we're play-acting, and we do it with love and joy and friendship. That's all I'm saying.

Love, Bo

● ● ●

To be an actor, you have to be honest.
If you can fake that, you've got it made.

-- George Burns

LIFE IN HELL

By Matt Groening ©1986

LIGHTEN UP, WILL YOU?

[from Human Kindness Foundation newsletter, Spring 1989]

> *A new lifer sat in with a group of cons who had done many years' time together. They would all just sit silently for awhile and then one would say "13", or "6", or some other number, and everyone would laugh hysterically. Later on, the new guy asked one of them privately what was going on. "Well you see, we've done so much time together we all know the same jokes. So we've numbered them; that way we don't have to repeat ourselves so much." The new guy thought it was pretty strange, but he wanted to fit in with the group, so he had this older con teach him all the jokes and their numbers. A few weeks later he was hanging out with the group, and he got his nerve up and said "23." Nobody laughed. One old guy looked at another and said, "Boy, some people just can't tell a joke!"*

The most frustrating thing about trying to write these newsletters is the "humor gap" that exists between writing and speaking. If you and I were sitting together talking, the heavy things would naturally and frequently be punctuated with a smile, a funny story, a hearty laugh or corny joke (as those of you who've been in my workshops may painfully recall). Most of those things don't translate very easily to the printed page, because they're spontaneous; they belong to the moment they're expressed. But the funny stuff isn't irrelevant or unimportant. It's at the very heart of the spiritual journey (seriously, now!).

Think about the great holy books -- the Bible, the Koran, Bhagavad Gita, Ramayana, Dhammapada, Guru Granth Sahib and so forth: Nary a laugh among the bunch of them. Now, I'm sure Jesus and Buddha and those other masters had great senses of humor; the best teachers I've met all had great senses of humor. It seems to be the very basis of an enlightened attitude. So what happened by the time it got into writing?

During the seven years it took to complete *We're All Doing Time*, Rick Morgan's cartoons became a key part of that process for me. The cartoons are absolutely essential in order for the reader to get the spiritual outlook I was shooting for. Yet of the thousands of people who write us and go on and on about how much the book has helped them, no one ever mentions the cartoons. It's almost as if they're only visible to me and Sita (and of course, Rick!). Maybe people who read spiritual books assume the message has to be heavy.

Sometimes I open *We're All Doing Time* and just look at one of the funny drawings for awhile, much like someone else may contemplate a powerful passage. Cartoons carry Truth in a wonderful way, they help us to smile at ourselves. They speak more to the heart than to the busy mind. But if my book outlives me, I'm sure that within a hundred years or so the publishers would leave out the cartoons.

It makes me wonder whether the original Bible had great cartoons or jokes which are now lost forever *(Jesus:...so the Pharisee says to the Centurion, "the duck? I thought he came with you!!" Disciple: Oh Christ, stop, stop. You're so funny, I can't take any more!).*

Though it may not show up in the written word, God's best jokes are all around us. Reagan was actually elected president. Twice. Native Americans are forever called "Indians" because Columbus was lousy at geography. Then there's the platypus. And look at the great sums of money curly-haired people spend to straighten their hair, while straight-haired people are spending their bucks on perms. Look at how you thought your last deal was going down before you got busted *(Hey, that's not funny!)*. Or spending millions of dollars so the Pope can visit the poor?

And don't you just love how the airlines, after two planes almost crash into each other, call it a "near-miss;" seems like a "near-<u>hit</u>" to me! And how about the 1988 nomination of Reagan

"No doubt about it, Ellington—we've mathematically expressed the purpose of the universe.

and Gorbachev for the Nobel <u>Peace</u> Prize? Two guys who kept building bombs although either country could already destroy the planet a thousand times over! And how come scientists never discover that soybeans or alfalfa sprouts are bad for us?; it's always got to be something like ice cream or chocolate or booze or pot. And how about the fact that most of the bloodshed in the world involves our biggest religions, which all preach love and mercy?

Let's face it -- this is a very funny world. We're crazy as loons, struggling for illusions which we can never get, on a planet that doesn't support the style of life we try so hard to create. As the great cartoonist Gahan Wilson once said, "Life essentially doesn't work. And that's the basis of endless humor."

Of course, whether life's ironies strike you as funny or not depends on your sense of humor. I didn't laugh much when I was an angry radical in the '60's. And when I was a naive "new-age" seeker in the early '70's, I was never sure what was okay or not okay to laugh at (heaven forbid I might offend somebody, or worse, piss God off!). Now that I'm not so angry or frightened, not only do I laugh a lot, but it turns out I have much more political and spiritual influence than I ever did in those joyless years when I was trying so hard.

THE FAR SIDE By GARY LARSON

Charlie Parker's private hell

In the same way our culture tends to mistake kindness for weakness, we also tend to mistake humor for several things it's not. For example, seeing the lighter side of something doesn't mean we "take it too lightly." Poking fun at ourselves and our inconsistencies, or even at others and their inconsistencies, isn't necessarily the same as ridicule.

Quite the contrary, humor is a tremendous safety valve for us as individuals and for the planet as a whole. Doctors are finally being forced to see the power of humor in medical treatment (and now are getting quite serious about it! God, we're nuts). And just imagine if Bush and Gorbachev were to spend the first day of a summit watching old Bugs Bunny clips or Richard Pryor movies, laughing 'til their sides hurt. Could they possibly be as hostile to each other? Humor brings our hearts together.

Often I'll do a workshop or a lecture, and my host will say, "Oh, you've just got to meet so-and-so, you've got so much in common!" Soon as I hear that, I get an "uh-oh" feeling in my gut, because "so-and-so" is almost invariably someone who's so heavy, so rigid or self-righteous that it amazes me people would lump us together. In prisons, so-and-so is often the resident yoga/meditation honcho who can twist his body into a pretzel and knows all the ancient texts, but whose heart is shut tight, thinly hiding a tremendous amount of anger and unhappiness right below the surface. I'm sure you know people like this too.

I suspect most of us don't *feel* a person, or at least we don't trust our gut feelings. We seem to take in a package instead -- the words, the reputations, the concepts -- and then file that person into the appropriate category in our minds without considering what our actual experience of them felt like. Maybe the assumption is that spiritual beings are all alike because the general principles are all alike. Bad assumption. Enlightenment is not heavy. Bear that in mind as you come in contact with friends, teachers or groups that try to convince you what terrible shape the world is in and how urgent it is for you to do exactly what they're doing. The facts they quote may all be true, but they've missed the deeper truth by a mile.

Mother Goose & Grimm   by Mike Peters

100

The point of this curmudgeonly diatribe is simply to say "Lighten Up." Maybe we don't say that enough in print. Constant seriousness usually indicates self-importance, and simply put, that just ain't gonna cut it for where we really want to go. Holy books and spiritual practices are great, but if you read a lot of holy books, try to balance them with Bloom County, The Far Side, Peanuts, Doonesbury, Life in Hell or whatever cartoons seem to poke the most fun at your own flavor of drama or self-importance (the titles above are the ones that do it best for me). Watch Saturday Night Live, The Simpsons, Cheers or Family Ties. Try to tune in when Steve Martin, Jay Leno, Richard Pryor and other great comedians do their thing.

Laughing is such powerful Medicine, especially finding the hidden humor in our inflated egos, constant rationalizations, and the tortuous things we put ourselves through in the proccss of "self-discovery." We live in a bizarre age, so it would be a shame not to enjoy the humor.

● ● ●

Herman

"This one comes with a lifetime guarantee."

The New Breed

The Don of the New Age.

Caldwell

DIRTY HARRY POPPINS

Caldwell

Cow Philosophy

You can enjoy <u>all</u> of life if you rest
in the confidence of the real
Immortal, Unchanging Soul.
You can realize that all of life --
even disease, death, heartbreak, prison,
everything we call negative and positive -
all of it is this wondrous mystical illusion
that arises
and

dissolves

in

every

moment

¤

EVEN "THE ONE" IS
ONE TOO MANY

[from HKF newsletter, Spring, 1990; transcribed from a talk at
the Seattle Church of Religious Science in November, 1989. The
unedited talk is available on the "Talks & Discussion" tape
which includes "Fearless Adventure Versus Endless Struggle."]

What is it? What is the Supreme Truth behind the mystery of life? That's the question we have all our lives. We do all sorts of things to find the answer, and we call it the Spiritual Journey, or Inner Journey. But frankly, 99% of the time, what we're calling "inner" doesn't even come close. It's just part of the outer. It may be the noblest, gentlest, nicest and most Spiritual reaches of the outer, but it's not the inner.

The *real* Inner Truth is unchanging, like a generator room inside of us. In that room, which powers our whole created universe, what's going on is just OMMMMMMMMM.... The generator is just humming. That's the Unchanging, the Eternal, the Immortal; That which was never born; which can never die; That which is beyond all form; G-D, we can't even spell it. That's Inner Truth. So the Inner *Journey* is about opening up to that Truth.

The inner journey is not about "becoming" Spiritual people. The inner is not about doing good. The inner is not about living a happy, compassionate life. Those are great goals, they're the most constructive parts of our outer, worldly lives. I'm not knocking any of it. I mean, I try to be a nice guy and recycle my trash and do good works; I love my family. You may want to finish your education, get a good job, travel, etc. Nothing wrong with any of it. The outer is very sweet and important in its own context. But let's not confuse it with the inner journey.

If everything is Spirit, how do we know whether something is connected to the inner journey or to the outer? Well, if it has a beginning or an end, a subject or an object, if it changes or grows or develops, if it can be analyzed or described, it's in the outer. It's still in time. The inner is not within time and space.

Even those of you who relate to reincarnation; somebody asked me last week in Calgary, "Are you saying that our souls don't develop? Our souls don't learn and grow over many lifetimes?" And I said, "that's exactly what I'm saying." The *mind* may learn and grow, the *personality* may learn and grow, but the soul is pure *Being*, humming along like OMMMMMMMMM. It's infinite and perfect already. Time and space arise out of it and dissolve back into it, mysteriously and endlessly. So what can it grow into -- a bigger infinite? It's beyond both creation and change, so there's nothing to do to it, for it, or with it.

So if everyone's soul is already the One Soul, and we're already complete and perfect, what's the difference between an enlightened being and the rest of us? The difference is simply that an enlightened being has dismantled the roadblocks we erect between our conscious minds and the Incredible, Infinite, Unchanging Goodness of our soul. So the journey to the inner is just clearing stuff away; it's a process of opening. It's not the process of *getting* or *developing* anything; but just gradually surrendering every tiny difference between *my will* and *Thy Will.*

God has a very warped sense of humor, really. The purpose of free will turns out to be to offer it back out of our own free will. That's pretty twisted. However, God does give us as much time as we want to exercise and enjoy our free will, until we see how our desires and fears keep screwing up our lives. And then we get so tired of the gap between *my will* and *Thy Will*, that we say, "Please, take it back. I've forgotten how to give back my free will. I really want to be in perfect harmony."

For example, this plant is sitting on the rug. It's not sitting there thinking, "I've got to keep on the rug. I've got to stay on the rug." And it's not thinking, "Man, I sure look cool sitting on this rug." It's simply sitting on the rug, perfectly *being* a plant sitting on the rug. Life works, or it can, in a way where we could be going about our lives with such un-self-conscious harmony.

And I don't mean that you don't get flat tires or hemorrhoids. I don't mean any of that. This plant can get mealybugs and then it's perfectly being a plant with mealybugs. If it's not watered, its systems will struggle to survive and then it will either get watered or it will shrivel and die, but all in perfect harmony, being what it is called to be, doing what it is called to do, dying as it is called to die. And then the essence that powered the plant moves on. The essence didn't really do, be, or die; it just powered a plant for a while. That's how it can be for our lives as well.

A lot of you start thinking, "He's talking about being totally passive, just sitting around and letting anything happen." But it's quite the opposite. I'm saying that as we stop getting in our own way, our lives can flow powerfully and joyfully on their own. Do we tell our bodies how to digest food? Do we command our eyes to transmit images to the brain? Of course not.

Yet our digestion performs miracles converting food into energy. Our eyes bring us breathtaking sights and brilliant colors, they adjust immediately to darkness or brightness, they protect themselves by blinking, they clean themselves with tears. Our bodies function in precise, elaborate, spontaneous ways without ego or self-consciousness.

Well, our minds and personalities can be just as effortless, so that we are not struggling emotionally and second-guessing ourselves all the time. Believe me, our minds and hearts know how to live a productive, enjoyable life like our organs know how to digest food and circulate blood.

So how do we discover this natural state of being? How do we move from self-consciousness to easy harmony, from my will to Thy Will? Can we achieve it through complicated philosophies which make our minds even busier? Doesn't it make more sense to narrow our sights just to the one moment we find ourselves in; to being a wide-open, in-tune, powerful human being right now?

But even so, how do we do *that*? It comes back to the inner/outer balance; silencing the mind through practices such as meditation. We don't have to "deserve" anything. There's nothing to *earn* in the Unchanging; it just IS; it already IS. The inner journey is simply to touch the Inner Truth in some way; just to *touch* the Unchanging, Eternal, Immortal Soul which IS right now.

Since most religions have fallen away from internal quieting practices and have become mostly group- and activity-oriented, they have gradually re-defined the inner as the highest, most ethical, lofty reaches of outer behavior. But I assure you, the loftiest heaven still implies hell. It is only in the Unchanging, the Eternal, that which was never created, that which cannot be uncreated, the OMMMMMMMMM; only in that, out of which everything and every moment arises and falls back; which is beyond good and evil; where Charles Manson and Mother Theresa are both dissolved in the OMMMMMMMMM; that the inner is experienced.

You could have a ten year period in your life which is the greatest. You've gotten that degree you always wanted, you're doing good works in the community, all your friends love you. You look good and you feel good and your kids are great, and you go into meditation or you go to retreat or something, that door into the generator room opens slightly and you notice it's going OMMMMMMMMM.

Ten years later in your life you look back.... "Oh my God... How did my life come to this? Everything has gone rotten for ten years. I've lost everyone I love, both my parents died in the same year, I was raped in New York, my house burned down." You feel like the book of Job all came down on you, and you can't take the pain of watching the news and reading the newspaper and seeing how much terrible cruelty is going on in this world. Then you meditate or take a walk or something happens and the door to your soul opens slightly again and you notice it's still going OMMMMMMMMM. Then you begin to have a true understanding of what "beyond change" is really about.

When that understanding finally seeps through all the levels of your psyche, like water filtering through charcoal, that's the basis of what you might call Spiritual Confidence, which enables you to do the "right" things, to be on the side of "good" as opposed to "bad", but without self-righteousness, without a sense of crisis or urgency. You can try to save the planet, work for peace, do prayers and affirmations, yet with an overall sense of humor, and the awareness that most of the time life doesn't happen the way you want it to happen, and it's perfectly fine with you.

Spiritual confidence in the *beyond* change, *beyond* time, is the basis of being able to do the outer world stuff without being taken in by the illusion. What you see around you is *not* the Spiritual Reality. Anything -- including the planet -- which can be made better or worse, destroyed or saved, is not the Inner Journey.

That's why it's hard for me to be interested in all the channelers, disembodied sages, gurus and supposedly alien beings who say things like "This is a crucial time for you people of Earth, to bring about a new dawn of humanity before you destroy yourselves..." and all of that stuff. That's mixing up the inner and outer in ways which reflect a lack of wisdom. World peace or a Golden Age are not the Inner Journey. There is nothing ever urgent or crucial about the Inner Journey, because what is Real is already at peace, and is beyond threat or destruction.

What the mystical tradition of every religion is about; the reason that Science of Mind and Yoga and Buddhism and all these Spiritual traditions have *practices* instead of just reading and thinking; the mystical basis that begins to awaken in us when we quiet our minds down from all of the outside activity, is that there are links between the outer world and the inner Unchanging Soul.

One secret link between the inner and the outer is the breath. It's a key. In each breath creation occurs, and life comes out of the formless. And it's everything we see, even all our memories of who we are and the history of the world, etc. In each breath it's all of it. And in each cessation of the breath, it's none of it. It's the OMMMMMMMMM. And that's why in a lot of traditions people learn to work with their breath in some way. Even common folklore says "Take ten deep breaths to calm down," etc.

I think it's interesting that medical science calls breathing "respiration." The root of respiration is "Spirit". Re-spir-ation. We re-spir-ate -- take in Spirit -- again and again and again, from the moment we're born, and what is it that defines when we die? It's when we stop breathing. Re-spir-ation, we keep doing it, we keep bringing in Spirit. We keep bringing in life in every breath.

Very simply what the human body is, ideally, is a living factory which converts the raw Unchanging Formless Spirit into compassion, which is the highest virtue of the outer world...loving kindness, whatever you want to call it. It's the human heart that actually does that. And in a reverse way we can also bring in all of the pain that we see in this world of change. Again the human heart and awareness is what converts it and is able to offer it up into the changeless; it's this incredible recycling factory, that's who each of us is, that's what the ideal is: That we can walk this earth recycling raw Spirit into human compassion, recycling human pain into raw Spirit.

And walking in this balance, you don't want to have too much focus in the changeless. It's just one toe in that generator room that reminds us of our genuine wisdom, so that we don't get caught up in "Oh, the world is coming to an end, we're destroying the world". Guess what? Whether we destroy it with bombs or pollution, or the sun dies a billion years from now, the world is in time. And if you want to talk about many, many lifetimes, that's still in time. Millions of years of reincarnation in the development of your Spiritual character, that's still in time. The real Inner Journey is just opening, just opening. It's not getting bigger. We're as big as big gets. We've got one soul and it's Unchanging.

I travel a lot, and I see a feeling of *lack* in most people who are striving toward Spiritual aims, and it breaks my heart. I want to put my arm around every one of you and say "That's not it. It's not striving to *get*. It's not striving because you're not *good* enough. It's not striving because you have to *change*. You're already safe, sound, comfortable, and infinite in the eternal. Like the affirmation in the church folder, notice it says we are "committing ourselves to know God." It doesn't say "for God to notice us". We don't have to get God to notice us. Each one of us has that generator room -- the Unchanging Formless Spirit -- in full, already, with nothing lacking whatsoever.

You can enjoy *all* of life if you rest in the confidence of the *real* Immortal, Unchanging Soul. You can realize that *all* of life, even prison, disease, death, heartbreak, *everything* we call negative and positive, *all of it is this wondrous, mystical illusion that arises and dissolves in every moment.*

It's this immense feeling of freedom, instead of feeling tiny and being so afraid that "if this happens to me... or if this happens to me..." You can live your entire life, through all your joys and sorrows, ups and downs, resting in the Bigness. And you can do that by narrowing your focus down to right here, right now, just doing the best you can with no sense of urgency, and having Spiritual confidence in the Unchanging Reality.

● ● ●

Dear Family,

Right now, this moment, I am as "happy as a baby in a candy store"! For the very first time, since I began meditation, Hatha yoga and pranayam techniques and exercises, I believe I have just meditated upon the "Eternal OMMMMMMMM"! At least I think I touched the Inner Truth in some way, because never ever have I experienced anything like it before. And I must confess I was frightened, but I hung in there.

I know you all are very busy freeing lock-in-souls (like mine) but I had to reveal my initial awakening to someone and thank

God for what I perceive to be the beginning of an Inner Spiritual Journey.

Thanking you all with the best of my heart, T

● ● ●

Dear Bo,

I've been receiving your newsletters for some time now, but this last one, Spring 1990 with "Even 'The One' is One Too Many", has finally prompted me to write.

I am not a prisoner, never have been. I'm single. I'm gay. I'm a university graduate (BA, MA English). I have seen most of the world and explored many of its cultures. And I'm very familiar with the basic tenets of the world's major religions, including Buddhism and Hinduism. I admire both, but cannot bring myself to believe in any sort of deity or cognizant afterlife. And it is the last that is giving me trouble.

Last year, I turned 50 and a few months before that, my best friend died. My parents are getting old. So, I have suddenly become <u>painfully</u> aware of my own mortality. I find myself triggered to think of my death by all sorts of things, from beautiful music to reading about someone who's been dead for centuries. I then get what must be an anxiety attack -- almost a panicky feeling of desperation. And the only way I can escape those depressing feelings is to divert my thoughts to something else.

I believe my attitude is not one of fear of my own death, but rather terror at not existing any longer after my death. I think it is more a feeling of impending loss than anything else, since it causes me to have to literally, physically alter my mental state to "get away from it". I would like to believe in something beyond death, but simply can't. I am a materialist, a realist in just about everything.

Until now, I have never been depressed for any period of time. I've always had a happy attitude and, indeed, enjoyed life. Maybe that's the problem? Maybe I've enjoyed life too much?

I would appreciate any advice you might be able to give me.

Sincerely, D

Dear D,

Congratulations. Isn't it wonderful that your own life and mind won't allow you to ignore the basic questions of your existence any longer? It's not required that you believe in anything or think in any particular way. Truth is truth. The issue is, can we see the way things truly are? Can we see who it is who panics when you think about death, and who it is who needs to define himself so rigidly ("I am a materialist, a realist..." etc.)?

By the way, you're not a "realist" until you can see what is real and what is not. The only true realists are people who are totally enlightened. The rest of us live by our imaginations.

You imagine life to be a certain way -- materialistic, without God, without afterlife, and so forth -- and now you are experiencing pain and fear. So you write to me hoping I can amend your imagination just enough to leave most of it intact but remove the pain and fear.

But your imagination itself *is* the problem. Stop imagining, and look at your life with a sincere desire to see the truth. That's the only way I can point out. The truth is, what dies is a tiny part of who we are.

You're frightened by death and non-existence; your fears are no more real than a child's fears of a monster underneath his bed.

The monster doesn't exist, D. I'm among the many people who grew up and looked underneath the bed for himself. Now I sleep well and have no fears of monsters which still plague you.

I don't ask you to believe me; see for yourself. Look under your bed. The way you do that is to quiet your restless, anxious mind. And even if you can't entirely quiet it, you can at least step back from it just enough to know you are much more than the body and mind you have always taken yourself to be. This takes work, but what doesn't?

If that's important to you, make room for daily meditation practice so you can see more clearly. The meditation section in *We're All Doing Time* is simple and a good start. If you like group support, take a course somewhere to get you off on the right foot. But you won't be able to solve your problem with thoughts and philosophies.

Your imagination of a materialistic universe has prevented you from experiencing untold beauty, power, magic, and mystery for fifty years now. *Thank* your pain and fear for forcing you to finally take steps toward truly being a "realist." If you think you have "enjoyed life too much," you have some really terrific surprises in store! I deeply hope you take the effort.

Love, Bo

● ● ●

If you let go, something will happen.
Fear is always anticipation of the unknown.
Most human energy flow problems relate to
the inability to relax.
Fear of letting go.
If you let go, something will happen.
Fear of the unknown.
Rational mind wants to make a deal:
first tell me what will happen,
and then I'll let go.
Fuck you.
No one knows what's going to happen.
Ever.
The future -- next moment -- is unknowable -- unknown.
Rational mind won't believe that.
He is afraid to.

-- Paul Williams, *Das Energi*

...the spiritual journey to me has never been a mass, conformist phenomenon. If I were the power-deity in one of those sacred spots, and I saw 5,000 affluent groupies trampling up to sit on me, I'd probably clear out until they had gone.

THE HARMONIC CURMUDGEON
AND OTHER TRUE SAGAS

My First Prison Workshop

Mark Twain once said, "When in doubt, tell the truth." I discovered the power of that advice in my very first prison workshop, on death row at Central Prison in Raleigh, NC, in 1974.

I had already been corresponding with prisoners and sending them a variety of spiritual books for about a year, but I had never gone into prison except to visit friends and relatives. This was the first time I was being asked to come in as some sort of teacher, and I was pretty nervous.

A psychologist at the prison had formed a small group of death row inmates who were interested in meditation and yoga. The psychologist also attended some of my classes at the ashram Sita and I were living in at the time. So a couple of times over the past year, he had brought me a cassette tape of his prison group asking a few questions, and I taped my responses to send back inside. The guys gradually became interested in meeting me, and after a lot of red tape, a two-hour meeting was arranged.

During the entire forty-mile drive from the ashram to Central Prison, my self-doubts bugged the hell out of me. I tried doing mantra, focusing my attention on each present moment, on the yellow lines of the highway, I tried watching the whole thing happen without getting attached, I tried breathing deeply and exhaling out all the doubt and anxiety; but nothing worked.

Despite my whole bag of yogi tricks, I kept thinking, "Who do I think I am, a little white guy from Miami, coming to death row in the racist South, to talk about peace of mind? How dare I preach at these black and poor-white inmates whose experiences I can't possibly understand? Why am I doing this? What business do we have together?," and other similar variations on the theme. My mind was a mess.

The prison was horrible. It was over a century old. Custody had no respect for the treatment staff or for programs. They treated the psychologist and myself like criminals. After a lot of hassle to get inside, one officer gave me the final coup de grâce as he opened the big ugly green door to the room where seven death row inmates awaited me: "You're going to be locked in this room for the next two hours with seven killers and no guards. Hope you enjoy it." Gee, that did a lot for my self-doubts!

There they were. One of the inmates, a black guy about seven feet tall, looked down at me and said to the psychologist, "Man, from his voice on the tapes, I thought he'd be a *big* dude!" I remember thinking, *Who could be a big dude next to you? You want me to be eight feet tall??* My mind was still a mess, and now I felt very small and very white.

We all sat down in folding metal chairs, the seven of them in a straight line facing me, and my psychologist friend off to the side. I had no idea what to say, but before I could've opened my mouth, one of the inmates -- a Black Muslim wearing all white and a lot of anger -- stood up and screamed, "WHO THE HELL DO YOU THINK YOU ARE, A LITTLE WHITE GUY, COMING IN TO A RACIST SOUTHERN PRISON TO PREACH TO ME, AN OPPRESSED BLACK MAN WHOSE LIFE YOU COULDN'T POSSIBLY UNDERSTAND?"

It was amazing. He shouted at me for about twenty minutes, using nearly the exact words which had rattled me all the way to the prison. Several other inmates motioned to me that they'd stop him if I wanted them to, but I nobly waved them away, as if I wanted to give the guy a chance to speak his mind. The truth was, I needed to buy some time, because this was quickly turning into a very bad day.

When he ended with, "SO WHAT BUSINESS DO YOU HAVE WITH ME?," I luckily didn't hesitate before I responded, "I don't know whether we have *any* business together. In fact, I was thinking those same exact things the whole way here."

His mind may have been prepared for a lot of responses, but not that one. He looked like he had just gone on "tilt." His fury and rage were suspended and we all just sat there for a minute or two, glancing around the room in silence. I slowly warmed up and began talking about the things which seem to be the same for all of us, of every color and set of experiences -- things like wanting to feel safe and loved and connected to life.

Funny thing -- I had no doubts anymore. I was simply a human being sharing some of the most basic, heart-to-heart ideas common to us all. It was a powerful workshop, and the angry inmate became a good friend by the end of our time together.

Love Thy Neighbor Because You *Are* Thy Neighbor

Although my prison workshops are always spontaneous, there are a few things I tend to do in most of them -- a simple meditation practice, some tips about breathing and power, and also a powerful eye-to-eye meditation technique which has never once failed to break down barriers between people even in the worst prisons, like Oklahoma State Penitentiary at McAlester.

My workshop at McAlester was held in the gym, which is always unfortunate for me because the acoustics are so bad. Besides the irony of having to *shout* about inner peace, it must have been 110 degrees in there, and we kept having to choose between the terrible noise of huge exhaust fans, or putting up with the feeling of being in a giant steam bath with all our clothes on. We'd leave the fans off for as long as we could stand it, then turn them on and barely be able to hear each other, then turn them off until we couldn't stand the heat again.

It was a rough way to spend a hot summer afternoon, and I was very touched by the endurance of the sixty or so men who hung in there for several hours.

McAlester is also (at least at that time, 1978), completely self-segregated. White prisoners sat on one side of the aisle, blacks on the other. So toward the end of the workshop, when it came time to do the eye-to-eye meditation, I found myself saying (shouting) "I want you to pair up with one other person now, putting your chair directly across from him as close as you can be without your knees touching. If you're black, pair up with somebody who's white. If you're white, pair up with somebody who's black."

The room became completely silent for about ninety seconds, the air filled with tension. I couldn't believe I went that far out on a limb. I could see how hard it was for the men to decide whether to follow my instructions. It just wasn't done at McAlester! How could I ask them to do something that just wasn't done?

Slowly, one large, muscular black man stood up and moved across the aisle with his chair in hand. He came to a large, muscular white man and put his chair down in front of him. That was it. Within five minutes, everyone in the workshop was sitting quietly across from somebody of the opposite race. Whew!

I asked them to close their eyes while I explained what we were going to do. Even that simple request brought about such tension! Closing your eyes in front of the enemy? How could you trust him? But they did it, and for the next twenty minutes or so they also followed every other instruction I gave:

> Partner A keep your eyes closed while partner B looks at you; now, B, see this person in front of you who has your exact will to survive, your exact drive to feel good and safe and loved, your exact desire to make sense of his life. See all the common experiences you share, of being hurt, of being lonely, of being scared, of feeling worthless, of praying for help, of feeling guilty and ashamed, of seeking relief, of yearning for peace.

> See that your partner is exactly like you, and appreciate that he trusts you enough to let you look at him while his eyes are closed. Realize that he *can* trust you, and you can trust him, because you see how much the same life is for both of you.

> Now B, I want you to give your partner the greatest gift in the world: I want you to keep looking at him, with total understanding, total forgiveness, total compassion, for anything he could reveal to you. Whatever stupid, violent, mean, crazy thing you could find out about him, you understand, don't you? You understand that life is hard, and we all screw up. Show him you understand through the power of God's love in your eyes.

> Now A, I promise you that B is doing this for real. What I want you to do now, before you open your eyes, is to bring to mind everything about your life that you want to get rid of; all your burdens -- your loneliness, shame, fears, secrets, yearning, weariness, all of it. And I want you to open your eyes and surrender it all into the eyes of Love. Your partner understands. He really does. You can allow him to see the real you more than you have ever allowed yourself to be seen by anyone.

The words may vary from time to time, because I make them up on the spot, but that's the general idea. Anyway, each partner gets to do both parts. After both parts are completed, I ask them to simply look into each other's eyes with no roles at all; just brothers on the path who have seen each other honestly. After about a minute of that, I ask them to bow slightly to each other in appreciation for the help they have given and received, I ring a bell and then it's over.

So at McAlester that day, we did the whole thing in the sweltering heat (fans off so they could hear me better). Not a soul seemed to notice the heat. They performed the technique perfectly, quickly getting past their racial tensions and extreme discomfort over looking directly into each other's eyes. It was easy to see that some profound experiences were happening.

The end came, I rang the bell, and nothing happened. No one moved. They all sat perfectly still, continuing to look in each other's eyes. Gradually, I saw a few hands reach across and shake hands or just grab each other's forearms, still unable to break eye contact, their heads nodding slightly to each other in acknowledgement of their brotherhood. They had been blown away by seeing their sameness. There was no way to deny it.

I've never seen a quicker or more powerful conversion from racism to brotherhood. All it took was taking a few minutes without words, without habits, to simply see more clearly who it is in front of us. It's *us* in front of us! That's why Jesus said to love our neighbors as ourselves. It's not a moral preaching; it's a statement of fact.

Thirty-Four Angels And A Monk

The best and worst meditation workshop I can remember was in 1981 at Bridgewater (MA) Hospital for the Criminally Insane. A psychologist there invited me to do a four-hour workshop. I didn't know it was anything other than a regular prison until I read the sign in the parking lot -- not that it would have made much difference, but it seems that it might be a nice thing to know in advance when my whole audience is going to be certifiably, violently insane.

The other thing I didn't know was that the psychologist had circulated the wrong poster about the workshop. My prison workshop was called "Getting Free," and was about the internal freedom which comes from quieting the mind. But I was also giving a prison *reform* talk at Harvard the next day, called "Toward A Consciousness of Crime and Punishment." For some crazy reason, the psychologist made copies of the Harvard poster instead of the "Getting Free" flyers we had sent him.

I *never* talk about prison reform inside a prison, because inmates aren't really in a position to do anything about it. My business with them is completely the opposite: To deepen their own peace and wisdom regardless of the injustice, cruelty or violence of their environments.

So there I went, under those circumstances, into a prison for the criminally insane, and on top of it all, for the first time, I brought a friend of mine who was a Buddhist monk -- orange robe, shaved head, the whole thing. We walked into the auditorium, I sat down on my meditation cushion on top of an old table, and closed my eyes to quiet down for a minute. I was thinking to myself, "Boy, this is a heavy-looking bunch; pretty rowdy, too."

Opening my eyes, I said "Well, we could talk about many things today: Meditation, yoga, spiritual training, quieting the mind, developing inner power..." and one guy in the front row stood up, waving that wrong poster, and said, "I WANNA TALK ABOUT GODDAMN CRIME AND PUNISHMENT!" I saw the poster and thought, "uh oh," and I said, "Well actually, that's the wrong poster. That's a talk I'm giving at Harvard tomorrow."

That wasn't the best thing to say! It turned out that those 35 men were representatives of all the angry ethnic and political groups in the prison. One guy said, "Oh yeah, well it's the fuckin' fascists at Harvard who need your 'peace of mind' crap! They're the ones who build these places!!"

And we were off and running. It was a wild verbal brawl, and I just went with it. They yelled at me, I yelled at them, my monk friend was ready to jump out of his seat -- it was wild. Every now and then, just to help me get through it, I would picture myself looking back at this and laughing someday.

After about an hour-and-a-half, the same first guy stood up and said the same comment about the fuckin' fascists at Harvard, and I realized we could go around in circles all day. So I brought it to a close and said "Look, I just want you to know I'm sorry for the misunderstanding, and I hope there are no hard feelings. I'm going to take a five-minute break, and if there's anyone here who would like to learn meditation and a few other silent practices together, come back after the five minutes. If nobody wants to, that's cool; I wish you all well."

Bhikku Piyavanno (nowadays known as meditation teacher John Orr) and I closed our eyes as everyone shuffled out of the room. When I opened my eyes about five minutes later, *34* of the 35 men were sitting in front of us once again, in total silence. I introduced them to Piyavanno, who had recently returned from eight years of meditation in a monastery in Thailand, and I went to the back of the room while he led them in a meditation. I figured it was more appropriate for him to lead the meditation that day, since he had spent eight years meditating and I had just spent an hour-and-a-half arguing.

I looked at the backs of their heads -- those crazy, angry activist convicts with tattoos and bullet scars all over them, many with their heads shaved, muscles bulging out from their t-shirts -- there they sat in perfect silence with their hands folded gently in their laps, trusting a weird-looking monk to teach them how to look into their souls; I've never seen anything more pure in my life. They looked like thirty-four angels sitting there. The scene was so powerful I felt like I could hardly stay in my body; I felt myself rising up toward the ceiling from the power of their openness, of their seeking.

It filled me with awe, wonder, and humility to see so clearly how we can't judge a situation at a glance. I thought the first hour-and-a-half was the biggest disaster I had experienced in eight years of workshops. Yet here was the most beautiful meditation I had seen in all those years. All of it was so perfect -- even the screaming and shouting which I feared was so "unspiritual" of me; somehow it helped create an honest link between us.

It convinced me more than ever that everyone is just looking for somebody who's genuine; everyone wants to meet somebody who'll be simple and straight with them. Once that's established, the sky's not even the limit.

"Hey Man, I Think He's A Yogurt!"

I had always thought how nice it would be to be more respected by prison administrations instead of being regarded as some way-out space cadet bringing in a weird program. But I got my wish once and never wished it again.

It happened in the Albany (NY) prison around 1978. The superintendent there knew of my work and was enthusiastic to have me do a workshop at her prison. The inmates didn't know or care about it in the least. Usually it's exactly the opposite.

In fact, the superintendent was *so* enthusiastic, she arranged the workshop in the gym, and *required* everyone in the prison to attend. A busload of young convicts from New York City arrived right around that time, and she herded them all into the gym as well. They came in and saw the whole prison population sitting in front of me, seated on a table, eyes closed, my legs folded in front of me. Those dudes must have thought this was a pretty weird orientation process!

So there we were, about 200 young male inmates, a dozen armed guards standing eight feet high on catwalks around the perimeter, and me trying to center myself and figure out why I didn't become a doctor like my mother wanted me to do. Acoustics in the gym were horrible and I had no microphone. The crowd was getting noisier and more rowdy by the moment, shouting things like, "HEY, WHAT'RE YOU DOING UP THERE -- SLEEPING?," and others responding on my behalf, "NO MAN, HE'S DOING YOGURT. HE'S A YOGURT."

As if things weren't bad enough, the final straw came in the form of about twenty young female inmates, led in and seated in one long row at the very back of the gym. So now, not only was no one getting ready to *listen* to me, they weren't even *looking* at me anymore. I had a gym full of young hormones going wild.

Like the tv ads for ginsu knives, "But wait; there's even more!" Also at the rear of the gym, off to one side, sat a small delegation of NY Dept of Corrections officials who came to see what my typical workshops were like. Good luck!

I sat in intense concentration and invoked an ancient, special mantra which links me directly to God (It goes like this: **"HELP!!!"**) A loud buzzer sounded, signalling the beginning of the workshop. I sat still, waiting for divine help to come, waiting for even a morsel of guidance. Five minutes. Ten minutes. The crowd gradually resumed talking, scuffing the floor, shifting in their seats. Fifteen minutes. The din once again became a roar, punctuated by occasional remarks directed specifically at me ("I THINK HE'S DEAD, MAN!") or at the women ("HEY BABY, I'M GETTING OUT SOON; WHAT'CH YOU DOING?").

Meanwhile, I was in severe negotiations with God. My position was pretty firm -- *I'm not attached to how this goes; if You don't move me, I'll sit here for an hour. I need a direct little push, damn it.*

After a total of about twenty minutes past the buzzer, a hand tapped me on the shoulder and startled me out of my bargaining talks with The Big Guy. It's amazing how many different dramas can be going on at once, because this was one I hadn't even considered. The hand belonged to the lieutenant in charge of the correctional officers, and he was clearly very agitated. He leaned over and shouted into my ear, "IF YOU DON'T START SOME-THING SOON, THIS PLACE IS GONNA BLOW!"

It wasn't quite the Divine sign I had in mind, but then again, He works in strange ways. And He hates to negotiate.

I opened my eyes and a lot of guys hooted and clapped, playing with the fact that I wasn't dead. I spoke a few words trying to quiet them down, and realized that I would have to give my entire talk at full volume. So I screamed about quietness of mind, and shouted about inner peace, and eventually there were only fifty or sixty inmates looking at the women or competing vocally with me in a room which amplified even the crossing of your legs into an annoying sound. I took a few shouted questions, yelling my best responses under the circumstances, and then called the discussion part to a close.

Thankfully, that's when I always invite people to leave if they've come only for the talk, or if they would feel uncomfortable following instructions about sitting still and closing their eyes and so forth. So, the place cleared out pretty quickly, leaving about seventy-five male inmates (the women had to leave in a group) scattered throughout the gym. I asked them to get closer together, and finally, we got down to the business at hand and had a good workshop for the next couple of hours.

They were earnest, they were interested. And on my part, I had a tremendous degree of respect and sympathy for the chaos they had to face every day in that prison. I just had a brief taste of it, and it was really something.

But the practices I came to share do indeed work. They worked for me, and those remaining inmates were impressed by that -- as were the officials off to the side. Once again, what I thought was a catastrophe was merely another perfectly choreographed production number to make things more real and immediate for all of us.

The Harmonic Curmudgeon

Wednesday, July 22nd, 1987. rringgg!

Bo: Hello?

caller: Hello, I'm calling long distance for Mr. Bo Lozoff.

Bo: This is Bo.

caller: Bo, my name is Eric and I'm devoting my energy for the next few weeks to the Harmonic Convergence. As I'm sure you and Sita are well aware, on Sunday August 16th we enter an entirely new age of mankind which will transform the planet...

Bo: Transform it into what?

Eric: Huh?

Bo: What's the planet going to be transformed into? A cosmic beach ball? A satellite dish? Michael Jackson's newest face?

Eric: Heh heh, I get it; you're making a joke. But seriously, the key to the total effectiveness of this transformation is whether we are willing to take responsibility for doing our part. Since you and Sita are prominent members of the spiritual community, I just want to touch base with you as to what you'll be doing, and see whether you'll use your mailing list to help send people important information.

Bo: What would you have me send?

Eric: Well, I mean information about the Convergence, letting people know that a great number of higher beings, astral teachers and alien guides will descend on Earth if we raise our consciousness enough to open the planet for their entry. That's why 144,000 people need to gather at 350 sacred sites around the world.

Bo: Look, I don't know anything about group decisions made by higher beings, but that sounds like extortion, like the time God threatened to kill Oral Roberts if he didn't raise $6 million bucks.

Eric: Why are you giving me a hard time?

Bo: I'm just being honest with you. The Harmonic Convergence is just a pain-in-the-ass media event as far as I'm concerned.

Eric: But why, brother? This more than any other time is when we need to pull together, to unite as one human family across the globe so that we can enter the Golden Age!

Bo: The thing is, I don't have that same ideal that you have of a "Golden Age." That seems awfully pretentious to me. I see a beautiful process going on in which suffering and joy are equally important and sacred; this is how we learn, this is how we become complete. I don't see anything "wrong" going on that we have to band together to change. Maybe there's a "golden age" happening somewhere, but I'd probably be very bored on that planet. I mean, what do people do -- smile at each other all day long?

Eric: That sounds very strange coming from someone whose life supposedly revolves around human service. Aren't you trying to relieve suffering?

Bo: Definitely; that's what gives meaning to my life. But for me, relieving suffering is very personal; it's a whole attitude. And a lot of that attitude involves not taking ourselves so seriously. Sita and I don't do human service because something "wrong" is going on, like God blew it and we have to straighten it out! We do what we do because we think selfishness and wealth are terribly over-rated, and we've found great peace through helping others. At the same time, we're basically hippies and non-conformists, and it goes against my grain for you to tell me I have to drop what I'm doing and hop on your bandwagon.

Eric: But right now we need to focus all of our energy on the spiritual process and call forth from within ourselves the very highest aims and motivations for our lives and for all of humanity.

Bo: But Eric, that's my whole point! What you're calling "the spiritual process" isn't a few hours of chanting or praying; it's got to be our very deepest attitude. It's got to include our being fun-loving as well as serious, it's got to be present while we watch stupid tv shows or eat junk food; there's no time out from the real "spiritual process". And If I could figure out a more powerful way to do it, I certainly wouldn't wait until August. I mean, are you going to save your spirituality up between now and August 16th??

Eric: You're mixing me all up. There's an event happening on August 16th that can change the world. I'm just trying to network with you to optimize the results of that event. Are you against world unity?

Bo: No, but I'll tell you what I'm against: Conformity. Especially conformity in the guise of spirituality. I've been teasing you, and I know you genuinely feel you're part of a process to bring people together, but don't you see that you're actually doing the opposite? I was working peacefully in my woodshop with all sorts of spiritual energy and good vibes, and you called to tell me 1) I need to hop on some bandwagon for *next* month's spiritual energy and good vibes, and 2) that no matter how I felt before you called, the place I'm standing is not as sacred as some volcano in Hawaii or pyramid in Egypt. Is that how you promote oneness?

Eric: First of all, we recognize that every place is sacred...

Bo: Oh come on, Eric! You can't have it both ways. Either those 350 spots across the world are more sacred than my workshop, or they're not. If they are, then God is discriminating against all my prison friends and countless shut-ins or poor folks who just don't have the bucks to travel. If these spots *aren't* sacred, then you and thousands of others are spending an awful lot of time and money in pursuit of some geographical self-delusion.

Eric: So you don't think there is such a thing as a "Power Spot"?

Bo: Sure, I think there are many spots on the planet which, depending on your own lineage, karma, needs, and development, can be very powerful. In the natural flow of your life, you may find yourself in one of those places, or let's say you get involved with a teacher who says "I want you to go to such and such place and sit silently all night," or something like that. That night may change your whole life. But the spiritual journey to me has never been a mass, conformist phenomenon. If I were the power-deity in one of those sacred spots and I saw 5,000 affluent groupies trampling up to sit on me, I'd probably clear out until they had gone.

Eric: But do you reject the idea that something special is taking place on August 16th?

Bo: It's not that I reject it; it's just that it's not so interesting. First of all, to me the spiritual journey has nothing to do with time. It's an ageless process in which time is one of the illusions we're trying to see through. August 16th is just a concept. If the concept works for you, then use it. But to mount a huge media campaign around the world for everyone to embrace the same concept at the same time is very alienating and intimidating. The Harmonic Convergence has become a short-term religion, and you've innocently slipped into religious fanaticism, which is probably the most divisive force in the history of mankind. All of this in the name of unity! And now you folks are giving Doonesbury, People Magazine and newscasters fresh material to make fun of "new-age" spirituality, and reinforce the notion that spiritual seekers are naive sheep who eat sprouts and chant at the moon. That's not a unifying force as far as I'm concerned.

Eric: But back to the event itself...

Bo: Back to the event itself, like any other mystical or cosmic event, it would work a hell of a lot better if we stay out of its way and just do our real spiritual work as best we can. On that level of reality, I don't know what the Mayans and the Gurus may have in mind for us. It's the kind of subject about which the Buddha used to say, *It's none of your business.* So spending a loving Sunday at home with our families, or volunteering at a soup kitchen, or digging our fingers into the beautiful earth of our gardens, or meditating quietly in the Eternal Mystery, we can be wide open to whatever it truly is. That's the real oneness, where we gradually cease to alienate people with be-ins, jargon, armbands or other paraphernalia, when we become truly simple human beings who cease to make distinctions about spiritual vs. unspiritual.

Eric: I really agree with everything you're saying, but still, a great number of higher beings for some reason have chosen August 16th as a day to come into our sphere, if we will take responsibility to change the resonance of the planet. Are you not going to do anything special on August 16th?

Bo: The truth? After all this, how could I help but pay a little extra attention during my meditation on that day? After all, what if I'm wrong about the whole thing? Have a nice day, Eric.

● ● ●

*Life is the sacred mystery singing to itself,
dancing to its drum, telling tales,
improvising, playing;
And we are all that Spirit, our stories all
but one cosmic story that we are Love indeed,
that perfect Love in me seeks the Love in you,
and if our eyes could ever meet without fear
we would recognize each other and rejoice,
for Love is Life believing in itself.*

-- from a Medicine story by Manitonquat

A lot of books and teachers tell you
how to affirm "I am a Godly person,"
or how to overpower negative thoughts
with positive ones.
But shouting that you're good, to cover
up a whisper that you're not,
is not the same as uncovering that
whisper, seeing that it's delusion, and
discarding it completely.

BE STILL AND KNOW THAT YOU AM GOD

[from HKF newsletter, Spring, 1990, condensed from tapes of
a talk at Unity Center in Arden, N. C., 4/1/90.]

It's interesting to notice the line in the Bible, *Be Still and
know that 1 am God.* There are so many other words that would
seem more appropriate from our usual attitudes about religion:
"Be *holy* and know that I am God," "Be *good* and know that I am
God," "Be *giving* and know that I am God," "Be *righteous* and
know that I am God," "Be *truthful* and know that I am God."
Why "Be Still?" What's the big deal about being Still? That's
wasting time, isn't it? How does that help us or help the world?

BE STILL AND KNOW THAT 1 AM GOD. There's no way
philosophically, psychologically or culturally to resolve why the
word "Still" is used there. If you want to find out what it's like to
get wet, you've got to go in the water.

There is a Stillness at the center of who we are. When we try
to remember or contact that Stillness, it's useful to find a quiet
place, or take the phone off the hook, or wake up before everybody else, or go to sleep later. It's useful to learn how to sit perfectly straight, how to sit in such a way that you can put the body
in park and turn the key off, so there's no attending to the body.
That's why I sit this way. The body is balanced. There's nothing to
tense up or or fall over if I were to lose awareness of my body.
It's like setting a vase on the floor.

So when we practice, when we're trying to get in touch with
the Stillness, it makes sense to find a quiet place, but ultimately it
won't matter whether we're running the Boston marathon or in a
crowded cellblock or sitting in a cave. There's that Stillness always,
because the Stillness is the infinite space, the Big Emptiness, in
which everything else exists -- noise, people, confusion, all of it.

If it intrigues us enough, we practice Stillness a little bit every
day, with no help; no group support; no external aids. Like Jesus
said, "praying in a closet." We sit down. We figure out what to do
with our bodies. And we begin turning inward to find the key to
this Mystery that bugs us. We begin the classic, most honorable
pursuit of human beings: learning to sit still and shut up.

Isn't that great? It's nothing that any of us idiots can't understand, no matter what capacity we have of grasping anything

theological or philosophical. "How do you find God?" "Sit still and shut up." "Oh, I can dig that. I can't even read and I can dig that. Thanks." We just sit still and shut up.

When we discover our Stillness, it begins to awaken in us the spiritual power we've always heard and read about. But first we have to quiet the mind and open the heart. To do that, we have to reduce the amount of noise that we carry around with us in the form of identities and fears and desires and greed and ambition, and self-reproach, the constant self-monitoring: "Oh, can I get some of that, can I avoid this, was I friendly enough, did I do it right, did I say it wrong, am I sitting in his seat . . ." All of that.

What I have to share with you, beyond all the words, is a taste of Stillness. Your own Stillness. It's not mine that you're going to catch, it's your own. And if you catch even a smidgen of it, it may entice you inward to catch a little more and a little more and a little more. We're all in the process of garbage removal. That's it. It's not *acquiring* anything, just removing obstacles to our Stillness.

I looked over the shelves in your church bookstore. There's a lot of good stuff there and a lot of garbage. That's nice, because it gives you the responsibility of discerning which is which for yourself. I'm not going to lie and say, "Oh, I honor and affirm everything that's taught in those books." There's a lot of garbage on those shelves. The reason it's garbage is, though it means well, it springs from an essential lack of faith in what you already are.

It's like there's this feeling in you that says "I'm not a godly person;" so a lot of those books and teachers tell you how to affirm "I am a Godly person," or how to overpower negative thoughts with positive ones. But shouting that you're good, to cover up a whisper that you're not, is not the same as uncovering that whisper, seeing that it's delusion, and discarding it completely.

Both "I am incomplete, I am not Godly" and "I *am* complete, I *am* Godly" are noise of the mind. That approach stems from the basic fear that if there is *no* affirming, *no* self-monitoring, *no* ego, *no* making sure, *no* caution; if we surrender into the Spontaneous Genius of being alive, that it won't be enough. That's a lack of faith, no matter how constructive or attractive its packaging. We just have to remove the garbage which covers our Godliness. We don't have to create it, strengthen it, or supervise it.

Spiritual life is always about becoming a Divine Nobody; no identities, no expectations, no goals, just a free-flowing expression of God's will, being magically created fresh in the image of God in every moment. A lot of the books try to help you become a good *somebody*. That's nice, but it's not the same as freedom.

It's Spontaneous Genius that we're after. I mean, let's face it, who can walk on water? Nobody can walk on water, right? That's how He did it. There was nobody there but God. There was Spontaneous Genius, and it came time to walk on water and so, walking on water occurred. Who can heal the sick and raise the dead? Nobody. Right! That's who did it! There wasn't "somebody" there, thinking "I think it would be a good idea now to raise Lazarus." There was just this Be-ing -- that's a verb, not a noun, this human be-ing. The noise of our desires and fears is all that prevents us from *being* such fearless expressions of Godliness.

I saw a list of about forty rules the other day. It was in a peacemaking newsletter. Things that we're always supposed to have in our awareness, like, if you have a difference of opinion with somebody, don't make them wrong, and remember to listen, and all of the things that you say yes, that's the way that human beings should relate.

But my God, there's no faith that that is how we relate when we get quiet. When we open up to our Stillness and surrender, We don't need to develop a *more* active mind -- "Uh, let's see, wait. Gee, I really disagree with her, but I don't want to make her wrong, so I'm going to . . . ." We're not trained horses! Life is an entirely different situation -- and a lot more fun -- than the peacemaking newsletter supposes.

Will you talk a little about your prison work?

Well, I have been *doing* the prison work for the last 45 minutes. Because all I do in prisons is what I'm doing on myself. This is what I do. Prison can turn out to be an interesting place to open up into the Stillness, because a lot of the social ties and obligations, a lot of the opportunities for fulfilling desires, a lot of the financial responsibilities, etc., that tend to distract us, or at least tend to be our excuses for not taking any time to become still, aren't available to people in prison.

People in prison have already had the family ties and social ties and objects of desire ripped away from them. If you're in prison, it doesn't matter whether you chose to get in, or whether it's even fair, whether you were framed, whether you're innocent or guilty. Wherever you are, we're saying you can use that place to get free.

There's a tremendous pull on the part of prisoners to discover that freedom in themselves. And I don't really care so much about sin and guilt, I'm talking about awakening. In the process of awakening, we experience the pain and the fruit of all of the seeds that we planted. And so I help prepare people for that.

In meditation, somebody who's killed somebody will probably go through periods of tremendous guilt or shame from having taken a life or from having lived a really bad life, a selfish life, etc. These are the layers of noise which cover over our Stillness, so they're bound to be experienced along the way. I teach people how to sit still through anything. So an overpowering memory, emotion, guilt, can rip through you like a tornado and you have developed the Stillness of body and the Stillness of speech.

The Buddha mentioned the Threefold Silence, or Noble Silence: Silence of body, Silence of speech and Silence of mind. Silence of mind takes a while, but we can achieve Silence of body (sitting down) and Silence of speech (shutting up) fairly quickly. I help prisoners develop those two silences so that when the really painful noise of the mind rips through like a freight train, they don't break down, get up, or scream out.

So they keep breathing and feel the pain fully. They see themselves clearly, feel the pain they've caused, and let it help them grow. Guilt can be useful if it's used constructively. Guilt can help make us more compassionate.

To me, the thing that matters is the Stillness. That's the pot of gold at the end. I'm not a psychologist, I'm not in the business of trying to help people analyze these things. I'm just telling them that these are probably layers that are going to be reached as they dive into their Stillness; I'm just helping prepare them for the shock. So we teach them how to sit still. We introduce them to reflective thought. We send them books, etc., all aimed toward finding their own inner guidance.

In talking earlier about uncovering those layers through meditation practice and things like that, into the Stillness, wouldn't you say that psychological and psychiatric work tends to uncover layers as well, and tends to do it many times more quickly? Is that not the path, also?

The "path" is simply to keep discarding false identities of who and what we are. If any tool helps you to remove layers covering your Stillness, then use the tool. It may be hard to discard identities if our minds are still screwed up about what our parents did to us, or screwed up about having been raped, or about having this happen or that happen.

So, if somebody tries to meditate and is unable to let it go that way, maybe therapy is a good idea as a temporary fix. Get this wrinkle ironed out. Then go back and let go of that abused child identity. "I am not that child who was abused. That's just a memory now. It's just clinging, and I can let it go, now that I've clarified what happened and how it affected me."

For some people, meditation does it all, and for some it's necessary for some kind of therapy. Journal writing, I think, is another good method. For me, speaking shows me where I'm at. I hear what's important to me come out, and it's always fresh. When I write, it's the same thing. I never know what I'm going to write about for a newsletter, I just write what's in my heart, and that's like therapy for me.

So, I think it's a personal decision as to whether anything is a useful tool or not.

At a point when psychotherapy or anything else becomes a crutch, an external authority or dependency, then honor it for what it's given you, and move on. For example -- and I'll probably get in trouble for saying this -- AA does a wonderful job of *beginning* to help somebody through a period of dependency on alcohol. But the vast majority of AA members latch on to that identity for a lifetime. Yet spiritual work is about gradually giving up *all* identities. Can you picture, "Hi, I'm Jesus and I'm an alcoholic?" "Hi, I'm God and I'm an alcoholic."

Or a codependent.

Sure. Or "I have PTSD," or "I'm a rape victim" or anything else. To whatever degree support groups and therapy help us to work through delusion and get back to self-reliance, they're enormously helpful, especially at a time of great pain or confusion. But let's not substitute one set of delusions and reliances for another.

Many support groups merely serve as group hiding places with an attitude like, "This is who we are, and nobody who hasn't been..." -- fill in the blank -- an alcoholic, a junkie, a convict, rape victim, abused as a child, etc. -- "nobody who hasn't been blah blah can understand what we've been through." Or, "I've been raped, and you haven't, and you'll never be able to understand what I feel. Don't you dare say you understand my pain." Again, substitute "a convict" or anything else for "raped."

There's a thing called empathy. Empathy is not just a word, empathy is a very profound experience. We can take someone else's pain into our hearts and feel it without having to experience the same exact source of the pain. If we're looking to divide our world, it's always easy. "You're Russian and I'm American, you don't understand my cultural experience." We can just divide it in any way. "I had a big car wreck and had this surgery and that surgery, this fear and that pain, and you can't understand..." But it's silly.

The aim of any spiritual work is to unite, not to separate, and support groups or therapy need to unite too, not just with people who've been through the same experience and not just to strengthen the ego, but to open up past the pain and be a healthy citizen of the world who sees that everybody is family, all places are home, and all experiences arise from the same Stillness.

What about things that control your life that you don't know? I was poor, so unknown to myself I made a commitment somewhere that I would never be poor. And for better than thirty years, money controlled me, instead of I controlling money. Someone pointed this out to me, and now my whole life has changed.

Until we are fully aware like the Buddha or the Christ, there are things in all of our lives that control us, simply because we're not aware of them.

A warrior king stopped on his way to a battle, and stopped to see the Buddha, and said, "I have very little time. I'm on my way to war and I might die, and I just want to know, can you sum up in one word what all your teachings are about?" And the Buddha said, "Awareness." Or, as Jesus put it, "Know the truth and the truth shall set you free." Awareness and truth are the same.

In this process of becoming still, little by little we let go of limitations, we let go of the things that control us. And we feel proportionately freer. It's unbelievable, the freedom that comes from not being controlled by so many things. Just walking around, it's like this extraordinary ordinary state. It's not that we've *gotten* anything, it's just being unfettered by thousands of little chains of desires and fears.

I feel a flow of power and fearlessness in my daily, trivial life that I never dreamed was possible to feel. Just being not so reactive to my likes and dislikes, being less demanding on how reality should work, being able to walk in a room and not have social fears of whether you'll like me or not, as well as the bigger things like not seeing illness and death as my enemies, etc. All of that noise, those desires and fears, not controlling what I do or say anymore. The power underneath is now just free to flow through me, and it's like, it just feels so good to be simply *alive*.

Gradually we break those ties that bind us, and we're freer than we were before, like you are now from that poverty thing. Gee, that's great; now you're free to be poor. [laughter] But it *is* great, to be free to be poor. Because now, you can take or leave wealth. You no longer require it. That's great.

Yeah, but when I came to this realization, the first thought was how many more . . .?

Thousands. Thousands. But you don't have to uncover them in one particular way, you don't have to bring them into rational awareness, and you don't have to resolve them one at a time. You can have a moment of meditation in which a thousand of them come up at once, and you see them without grabbing or flinching, and they all just leave. And you get up from that single meditation, and you're like thirty pounds lighter and freer of past burdens. So, it happens. And then there might be one that you're working with for 35 years.

Remember, the peace which surpasses understanding does *surpass* understanding. The New Age culture seems to say that if you think good thoughts and if you free yourself through therapy or whatever else from these things that are controlling you, and if you get yourself balanced between inner and outer, you'll be at peace. I want to remind you, the transcendent is *transcendent*. It isn't a matter of *any* formula.

What can be understood is not the Stillness, and the Stillness cannot be understood. So once again, the trick is to do whatever therapy or self-examination or wholesome lifestyles we need to do, just enough to then move beyond them.

Some teachers, even doctors, say that all illness is just "dis-ease," and even AIDS or cancer can be cured by loving ourselves unconditionally.

I would be cautious about those teachings. On one hand, our minds and Spirits are certainly stronger than any bodily illness, and anything *can* be healed. But that doesn't mean illness is wrong, or that *everything* is supposed to be healed. If something is wrong about dying at age thirty from AIDS, then tell me, what's the "right" age to die? Is it 80? Go ask a 79-year-old! And what's the "right" cause of death? Heart attack? Train wreck?

It's the most natural thing in the world to want to feel good and stay healthy and live a long life, and we should use any reasonable powers of mind and body to do so. That's where some of those teachings come in handy. But don't get drawn into the notion that illness implies failure on your part, or that death is a tragedy. Illness and death come to us all, at many different ages and in many different ways, *and* for many different purposes.

Haven't you seen illness and death bring enormous amounts of love, patience, humility and forgiveness into our lives and the lives of our families and friends? Illness and death are not the enemy.

In terms of strategies, being seriously ill seems like a powerful time to quiet down and look into our Stillness. If it happens to be true that we caused our illness by stress or a lack of love for ourselves, we'll see the truth of that as we quiet our minds, and we can do whatever we need to do about it. That seems more helpful than *busying* our minds with a million affirmations and positive mind-games which may or may not be on target.

I just keep getting back to the one Stillness as the source of our very best guidance. I know that Stillness personally. And I know it in a way that I know that you have that Stillness too. I know that it's not just mine -- it's laughable to think that it could be. When you're in the Stillness, there's only one of it. So, I say look, I found the Stillness, not my Stillness, I found *The* Stillness. The Stillness is in you, too. Be Still, and know that You Am God.

All the universe is but a sign to be read rightly;
colors and forms are only put here to speak to us;
and all is Spirit, there is nothing else in existence.
War and peace, love and separation, are hidden gateways
to other worlds and other times.
Let us not grow old still believing
that truth is what the most people see around them.

-- Wm. Buck, The Ramayana

SONNY BOY

[this song was written for
the occasion of our son,
Josh, leaving home]

I watched you being born, I saw the first time you breathed;
   I Held your tiny hand and I could hardly believe it.
Seemed like it would last forever back then,
   But now it's in the past, though I see it all again and again.

[refrain:]
     Sonny boy, I know that you can't stay,
   you have to find your own way, and I love you.
    Sonny boy, I know you'll take your stand,
  and you will find a good man inside of you, Sonny boy.

You were Superboy, Bionic Man, a Light just running free;
   I helped you check your height by making notches in the tree.
Your changing cast of characters I thought would never end,
   Now they're in the past though I see 'em all again and again.

[refrain]

In your teens, across your face the pain and wonder flashed,
   I felt the hurt in both of us each time our tempers clashed.
You went from little boy of mine to being my best friend,
   Now that's another time, but I see it all again and again.

[refrain]

Many years from now, though it'll seem too soon,
   In some dusty box somehow you'll find this little tune.
Your own kids may be grown & gone, you'll wonder how & when
   You forgot this little song, then you'll smile
                   as you hear it again.

[final refrain 2x]

GRIEF IS JUST LOVE
WITH A BAD REPUTATION

[from HKF newsletter, Fall 1989. This article brought the most response we've ever received, and was reprinted in *Utne Reader*.]

Josh, our only child, has left home. He's a bright, handsome, healthy, kind, talented eighteen-year-old, and now he's off to find his own Great Adventure. For now, that means living in L.A. to further his acting career which he's been pursuing since the age of nine. Sita and I are so proud of him and happy for him, and happy too for the world, because he'll surely be sharing his gifts to make it a better place. At the same time, our hearts are broken into a million pieces over the loss of our child into adulthood. Our child-raising years are over, and they came and went so fast we can barely grasp it. I don't think I've ever felt more pain, even over my father's death.

Yeah, yeah, Sita and I know all the standard consolations our families and friends have been offering: "Oh, you'll see him a lot!" "He'll call!" "You'll always be his parents." "You'll love each other even more," and on and on. And you know something? All those things are true, and they don't take a damn thing away from our hearts being broken. Because there's nothing wrong with our hearts being broken.

There's nothing wrong with feeling agony over the passing of Josh's childhood. There's nothing wrong with opening the drawers to his dresser, seeing every drawer empty, and gasping in pain like my heart is being wrenched right out of my body without anesthetic. I built that dresser, along with his bed, by cutting dead cedar trees, milling the boards and crafting every little bit of it with love for my precious boy.

There's nothing wrong with me and Sita sitting silently in the evening, holding hands and allowing the tears to flow down our cheeks as we listen to the aching emptiness in our home -- the home we all built together, nine-year-old Josh taking a million swings at each nail on the roof and bending more than a few of them beyond belief, Sita always keeping one eye on him no matter what else she was doing.

There's nothing wrong with letting your heart break, because it's always Love that breaks it. Each time it breaks, it grows back bigger (if you let it) and then it can hold even more Love. Then it breaks again, grows bigger again, and on and on. That's how we gradually surrender all the boundaries we place on Love, so that one day we can open fully into the boundless Heart of God.

If we avoid intensely painful experiences, we give up a great deal of spiritual power. The pain of our hearts stretching past the breaking point is one of the most meaningful spiritual initiations of a lifetime. Who ever said that life is supposed to be just happy or neutral or even bearable? Life is high drama, tragedy, comedy, adventure, mystery! We can't cross the Ocean of Existence by hiding in a safe little harbor! As George Bernard Shaw put it, "I want to be thoroughly used up when I die."

There's a spirituality on the rise these days which is terribly lopsided toward positive feelings and experiences. It started out all right about ten or fifteen years ago -- encouraging people to be more positive and stop causing so many self-created problems in their lives. But somewhere it blurred the line between self-created pain and natural, important pain.

Now its main message seems to be to avoid pain and negativity at all cost -- avoid, ignore, deny, re-define -- anything so long as you stay positive. You're not supposed to say "oh shit!" when you get a flat tire or hit your thumb with a hammer, you're supposed to say something like "oh well, let go and let God." You're supposed to stick countless affirmations all over your refrigerator door to keep brainwashing yourself with positive thoughts. There's a whole raft of books and cassettes these days which basically teach you how to distort the realities of your life until they all look positive.

But why? When we really know that it's all God, we can play *all* our parts honestly, saying "Oh shit" at the flat tire and "how wonderful" at a wedding; we can say "damn it, look at those gas prices," and "thank God Johnny made parole;" we can say "I've been depressed lately," or "this is a great period in my life," with equal wisdom. And we can allow major milestones, like our children leaving home or the death of a loved one, or being sentenced to prison, to help us explore the profound mysteries of love and grief no matter how long it takes or what it looks like to our friends. We don't have to take advice like, "Okay, listen, you've had a good cry, now it's time to get on with your life."

Clinging to the positive side of life is not spiritual wisdom, it's spiritual wimpdom. The true seeker sees that neither positive nor negative, nor life nor death, are what they seem. As Walt Whitman said, *Every moment of Darkness and Light is a Miracle*. So when you get kicked in the stomach, you don't have to force a smile and say "my, what a miracle!" You can double over and go "ooooff!" because doubling over and going "ooooff!" is a miracle too, and it's a lot more honest one.

Obviously we don't walk around hoping to get kicked in the stomach or run over by a train, but life will bring us many natural moments of pain and struggle anyway. We lose people we love, we get injured, sick, betrayed, lonely, afraid. Even Jesus experienced those natural human struggles.

True spirituality allows us to experience *all* of life -- not just the easy parts -- with fearlessness, respect and honesty. One prisoner used to sign all his letters to me, "loss and gain, pleasure, pain, all the same." Life really *is* a miracle, just as it is, without dressing it up in funny hats or pretentious affirmations.

There's a story about the ancient Tibetan guru, Marpa. When his son died, Marpa cried for days, weeping and wailing in absolute agony. His students, though compassionate, were amazed to see an enlightened being in such an intense state of grief. Finally, a senior student approached him and said gently, "Master, you have taught us that everything in life comes and goes, and that it is folly to try to hold on to anyone or anything. You have taught us that these bodies and these identities, and even birth and death, are nothing but illusion. How can you carry on like this over the loss of your son if it is all just illusion?

Marpa looked up and replied, "Yes, it is indeed all illusion, but this is **heavy** illusion!"

I was in my early twenties when I first heard that story, and my understanding of it for about ten years was that Marpa admitted to being thrown off-center by the heaviness of his son's death. But as I grew older and opened my heart further, I came to see that there's nothing off-center or unenlightened about carrying on as he did. Life is indeed an illusion of sorts, but sometimes the illusion is light and happy, and sometimes it's heavy and sad.

Liberation means freedom, including the freedom to laugh or cry as each situation warrants. It's about living in Truth each moment of our lives, not imitating a bland concept of enlightened behavior. As an old saying goes, "Before enlightenment, chopping wood and carrying water. After enlightenment, chopping wood and carrying water." The differences are tremendous, but not necessarily visible from the outside.

Besides, as pain and pleasure get really intense, they become mysteriously similar. Isn't it hard to tell when someone is crying tears of agony or tears of joy? Many times, even the one who's crying isn't sure. Agony and ecstasy are forever intertwined. If we avoid the agony, we push away ecstasy as well. I've been in ecstasy several times, and I've also looked very closely at the nature of grief while right in the middle of it. The core of each is the same. Look for yourself.

Grief is just Love with a bad reputation. Really. It's forceful and a little scary because it's so internal and undistracted. It's definitely trying to break our hearts, but that's good, not bad. We say that grief is a "sense of loss," but what does "loss" feel like? What's the feeling made of?

As I look through our family album and see a youthful Bo and Sita holding our beautiful baby boy, and I face the incomprehensible fact that those sweet, sweet days are gone forever, what is that lump in my throat and pain in my heart? Isn't it made of love and joy and gratitude and awe and wonder?

So, these days we ache, and I wouldn't trade it for the world. It's so much more powerful than feeling superficially positive. It's an ache filled with nostalgia and wonder about how life rushes by, no matter how happily or how sadly we live it.

Most of us had pretty shitty childhoods, didn't we? I don't even remember the day I first left home at sixteen. I just wanted to get out of there. I certainly never helped build the family home or sat around playing rock and roll guitar with my dad, like Josh did. My dad was in his forties when I was born, and he was paralyzed from the time I was nine until he died fourteen years later. My mother worked all the time to take care of him and us four kids. My brothers and I unloaded trucks or did construction as soon as we each got big enough to work.

You know what I'm talking about. Many of the people reading this had it a lot worse than I did. So you just couldn't wait to get old enough to leave and find something better, and there's this little part of your mind which hates childhood itself for having been so painful. And you think maybe your heart wouldn't be holding so much hurt if things had been better.

Well, Josh had a *great* childhood. When he was born, Sita and I had a chance to *be* the parents we wished we could have had -- youthful, healthy, hip, loving, supportive. Josh has been appreciated, respected and enjoyed every day of his life. Imagine how much it hurts to see Time march brazenly into our cozy little home and split up our threesome forever.

So if life hurts when it's this good, and life hurts when it's so bad, it's hard not to be filled with wonder, isn't it?

The bottom line is, we can live life fully as ordinary human beings, and at the same time see the bigger, transcendent picture. We can face success, failure, health, illness, birth and death as mortal humans, and simultaneously as immortal souls. We can be free enough to enjoy our highs, endure our lows, cheer our victories, and bitch about our defeats, all with an underlying freedom and humor.

Seeing the way things really are -- which is a good reason to quiet our minds and clear our vision through meditation, breathing, prayer, study, etc. -- we can play our parts with great power in every stage of our lives. We can live out a full, uncensored human experience in a way that brightens our Light as we get older, because even though the body decays and falters, our hearts and souls can be free of fear, aversion, and the countless limitations we imposed on ourselves before we knew the score.

Tonight, Sita and I can be free enough to feel the joy of God, and also ache for the absence of our son. What a full plate!

● ● ●

Josh Lozoff, 1990

True love hurts.

-- Mother Theresa

A superficial consumer lifestyle isn't really enough for anyone... but because of what they've been exposed to, ex-cons, war vets, victims of rape, abuse, etc., may feel the emptiness of it sooner and more deeply than people who haven't had such profound experiences.

NEGATIVE & POSITIVE PROFUNDITY

[from Human Kindness Foundation newsletter, Summer 1988]

> *Since I've been in this place, Bo, I've seen nice young kids get gang-raped, I've seen human beings be bought and sold and traded for packs of smokes, I've seen guards pull shit that was worse than most of the crimes us convicts ever committed, I've seen a system that makes a joke of fairness and rehabilitation. Now I'm supposed to get out, get a steady job and an apartment, and pretend everything's okay, right? Well, it ain't okay. It's just like getting back from 'Nam. This daily bullshit don't make sense anymore. There's gotta be something bigger than a paycheck and going bowling with the guys, you know? But I don't know what it is.*

Life gets lived on a lot of different levels. The modern consumer lifestyle which gets pitched to us day and night through tv, movies, newspapers, and magazines is not very deep. It's a world of wanting and getting, buying and selling -- because that's what makes consumerism work. But have you ever noticed that after somebody has a heart attack, or loses a child, or goes through anything really heavy, their outlook can change overnight? They see life on a deeper level than before. They tend to think about the bigger things and not care so much about what color their cars are or whether last year's bathing suit is still in style.

Well, prison life, too, is lived on a deeper level than the lifestyle that comes across on sitcoms. Seeing the very worst of human nature, having to live in the midst of constant fear, despair, violence and terrible waste of human talents, is a profound experience. It may be horribly negative, but it's profound.

I have a hunch one of the most common reasons for recidivism is that life on the streets is too blatantly superficial for many people who have experienced such darkness. Ex-cons are expected to fall into line as normal conformists and consumers much like Vietnam vets were expected to do, but in both cases, that lifestyle may not heal their wounds. Negativity has opened up a very deep place in these people, and suddenly the negative forces may be gone, yet they can't find any encouragement or assistance to fill that deep place in positive ways.

That's one of the reasons I'm very strong on human service

work. Whether it's a fulltime job or an hour a week as a volunteer, feeding the poorest of the poor, housing the homeless, rescuing the trapped, working in some way to lighten the load of others, is perhaps the greatest healing force in the world. There's magic in it. It fills that deep, negative place with experiences of real human dignity, hopefulness, compassion, and gratitude.

I know it may sound strange that picking up diseased, dying beggars off the street can somehow remind us of human dignity, but just ask anyone who has done it. Helping others fills up a lot of empty spaces in our hearts.

Applied to prisoners and ex-cons, service makes even more sense. Besides healing those personal wounds, they get a chance to make a payback for some of the negativity they may have brought into this world (yes, even the crimes you weren't busted for; we're talking cosmically here, not legalistically).

In every community in the world, there are needs which aren't met for some people. Ex-cons can live a very enjoyable life, and still be part of the forces which try to meet those needs.

Prison rehabilitation programs generally focus on skills and education. Skills and education are wonderful, they're important, but they're not the biggest issue. A tremendous number of skilled and educated people commit crimes, and an even greater number, though they may not break the law, are generally unhappy and can't figure out how to make their lives work.

The idea isn't just to get out and stay out. The best idea is to take a different look at how life works and doesn't work. That way, when things go wrong in ways that skills or education can't fix -- as they surely will every now and then -- the first impulse isn't to knock off a convenience store or blow somebody's brains out. People with deeper values already see the world very differently than that.

As a society, the overall image we tend to project is pretty lightweight in terms of human values. For example, read any article on lottery winners, or watch any game show on tv. When winners are interviewed about what they intend to do with their winnings -- even when it's millions of dollars -- almost never will you hear a mention of giving to worthy causes or creating their own charities, or doing anything at all that could make a difference in their communities or the world at large.

That's not what the interviewers or the audience want to hear. Look carefully at the Publisher's Clearinghouse Sweepstakes prizes next time you get one in the mail. Ed McMahon is happy to give examples of ways you can improve your life if you win the jackpot: Luxurious yachts, vacation homes, world cruises, fancy sportscars. But not even one line on one page comes close to the idea of spending part of it to help the world. Yet most of us know that would bring us more lasting joy than ten Ferrari convertibles.

So I guess part of what I'm saying is that prisoners and ex-cons need to live with deeper values than many "free" people in our society. Don't get me wrong -- a superficial consumer lifestyle isn't *really* enough for anyone, and people find that out in many different ways. But because of what they've been exposed to, ex-cons, war vets, victims of rape, abuse, etc., may feel the emptiness of it sooner and more deeply than people who haven't had such profound experiences.

And although people on the street may come into contact with many opportunities to consider some sort of human service work, such opportunities aren't usually presented in rehabilitation or re-entry programs.

If you're in prison or getting out of prison, the simple message is that you may need to be a wiser, more caring human being than may be "required" of you. You don't need to be some kind of goody-goody who stacks the chairs after church every Sunday. You don't need to lose your sense of humor or playfulness. But you may need to be more philosophical about your life than your old friends or family members are about theirs.

For your life on the streets to make sense, you may need to think about pay*back* as well as pay*check*, about values as well as valuables. Take a while to think about the quote from George Bernard Shaw at the end of this newsletter (page 154). I think we've all been "a feverish, selfish little clod of ailments and grievances" at various times in our lives, so we should be able to remember that it doesn't get us anywhere.

Self-honesty, courage, kindness, sense of humor, and sense of wonder are every bit as important a checklist as the more "practical" things like job, apartment, transportation, and lover. Millions of miserable people have jobs, apartments, cars and lovers. But I challenge you to find me one miserable person whose life expresses self-honesty, courage, kindness, sense of humor and sense of wonder.

And of course, all these things apply even to someone who's never going to get out of prison. There are a lot of things prisoners can do to express kindness in the world while they're still locked up. Don't wait for the system to hand you ideas, because that could be a long wait. Quiet your mind a little, look into your own heart, and get some feeling about giving help rather than asking for it. I swear to you, there is magic in this world, and service is one key to unlock it in our own lives.

● ● ●

Dear Bo,

I am presently on my 17th year for a double murder, I accepted this guilt many years ago, and worked my way into understanding just how much hurt I have caused so many people in the past.

I cannot simply write someone's family and say I am sorry. Sorry didn't do it. I did. I would like to find a way to make it up to not only the families but to society also.

I spend 20 minutes twice a day in meditation, I know the answer is to be found somewhere within myself and that only I can find it.

I want to thank you for your books, We're All Doing Time *and* Lineage and Other Stories. *I really do appreciate them and their wisdom.*

I also appreciate the opportunity to write to you and thank you for all you have done for the men behind bars everywhere.

Setting Still, M

Dear M,

I was very touched by the honesty and directness of your letter. The situation you're in is not new -- people throughout history have committed murder before they became spiritually awakened, and then tried to find ways to make "payback" for what they did. Some of the greatest saints were murderers first.

To answer your question, about finding a way to make it up to "not only the families, but to society also," the answer is simple: Devote your life to helping the world be a kinder, more caring place. That's the payback. That's why we encourage meditation and so forth -- to keep a clear mind and open heart, and be a good force wherever you are. Be ready to live and even die for what's right and what brings the world closer together instead of splitting it further apart.

But the bottom line is, it's up to you in each and every moment -- not in a heavy, self-righteous way, but rather full of life and good humor -- to bring Light to whatever's going on. Your letter itself is a good start. If you can just be this simple and caring during every minute of the day, you'll be making up for what you did.

I don't know the situation enough to say anything about contacting the families one way or another. But don't rule it out. Just bring it up into your mind every now and then as your mind gets clearer from meditation. Don't think of such things as "decisions." They're actually "recognitions." We have to clear our vision well enough to recognize the truth of what we need to do.

All the best and all my love to you, brother.

Love, Bo

● ● ●

Dear Bo,

I read your stuff and really like your energy a lot, I mean you're obviously good people and all, but man, all I really need is to get out of this place. What's wrong with warm bodies, cold beers, and fast cars if you're not hurting anybody to get it, huh?

I've screwed up in the past and I'm not blaming nobody but myself. But man, soon as I hit the streets, it's a good time I'm after, and I don't see nothing wrong with that. Do you?

With respect, Y

Dear Y,

There's nothing "wrong" with it, but there's also nothing wrong about cutting bread with a dull axe instead of a good bread knife; it just doesn't work as well. A happy life takes tools and skills just like anything else.

No matter how much you may enjoy dreaming about a warm body, a cold beer and a fast car while you're locked up, none of those will *keep* you happy if you don't have other, deeper stuff going on in your life. Bodies get cold, beers get warm, and cars break down.

Why does life work like that? Because each one of us is supposed to be a hero, a noble figure crafted in the image of God -- not just selfish pleasure-junkies forever chasing everything that the advertisers cram down our throats, or every sensual whim.

We're supposed to be alert and good-humored, generous and compassionate, courageous and open-minded. We're supposed to leave things better than we found them, leave people happier for having met us, leave the Earth more alive rather than closer to destruction because of our presence.

If you want to be an outlaw to those natural laws of life, go ahead; no one will stop you. But it's never going to bring you lasting happiness. "Looking out for #1" simply doesn't work, inside or outside of the joint. People like me didn't create that truth, we just realize it and pass the word.

Good luck doing whatever you do, Bo

● ● ●

"This is the true joy of life, the being used up for a purpose recognized by yourself as a mighty one; being a force of nature instead of a feverish, selfish, little clod of ailments and grievances, complaining that the world will not devote itself to making you happy. I am of the opinion that my life belongs to the community, and as long as I live, it is my privilege to do for it whatever I can. I want to be thoroughly used up when I die, for the harder I work the more I live. Life is no 'brief candle' to me. It is a sort of splendid torch which I have got hold of for a moment, and I want to make it burn as brightly as possible before handing it on to future generations."

-- George Bernard Shaw

Go all over the world,
correlating happiness and unhappiness
with kindness and unkindness.
The results will be overwhelming
across all nations --
happy people value kindness;
unkind people aren't happy.

PRISONS AS CENTERS OF KINDNESS

[from Human Kindness Foundation newsletter, Fall 1988]

> *" If not you, who ? If not now, when ? "*
> -- Hillel

Kindness is one of the natural laws of the universe. Everybody would like to feel it; everyone likes being around it; living without it leads to unhappiness and even poor health. We award the Nobel Peace Prize to Mother Theresa for her kindness; we teach our children the virtues and benefits of it.

But when some of those children grow up and break our laws, we lock them up in places where kindness is rare and is considered naive, weak, or even impossible. Staff and inmates alike put on self-protective masks of toughness and cynicism, even though no one can really thrive in such an environment.

Wouldn't it seem more reasonable to put outlaws in a place which *cherishes* kindness, reminds them of how important it is, and affords them opportunities to develop and express it?

If a twenty-year-old idealist, or a bleeding-heart liberal, or a preacher who'd never been inside a joint, had said what I just said, we could dismiss him as somebody who doesn't understand the realities of life inside. But I do know how tough it is, how scary it is. I've been both an outlaw and a prison worker. I've been inside over 300 prisons, and know many thousands of prisoners personally, including a couple of cousins, an uncle, and a brother-in-law.

Knowing all the difficulties involved, I still say the time has come to take this next step toward being a more mature civilization. Each of us has a part to play in taking that step; we can't pass the buck to the other guy and say we have to wait for him or her. All of us -- prisoners, prison workers and the general public -- must begin, one by one, to see how crazy it is to attempt rehabilitation without valuing kindness above all other forms of training, education or therapy.

Conservatives and liberals alike have designed prisons to be narcissistic environments. Whether negative or positive -- from basic survival to getting a college degree -- an inmate's attention is focused intensely on himself. And in dealing with inmates, most of us tend to reinforce the narcissism.

After a while, it's easy for a prisoner to assume the role of always being the needy one, always the one on the receiving end, the assumption being that he or she isn't expected or able to give anything. Then the prisoner may get out, and we complain that he or she just can't seem to get along with people or be comfortable in a job or romantic relationship -- all of which require good "giving" skills, all of which require an element of kindness.

We tend to regard kindness as a "soft" issue, not a "hard" fact like the need for education or training. But kindness isn't just a corny moral or religious value; it's as scientifically verifiable as gravity. If you doubt this, then do some research: Go all over the world, correlating happiness and unhappiness with kindness and unkindness. The results will be overwhelming across all nations -- happy people value kindness; unkind people aren't happy.

As the 20th Century dawned, we left behind the notion of "insane asylums" and gradually acknowledged the need to treat mental illness with compassion, creativity, and hope. Now the 21st Century is dawning, and it's time for us to take the same step with criminal behavior -- leaving behind prisons-as-warehouses, and acknowledging the need for facilities which surround inmates with kindness, fairness, and encouragement to change for the better.

As my part in taking that step, I include the following "letters" written to the prison system, prisoners, and society.

● ● ●

Dear 20th-Century Prison System,

You can't "correct" prisoners or help them correct themselves by creating cold, impersonal environments which focus, at best, on skills or training rather than on basic, human-to-human interactions. When we put somebody back out on the street, we have to hope he or she is a more caring human being. You can't "train" or "educate" a sense of caring. It has to be shown in the environment itself, and in the way you do everything you do.

You send absurdly mixed messages out to prisoners. In many places, you call them "Mr. ___," which, according to the outside world, is a term of respect; but in prison it seems instead to be a reminder that you don't want to be personal or friendly. You insist that guards be called "correctional officers," yet you don't allow them to form friendships with inmates.

You say you want inmates to develop stronger social values, yet you forbid best friends from staying in touch with each other when one gets transferred or paroled. You claim to encourage sensible planning and reliability, yet you maintain an atmosphere in which a prisoner can be transferred to a new location without warning, or lose his job or all his prized possessions in a shake-down, with no explanations, apologies or negotiation.

You expect ex-cons to be responsible, yet while they're inside, a bell or whistle defines every moment of their day. You claim to encourage future social decency among your inmates, yet you maintain an environment in which it is dangerous to speak out, help a friend, or show one's true feelings about anything.

The thousands of prisoners I've known who truly changed their lives in prison seemed to do it, for the most part, *despite* your system rather than because of it. Why are you so resistant to change? Why do you remain so difficult? It's bad for you, bad for your staff and officers, and bad for the people you hope to "correct." If you won't change, then it's up to your staff people to wise up and make you change bit by bit, by expressing true kindness, more common sense, and abiding by the spirit of your rules rather than the letter of them.

And if they get fired for doing so, it's time for them to go to the media and let the public know what's going on behind the walls. It's time to let this era of incarceration fade into history.

There is absolutely no conflict between running a kind facility and running a secure one. Kindness is an attitude which can underlie even the strictest rules of custody. A facility expressing kindness, fairness and encouragement can also be a facility which maintains no-nonsense policies about escapes, contraband, and general inmate behavior.

The vast majority of prison inmates would love the opportunity to turn their lives around for the better. It's time you, the system, opened your heart to that yearning instead of treating your programs and program specialists like nuisances or token legal requirements. Change is inevitable, because the system doesn't work. Why be dragged into this change kicking and screaming, instead of being at the forefront of it?

● ● ●

Dear Prison Inmates,

What if the system doesn't change anytime soon? It would be easy to lay this all off on the prison systems and say, "look here, you've got to run our prisons with more kindness." People have been saying that for years, and we're still waiting for it to change.

But you too have a responsibility to help make the world a better place. As terrible as prisons are, your behavior toward each other is just as terrible. Even those of you who "do your own time" look the other way when a Brother or Sister gets ripped off, raped or even killed. This allegiance to the stupid "Convict Code" set down by a small number of 1940's petty gangsters, allows the tone of prison life to be set by a small minority of the most brutal convicts in the institution.

You must develop a new "Convict Code" based on respect, tolerance, and mutual support -- where a con can trust that cons watch out for each other and allow each other to live in peace and self-dignity; where if a gang of ten threatens you, you can count on a hundred -- of all races and creeds -- to stand with you and say "That kind of stuff doesn't fly here any more."

I know this isn't an easy task, and most of you just want to get out of prison alive. But if your prison life is "Hey man, I'm looking out for number one, and I just want to get out of here in one piece," then that's pretty much how your street life is going to be too. It's an empty way to live. Anywhere we ever are, there are going to be values like kindness to stand up for, sometimes to suffer or even die for. That's how we gain the self-respect which can hold up anywhere, under any circumstances.

I've talked with countless prisoners one-on-one, and every one of you wanted to treat others with respect and kindness and be treated the same way. But when you leave me and go back out into population, you cop your old attitude. It's sort of like, "Well, I ain't gonna be the first one to turn over that new leaf; I'd get stepped on."

I know cruel things have happened to each of you. But none of you has been beaten, scorned, punished or laughed at more than Jesus was. No one of you has given up his very life for the good of others, as did Mahatma Gandhi and Martin Luther King.

Yet those men, even in their humiliation and deaths, showed such greatness of the human spirit that they continue to inspire us long after they passed our way.

Whatever you've gone through, whatever you've suffered, however much suffering you've caused to others, none of it prevents you from caring about the people around you -- not only inmates, but guards, staff, etc. You have to break the circle of pain and selfishness or forever be lashed to it.

You tell me you really want to change your life for the better. Then do it. Don't rip anyone off. Stop lying. Trust somebody until they prove you can't. Cautiously open up your honest feelings with the people who seem like they want the same thing. Don't manipulate or lay guilt on your family, friends, and outside organizations. Don't harden yourself to suffering just because it's painful to deal with.

Put dope and booze behind you so you can pay clearer attention to the changes you want to go through. You and I have had enough dope and booze. Some of the experiences we had on drugs may even have been important for us, but there comes a time when you have to move on.

And look into this idea of kindness. Kindness is a great mystery. It heals so many old wounds and hurts we can't possibly count them all. Take up the challenge of how to become a truly kind person without being exploited or abused in a place like this.

Look around for ways to express a little kindness around the prison, the outside community, or the world. Discover the magic!

No one can ever do that part for you. And it's never going to be any easier wherever you are. People who wait, tend to wait forever and die waiting. Take responsibility instead. Then you'll begin to feel the self-respect and self-dignity you've been writing to me about for so long.

● ● ●

Dear Society,

Probably every community in the world has needs and problems which could be met by the involvement of prisoners in a nearby institution -- men and women who really need to experience the thrill of helping out. It's time now, in our social development, to begin recognizing this natural pool of volunteers rather than trying to forget they exist.

It's time to remind the authorities that prisons are part of the community, and to begin discussing ways prisoners can contribute to community life even while they're inside. We have to remember that every human being needs to feel useful, and therefore we need to present as many opportunities as possible for prisoners to experience their usefulness. In this way, the community becomes part of a person's rehabilitation, which is as it should be.

Many people feel that things won't get better until we tear all the prisons down. I say that's a cop-out. It's obviously going to be a long time, if ever, before such profound changes take place. Meanwhile, hundreds of thousands of human beings live in prisons as they are, and we can begin making a real change in their lives without waiting for such major breakthroughs.

Let's help prisoners to change their hearts, and people in the community to change their feelings toward prisoners. What better way to show the unnecessariness of the present system?

Kindness toward prisoners isn't pity, and it's also not gullibility. Kind people sometimes have to lock people up, or refuse to let people out on bail or parole, or remove them even from the mainstream prison population if they continue to be dangerous. A great Indian sage once said, "Do whatever you must with people, but never shut anyone out of your heart."

Most prisoners have been shut out of society's heart for a long time. Many have *never* been in an environment of kindness and encouragement. Many have never experienced the satisfaction of helping others. This is what it will take to make us safer from crime. I don't know whether our prisons will ever be empty. But I know we could drop the recidivism rate from 70% to 10% if we dropped our "out of sight, out of mind" attitude and focused some creative attention on the humanity of the people we lock up.

● ● ●

Dear Bo,

Thanks for your recent newsletter. I agree with you 100% on your comments concerning the "Convict Code of Honor." It is not worth to live by and it is certainly not worth to die by. I recently did some research on it, and I thought your readers might like to know its true history, and maybe help them make up their minds about abandoning the code (as I have).

You have it partly correct when you state that this so-called code of honor was established by New York's petty criminals during the prohibition era. You could add that this took place because at that time, it was one of the rare periods when the city of New York was trying to get its cops to live up to the same laws as the rest of the citizenry. So they imprisoned a large number of cops for such crimes as bribery and extortion. These former cops kept up their previous profession in prison and they established this so-called code, in order to protect their activities against other prisoners. The Convict Code only works against prisoners, and as soon as we realize this, the better.

Sincerely yours, F

● ● ●

Dear Bo and Sita,

How's it kicking for you two? I'm doing fine. Just for a little update. I worked the program here so well I made it to minimum security. A concentration camp. I now eat, sleep, and work for the Nazi's. It's no big gooey shit though. But that last newsletter was full of shit (Fall 1988). Man I really hope you didn't write all that dribble. And I'm sorry to knock whoever it be, that has written such a whitewash.

Sure I'm for kindness. Lots of it. Sure there's guys here that would flip out just to have some shine on their dreary existent ways. But as Richard Pryor once said, "Now I know why they build prisons!" If ya think about it, Ronnie Raygun let all the mentals out because he thought we as taxpayers shouldn't pay their ways, they came here. And, just your average run of the mill psycho.

Do you really understand the reason for gang rapes, senseless stabbings and your run of the mill mayhem? It's done because those that engage don't give a shit. If they did, they wouldn't be here. And the warehousing is just a crap. Hell, I'm doing time in here, and my thought of the overcrowding problem is to knock down the walls on the buildings, put up two fences parallel to each other, dig some shithouses and issue a herd of tents. I promise the recidivism will be less than your pansy 10% estimate. Try to escape you are shot climbing, fight, you die. Just generally fuck up, you're shot.

No, Bo, I respect you for what you are trying to accomplish. You should have commendations running out your ears. I love you and Sita with all my heart. But you're working this from the wrong end. I'd say at least 85% of the people locked down don't even know what <u>morals</u> are. Let alone care if they did. Most of the people locked down want that free ride, and all the trimmings.

I'm sure you realize the twin unities. It's easy, ya blow it, ya pay. Don't cry, don't be a wimp. Hell, Gandhi knew that. Sure the whole world could use some kindness. If it was something to be shoveled, I'd do it, 12 hours a day. But it isn't. And just saying to be kinder isn't going to cut the mustard either. If there was maybe a few more outbursts, maybe the no good lazy people in this country would get off the couches and demand something done.

Before any massive change in this small world comes about, a dumb government somewhere will become overly paranoid and lash out until it all goes to shit. Fear is what's stopping your desire for kindness. If the jerks locked down would stand up and take it on their selfs to get it together, these festerholes we call humane prisons, would close up and the people running them would be on the breadlines just like the rest of us.

Until then ya just can't keep giving. Ya see, I give, I give till it hurts. I'm 210 lbs. of mean. But I control it, I face my fears, I don't spread fear (I should sometimes), instead I give myself, whatever I have. I only affect a few that care to venture around me. Most are scared. But those that aren't only come for that little ray of shine that I throw on them. Then they are gone. People don't care any more.

Sure, sure, there's always an exception to the rule. That's nature. But I don't care how much awesomeness shines within any given being. Even the masters didn't captivate and teach the masses. That's nature. That's the benefit of being unique. "How do ya catch a rabbit?" "Ya sneak up on it." Change only comes when the masses want it. Right now, the masses want a free ride.

They'll get it. Ya can only eat so much before ya move on and eat somewhere else. Right now the meal is on, getting good and ripe.

"We come into this world alone, we depart alone." That's about the most wisest thing to be said. What ya do in between is a lost cause. People will suffer. That's nature. It's a cruel tradeoff. But ya can't beat it. I don't care how big your stick is. If you're really interested in helping us to make it better for our own ways, give us something to bite our teeth into. If yer not hardcore, let it be known. If you look into those walls and breathe that foul air, hear the pain of defeat, taste the swill of hopelessness, touch that last beat of the strongest heart, you will see it there. I feel it. It pumps through my veins.

I don't know what you see when you enter one of these sanctuaries, but I'd say we actually got it good. Three hots & a cot. Can't beat that. The rest of it is just a mental trip each individual puts himself through. You say you've been tripping around our little globe, Bah! If you have, then you know we in here are probably "in better" than most of the third world countries. Hell, we're doing better than most of the people on the streets. It's a joke. And we have plenty around here, "Come to prison and get a degree!" "Go to prison, meet a few good people!" "Go to prison, gain that extra pound!" "No sex is safe sex!"

I don't know Bo, maybe I'm wrong, but I walked an awfully long block to get here. If I've missed the mark, please let me know. I hate to think that I've come across like a warmongering full blown headhunter. But sometimes ya have to be tuff in life. All of the greats were tuff at one time. You said it yourself. They didn't sugarcoat, they gave the ultimate hit.

OK, so you may or may not think yourself a master blaster. I do. That's what it's about ain't it? Those of us that you reach and guide with your small little newsletter need something to spread. Do ya really take us to be as naïve as to really not already know what you're talking about in your newsletter. And the system does work. But people are too lazy to work it. I'm proof it works. You're proof it works. It's just working it that has to be done. "If not you, who? If not now, when?" Have ya bitten yet? Those who bite, get bitten, those who don't damn near get eaten alive!"

If ya want a little human-to-human interaction, well this is my thought, "Sure you convicted (fill in with your crime), I'll give ya some interaction, I'll stand on your neck until it hurts, I promise to talk the whole time, but what you did is wrong, now it's time to pay the ferryman. I promise that when I'm done yer neck will be 4 inches longer and you'll really know the true meaning of existence."

Man I live this rodeo. I made the choice to come back. Ya can't get to somebody from out there. That's how I thought. I know better now. You got to me. But this is one time you really got me. It takes a lot to make me feel the sense of pain. Oh sure, I can feel the physical just like everyone, the mental pain I have had to endure is enough to break a normal person.

Envision the pain Bo, you would feel if you lost Sita to a murderer. One that had beat her, so severely, then just for fun carve on her. Then realize she laid there for over four hours before she died. Now that you have felt your anguish, feel the suffering that she would have had to be going through. Then see the man come and say, "Get up Boy! That's life, go get yer helping of shit, gulp it down, then get yer ass back in there and give em' hell!"

I would say, "Where do I go from here Bo?" But that man was right. I've been eating my shit with vigor and I'm trying to get back in there and give em' that hell. But one needs that shove in the right direction, once it's determined that this or that is the way, one likes a hand to hold on that narrow path. It's an illusion I know. But you are feeding my illusion. You are feeding a lot of them by your helping hand.

I had to fall back and take a look at the path you want me to follow. I wanted to cry for you after I read that newsletter. But instead here I am writing this crazy letter. I have become more aggressive in my endeavors. You did it to me! So hey, how about lightening up on the woes of how bad we have it in here? Okay? How about giving us fish something to take to the school? Please? If I have offended you in any way, I'm sorry. That's not my intention. If I am reading your message wrong let me know. But I do spread myself out as far as I can. I already got that part. If I am to shovel it, I need to know how.

"Remember when you were young? Ya shone like the sun." You have set a standard which others have followed. Don't stop there. Please? Well I guess I'll go for now. I see you're on your *way out again. Please take care, enjoy.*

Love ya for life, D

P.S. "You can see you have made me angry, so I suppose you have begun to reach me. Now I must have made you even more angry. Fall in love with me!" Take it easy!

Dear D,

Yeah, I wrote that dribble. And what's worse, I stand by every word of it. Nowhere in there did I say it's easy or everything's going to work out just fine. I'm not a social worker.

If life were no more than what you see, then maybe you'd have a point. But life is a lot more. It's even a lot more than Sita being raped and murdered and carved on "just for fun". Did you think you'd shock me to my senses by that example? You don't get it. This spiritual path is a lot tougher than you think.

What does the attitude in your letter accomplish? You think of yourself as a "realist" or some bullshit like that, but all you're doing is justifying bitterness and pessimism. In the fall newsletter, I said quite a bit about taking responsibility; I wasn't letting convicts off the hook or encouraging them to enjoy the free ride. But at the same time, prisons make it as hard as possible to turn things around for the better -- and that's just plain stupid. The newsletter encouraged everyone to get up off their asses and work toward the change they want without waiting for anyone or anything else. What do you have against that?

You're dead wrong that most convicts don't have any moral values and don't want their lives to change for the better. Without values like kindness, courage and so forth, NO ONE can be happy. And everyone secretly wants to be happy, D. A lot of people -- like yourself -- are just afraid to reach for it any more because they've failed so many times.

I'm not saying every one of the "masses" can be reached or changed. Frankly, that's none of my business. My business -- as is yours -- is to be an expression of the biggest truths in everything we do. That's what the newsletter is about, and it helps a few people here and there to change their lives for the better. I don't think your way of standing with a foot on somebody's neck really works. There are already too many feet on too many necks in this poor little world of ours.

Even if it prevented future crimes, that's still not my ultimate goal. Remember, I'm a holy man, not a corrections counselor. My goal is to help people see beyond the painful illusions all around us. And you ain't seeing that yet, not by a long shot. So you're arguing with the wrong guy. If you want to argue correctional treatment, go find somebody in that line of work. If you want to take a chance and look within your heart to find a doorway to the miraculous, endless Spiritual Adventure, well, that's more up my alley. Try the newsletter again from that angle.

Your brother through thick and thin, Bo

[the following letter was received the same day my response went out:)

Dear Bo and Sita,

I'm sorry about my last letter. I had no right to rain on your rodeo. I guess I was in an idiot's frame of mind. What you are doing is well needed around here. As soon as I mailed my last letter I felt like an idiot. So to make myself feel a little better I tried to spread a little kindness on the cops in a subtle way. It worked on real people.

But the freaks I live with didn't give a shit about kindness. They want theirs and an easy way out of here. So much for spreading sunshine in an overcrowded rat race. The cons are the downfall of their own system. A week ago I was moved clear across the state to an honor camp. Yah, sure, I have 4 years left. But like I said, you can work the system if you play by the rules. The rules changed here. It's a work camp, but it's still the same as behind the walls. Everybody looking for that easy score.

I tried making the crew I'm on a happier one. Ha. The Boss-man tuned in, but the cats I work with didn't care for spreading the rays. They'd rather sling horseshit. So I'll let 'em. I'm big enough to make them happy, but that's plastic. They got themselves here, and I'm sure they will get themselves out. They live in a plastic world and it will melt down in its own good time. A plant can only grow on its own. Add a bunch of shit and chemicals to it and it will kill you. These guys eat up all the grow lights, herbicides and chemicals that they think will make them grow the fastest and easiest. I can't change that for all the trying.

I feel defeated. Out of all the people here I can't even relate to one person. Sure I can sit and jaw all night, but when I try to point toward one direction I'm a weirdo, weak, stupid, or off in left field. Nobody cares to see themselves. I don't know what to think about something of that nature. I guess I was self-centered for so long all I ever seen was me. Now me is tired of riding in this rodeo. But my ride isn't over, so I'll keep on plugging.

I'm very sorry about my last letter. I see what it is what you were trying to get across now. It got across here. So please let me know how things are. I'm going back to being a watcher instead of a doer. It still hurts, but the pain isn't as sharp.

Love and peace, D

[this came the following week:]

Dear Bo,

I just received your letter. I beg your forgiveness. I started this gloom and doom with mere words. Not seeing the truth. What I tried to convey in the depiction of brutality, is what has happened to me. At the time of writing that letter I had fallen into a dark hole. The powers that be was too much for my weak mind. Timing in life wasn't on my side.

I know you're not a social worker, or a corrections counselor. A holy man in the third degree is how I see you. Someone I learn from. But to forget my past is a hard thing to do. I lost my woman in one of the most heinous ways a human can leave this existence. I came to prison to complete the known human cycle. Revenge. But what I found here was not revenge. I found me.

At the time of that <u>dribble</u> I wrote, I had lost myself back to the ignorance that had brought me here. After I had mailed that garbage I had regretted it from the time I walked away from the mailbox. Words of aggression has never helped humanity. I know this. I know the truths. My mind is my enemy, not you, not any-one else. But in my battles, I am not always the victor. In this boat of words I have found the way to the top in myself. It is a lonely place. But that's the nature we take when we are born to this world. Looking for that shoulder to cry on either by meekness or aggression as I so stupidly did, is a cop out. There is no way to bring my peace back.

I have been searching in hopes my woman might magically appear in front of me. It was the only thing I had to cling to that I thought would keep me sane. I know now the matter of my sanity isn't the problem, my mind is as strong as I am physically. Sure, I must find the way to make my gear shifts smoother, not to grind them.

You say you are a spiritual revolutionary. No, you are just a spiritual man. Revolutions are never won. Both sides lose in war. We both know this to be true. You have overcome the fight by not fighting, me, well I am just student. I have looked to you for my guidance, maybe my letter portrayed you to be some kind of counselor, that was not even in my thoughts. Arguing with a teacher is a non-virtue. That is why I regretted this whole incident. I feel the same as if I had lost my woman all over again.

It is said that suffering is the way we learn. To overcome suffering is the way to happiness. It is a tough road to haul. I realize now my path is tougher than others' is, that we are individuals not clones, and we don't share the same exact existence. How easy it would be if we did. In my mind's confusion I saw an illusion last month. I couldn't see through the mire of what I've been seeing between the thought of I to be a some kind of leader of humanity. I am just a pawn in life. We all are. I am just a feeble young man on a lonely path that is unknown, with no one to lead me or hold my hand or to follow.

I went at it the same way I did my whole life. Wide open. Big mistake. It is not a super highway, but a small foot trail. A bulldozer only rapes the land. I will now slow down, now that I have burnt my trail. My revolution is now over. No longer to be the headstrong impetuous idiot, that charges in guns ablaze, and looking the fool when the smoke clears. I value your words and guidance. Please accept my apology.

Love from my heart, D

Dear D,

Got your second letter after I sent off my reply. Please don't feel bad about your first letter; I'd rather we always be straight with each other than nicey-nicey (as you can see in my reply to you, I can dish it out too).

The profound pain you have experienced is beyond any of our abilities or attempts to understand. But we *can* come to see clearly that even such horrible pain is part of the Great Mystery. We can be humbled and awed by it rather than destroyed.

I hear what you're saying about having no one you can relate to, but I really want you to try to understand, it's the same way on the street. Sure, there may be more people who talk a good game, but the true spiritual journey is always rare and individualistic. And the way you look around in prison and see the needless things people do to bring pain into their lives -- well, that's the same out here, too.

But the real message of my teachings isn't to pine for some fantasy world where everyone gets along and acts supportively. I'm still asking you to quiet your mind down and start tuning the whole game inward to a more mysterious place. There's a place in you that was never born and can't die, and isn't a separate little being crying out for friendship. I swear to you, that place is within you. Let your frustration point you inward to find it.

I Always Love You, Bo

[seven months later:]

Dear Bo,

How are you doing? Me? I'm still doin' it. I have changed tenfold. Pat yourself on the back. This is one of the most weirdest months in my life. I start it off by a call that a close friend has been killed. Her 13-year-old finds her mother minus a face. Nice thing to wake up to before oatmeal and Woody Woodpecker.

Then I turn 29. For the big event my father comes to see me. First time in about 4 years. My, my what a nice day it was. A twinky with 29 matches. Best B-day cake I can ever remember. A rare find for my present. The bros gave me a Massagara rattler for a gift. Made a pretty skin and earring buttons. I caught a copperhead last Friday night that is the catch of the decade as far as copperheads go. If I hadn't been quicker and had the fear element still in me, he (or she) would have caught me. I almost stepped on it. Buddha says things will pop up to those who wait. I have been waiting for that copperhead since winter.

Then just yesterday I get another call. One of my best friends had his 10-year-old daughter taken from his house in the middle of the night while the whole family slept and she was killed 500 feet from her bed. It's a beautiful world we live in. I am down to 195 lbs. and can run a rabbit down. No bullshit. This Daniel Boone country is some crazy stuff. I'll be here for three more

171

years. I got a six month time cut this month.

Buddha and I kick it every day now. My bro's don't understand, but they don't give me any lip either. They hate to go head to head with a mind that has no locks or fears. Plus they hate the idea of what's behind a guy that sits for hours then feeds the songbirds by his hand and then shucks a pit viper of its bark all in the same day. Some have expressed this but have left out that it seems weird or whatever.

Everything is starting to come to me like drinking water. It's a thing that is needed. I just have one question I can't get an answer to that I have been working on. Part of the path says to meditate on the suffering of the world, past, present, and future. I am feeling more of it every day. I breathe it, eat it, sleep it. I know that to come to the total feeling and wisdom of that magnitude of suffering takes time. I don't rush it. I also see as I go I learn in leaps and bounds.

But Bo, is there a point where I will no longer feel or need to feel this suffering? And if there is such a point, what's there? And please don't tell me to wait and find out myself. I'm going to find out anyway. I have so far. But just this time, can I have a helping hand? And remember, the Romans lopped off the heads of bearers of bad news. Well, I've got to ride. C-ya.

Love, D

Dear D,

You ask if there's a point you'll no longer feel or need to feel the suffering. My answer is, there's a point when you won't have that question; when you won't mind the feeling, and you won't worry about not having it either. As Nisargadatta Maharaj said, "Pain is pain and it has to be endured. There is no such thing as overcoming pain."

There are a few little tips for this process, though. For example, the "right" way to feel suffering is in an open way which winds up giving you more compassion for <u>everyone</u>, including the people who cause suffering. Meditating on suffering is not for the purpose of feeling heavy or depressed. If that happens, you're not getting a big enough view.

Ultimately, suffering and joy will come and go because they're both natural parts of life. Both will be intense, because your awareness will be so clear. And yet you'll be attached to neither, because in your clarity you see it's perfectly fine to experience all of reality.

I think you're well on the way, brother, you just have to hang in there. I have a favorite verse from an old Leonard Cohen song called *Teachers:*

Teachers are my lessons done?
I cannot do another one;
They laughed and laughed and said,
"Well, child, Are your lessons done?
Are your lessons done?"

I love you, brother, Bo

● ● ●

My religion is very simple. My religion is kindness.

-- The Dalai Lama

Part Two:

DEAR BO . . .

Still round the corner there may wait
a new road or a secret gate;
and though I oft have passed them by,
a day will come at last when I
shall take the hidden paths that run
west of the moon, east of the sun.

-- J. R. R. Tolkien

SECRET GATES, HIDDEN PATHS

Dear Bo,

We got your Christmas newsletter and I feel compelled to write, even though I know you don't need this kind of mail, as you get so much from people on the inside. But you say "real life -- is always right on schedule."

Well, since August 25, our 27-year-old son is in the hospital extremely ill. He has had a colostomy and then an ileostomy and both times he could have died. He doesn't know if his sickness -- Crohn's disease -- will return or if he will ever have his intestines reconnected to the bit of bowel he has left, otherwise he will live the rest of his life evacuating his stool into a plastic bag. He lost so much weight that the nerves in his legs got pinched and had to be operated on to free them from the pressure. We will know in about three months if these operations worked -- if not, he will drag his toes when he walks.

I could go on, but you can get the picture. There is no way that this young man deserved this suffering. No stories of previous existences can change this conviction for me. You only change the time frame, the problem remains the same.

The only way I can deal with this is to believe, with the scientist in Woody Allen's latest film, "September," that the universe is random, morally neutral and incredibly violent. Any idea that there is a plan makes me tremble with anger and shame at such a cruel planner.

Yes, I am grateful that he is still alive and I hope that he can put his life together but I can't see it as a manifestation of divine love. Like some little Ethiopian child, he is a victim of a cruel arbitrary existence.

In spite of all this, I am grateful for your work and publications. They mean a lot to me as, of course, they do to my wife.

With love, I

Dear I,

I understand your feelings, I really do. I grew up with a paralyzed father, and also I've personally gone through a lot of surgery and pain and limitations which at one time led me to scream at a

Jehovah's Witness on my porch, "Well, if there *is* a God who lets all these things happen, then I *spit* on him!" Please understand that my Christmas greeting didn't mean to imply a Pollyanish or simplistic spirituality. I *know* how profoundly life can hurt us.

I also agree with your gut feelings about the multitudes of spiritual loudmouths who may be quick to tell you "it's all for the best" or "God must have a reason" or "it must be your son's karma from another lifetime." I think that 99% of those people are merely parroting spiritual slogans which arise from their own fear and aversion. It offends me as much as it offends you. They don't want to feel your pain.

But what I ask you to consider, in your deepest heart, is that there is indeed the other 1% -- the truth which the 99% are imitating. Though nearly unbearable for us to accept, there is a truth and wisdom behind such suffering as you and your son are experiencing. I didn't read this in a book or hear it in a lecture. I slowly opened to it through a lifetime of pain and anger. I experience this truth as clearly as you see your image in a mirror. It's not a concept. The people who mouth the empty words are using concepts, but I'm not doing that. I'm sharing very real experience and insight because I do understand and I also see the other side of the pain.

Life has more purpose than physical health and mobility. The deep humility which can emerge from being stricken with disease is rarely found in healthy people. Severe limitations can foster a level of inner wholeness and joy which healthy people rarely glimpse. The social alienation which arises from being bedridden can open the mind to a sense of the Great Mystery which is rarely experienced by healthy people.

And it still hurts like hell to watch a loved one suffer, and it prompts us to do anything we possibly could to make it go away. All those things are simultaneously true. I remember when I was a kid, I'd make about a dozen deals a week with God, like "If you make my daddy better, I'll..." But my daddy never got better. He was paralyzed for 14 years and then died.

What's hard to notice all those years is the compassion and patience and courage and humility we were all developing because of this terrible situation. I didn't notice how incomparably sweet our feelings had become for this pained little man of such boundless endurance; how much we learned to savor the preciousness of our time together, no matter what the circumstances. Looking back at my life right now, I wouldn't re-create it any differently if I had the power. My father wasn't "punished" or "victimized" by an arbitrary and unfeeling universe. He experienced one of the innumerable, equal scenarios we human beings may experience. We each live out our own unique stories, and what we do with the scenarios we're given is what makes our lives fulfilling or empty. There are thousands of affluent people in perfect health who suffer daily much more than my family ever did.

I said earlier that the attitude "it's all for the best" comes mostly out of fear and aversion. Well, I also think the opposite attitude comes from the same place. The current popularity of "When Bad Things Happen to Good People" seems to reinforce your feeling that such things happen randomly in a violent universe. But isn't that just another way of legitimizing anger and ducking the profundity of the real truth? It's like letting God off the hook just because the pain is too much for our faith to bear. These parts of our life stories are our "dark nights of the soul;" they're our agony, our scourging and crucifixion. This isn't the time to give up our faith or prayers; quite the contrary, this is what faith and prayers were created for.

What you're feeling right now could be yours and your family's inducement into enlightenment; what stronger human emotion exists than compassion for a suffering child? The power of your feelings, if you open to them fully rather than closing around them in anger, can crack your heart wide open and bring you directly into the agony and ecstasy of Christ on the cross. At that moment, you'll never again need words to grasp why these things have happened to you or to him.

We're all going to get sick and we're all going to die. Some of us enter those stages quite young, some quite old. There's no "right time" for catastrophe. It's latent in every moment, in every trip to the store in the family car, in every peaceful night's sleep as billions of organisms migrate through our bodies. But I swear to you, from the bottom of my heart, "He marks the sparrow's fall." "He counts the grains of sand". There isn't a slip-up or unattended moment **ever**. Some of us must must gentle our souls in the crucible of pain, but one day we discover it's all right. It's not only all right, but it's as miraculous as the birth of a baby.

I know words can mean less than nothing during pain such as yours. Beyond all the words, please know that Sita and I offer you our deepest love and friendship for your passage through these times. We hold you all in our hearts.

Grace surrounds you, Bo

Dear Bo,

We were all touched and moved by your strong, beautiful letter. It arrived last Monday, the same day J called us to say that the surgeon was talking about a third operation which would leave him permanently with a bag hanging from his abdomen, probably also impotent and with bladder troubles.

During the week we have been working on alternate sources of help and a number have turned up. As well, the physician who is also on the case has proposed an alternative with medication -- it will take twenty weeks but it gives us and J hope.

Your letter is particularly helpful because it helps us face the worst possible scenario. Maybe it is time that J's getting well is not the most important thing happening here. But you also understand that we will keep trying until it is clear that nothing more can be done. One of the hardest things is to know when to strive and when to accept. The sense that all is well is hard to come by when a whole lifestyle seems to have failed. J was the first vegetarian in our family (although he later returned to some fish eating). He has not smoked tobacco or anything else for several years, nor taken alcohol (all his own decisions). He is a Karate teacher and regarded by the people in the dojo as a strong, responsible person. My wife has devoted a lot of time and effort to the study of nutrition, practicing mainly macrobiotic cooking. For J to be struck with a vicious disease in his bowels is like a rejection of all this care and effort, it's like a non-smoker getting lung cancer. Cause and effect do not seem to work here.

Of course, what we expected doesn't matter, what is is what happened. And while I am deeply affected by your letter, for a good deal of what you say, I'll just have to take your word. I have not heard from God. I am not a regular meditator but I do get myself in a sitting position several times a week. I believe I am listening attentively, but I hear nothing. And if God marks the sparrow's fall then he will understand my anger and dismay.

On the other hand -- and it's a great irony -- the best chance of recovery, as Bernie Siegel proves with statistics and experience, comes from a positive outlook, so we're working on that, too.

You are very generous and sincere with us. Your letter will be read many times by all of us. I can't pretend to believe something I don't, but I recognize the authenticity of your experience and respond to it with love and gratitude.

I

Dear I,

Well, it's touch-for-touch now; you were touched by my letter, and Sita and I were very touched by your letter -- especially your openness and self-honesty. And one thing you brought up that I wanted to acknowledge -- the issue of not knowing "when to strive and when to accept." I want to sit next to you on that one because that's such a powerful, fundamental issue for us all.

I just want to be sure you know that I'm with you all the way in your "striving." To me, the striving and accepting are not in opposition to each other at all. If I were in your position I would be doing *everything* within my power to find alternatives to the surgery and to relieve my son's pain and suffering completely if at all possible. I'd probably try every form of medicine, healing, healers, or even voodoo that promised any hope whatsoever. But the "acceptance" is <u>simultaneous</u>; it undergirds all of your effort in such a way that there's no sense of failure if everything we try seems to make no tangible difference.

That's really the core of the Bhagavad Gita -- try like hell, but entrust the fruits of our efforts to God. Or Jesus in the Garden of Gethsemane praying "If it's possible, Father, how about cancelling that whole crucifixion thing? If not, I'll do it as you wish."

This is where striving, acceptance and Bernie Siegel's advice on positive attitude all come together -- essentially by never being separated in the first place. For an opposite example, consider your feeling of irony and failure about J's wholesome lifestyle. *No* lifestyle or ideology can ever fully address the Mystery, the wonder, of our lives. Your mind subconsciously created some false assumptions way back when. Your mind separated catastrophic illness from a wholesome lifestyle. Nature didn't make that distinction; your mind did. Nature may *suggest* that vegetarianism and such-and-such are good ideas, but it never gives us any guarantees. Nature is the realm of all possibilities, and therefore always a realm of wonder.

What I'm trying to say is that **nothing failed**. As hard as it is to consider, *nothing went wrong.* This is life; this is the Great Mystery unfolding.

I also agree with you fully that God will understand your anger and dismay. My only concern as your friend is not that God will judge you, but rather that your anger and dismay may tend to get in the way of the profundity which is available to you right now. I don't know how else to say it. The kinds of things I'm talking about aren't merely words or ideas to make you feel better or to help you "cope" (God, I hate that word!).

Let me offer a practical suggestion: You mentioned that you sit a few times a week and that you "listen attentively" but haven't yet heard anything from God. I encourage you to sit very still and breathe in and out the heart-centre, opening yourself to all of your pain, anger, and so forth more fully than you ever have. Sit perfectly still, but allow the feelings, especially your empathy for J, to keep growing. Feel the sensations in your heart. Don't redirect them or limit them or say "this is enough for now".

My contention is, your compassion for J is literally unbearable; and if you allow it to reach that point, your agony will burst the limits of your mind and you'll experience communion with God. If you make such a breakthrough, you'll become a formidable healing force in J's struggle. I'll be pulling for you, my friend.

All my love, Bo

Dear Bo,

It's tremendously helpful to hear from someone who has "been there" and has moved further down the road. You have gone so far into the mystery of pain and suffering that you seem untouchable -- that is, beyond being wrecked and demolished by it.

For my part, I am holding on to hope. J is doing better. He has four outside people going in, doing self-hypnosis (for the pain), visualization, acupressure and another form of body work. They are all positive, loving and competent people. He feels really helped by them and, even better, he feels more in control of his own recovery than at any time since the summer.

In this frame of mind, I am more ready to work at Shakti Gawain's method for getting in touch with my own higher self, than I am at pressing further into the pain and uncertainty, but I know that I may have to.

Although my wife has long been your supporter, I have always admired the work of the Prison-Ashram. We sent one of your Christmas letters as our own greeting the following year -- the one about Jesus hanging out with innkeepers and prostitutes and so on. I guess we are separate but equal -- my wife sends contributions and I send quibbles.

But you have helped a rather uptight Anglo-Canadian who has lived too much in the rational side of his mind to open up to some vital realities and I am truly grateful.

Much love from all of us to you and Sita, I

[a year later:]

Dear Bo,

Things are much better here than when you and I exchanged letters in the winter of 1988. The ordeal lasted for another six months and left J with a permanent ileostomy, but he has recovered his physical health remarkably and learned to live with a bag. He has even returned to karate, both practice and teaching.

Psychologically, I would say we're all still recovering but, as you know, all that suffering is a great teacher. I really related to both kinds of message which you have sent out in the last few months -- the "how heavy the illusion is" about your son leaving and the serenity feelings which you describe in the latest letter.

While I believe in free choice, we have almost too many choices around. Through my wife, I have gotten interested in shamanism. It's the only time I have had any kind of direct experience of another level of existence (outside my dreams) and it was pretty faint at that. But I have a lot of trouble with the "I can make it rain approach." I don't want to trade in an angry old partiarch god for some new rain or volcano god who has to be placated. I want that good old oceanic serenity and the hell with it! Keep up the good work, Bo.

Love from us, I

● ● ●

Dear Bo,

I am confused. I am going to be 20 next month, and I am serving two life sentences for homicide. I was busted at 17 years of age.

Since I came to prison, I have been engaged in a conscious search for truth. I have found that it can't be found by looking outside, but by looking inside. I have also come to the conclusion that there is only one basic undisputable truth: I Am. I am a part of a greater consciousness or life than this body or mind. So, all this is nice but when I came to this realization via a practice of yoga and meditation which I learned in the martial arts, I thought I was really getting somewhere.

Then I was given your book, Lineage and Other Stories; *it totally blew my mind. The story about the preacher's visit from Christ...I wish I could describe what I want to say. This may take a little while to explain. Please bear with me.*

I spent the last six months in I.M.U. (Intensive Management Unit) *for refusing to go to P.C. This gave me plenty of time for meditation as I was locked down 23 hours per day. Now I gave in and am in P.C. -- A very big blow to my pride. I promised myself I would never be in P.C. ever. But this is just something I will have to learn to live with. Not to mention all the snitches in here.*

I grew up as an only child with parents who were fanatically over-zealous in their faith. They believed in hellfire and brimstone Christianity to the point of hypocrisy. It became abusive. The abuse and mixed signals of love-violence fucked my head up really good, or bad, but I've come to understand and resolve the futility of that conflict. Unfortunately, I had to come to prison for killing two people before this happened.

Now here's where my confusion kicks in. I've been learning the martial arts from another inmate and have become pretty fair at what I know, but I am beginning to question my Sensei's teachings. He sees, as you, that all major beliefs point to the same thing, which is unity or self or whatever terminology you prefer. He combines certain aspects of Zen, Tao, Hinduism, Buddhism and others, and rejects Christianity as a manmade religion to control people by teaching obedience and pacifism.

I agree with this, yet I find certain aspects of Christianity to be truthful. So the logical conclusion is that Christ most likely did teach real truths based on his personal enlightenment, but these teachings seem to have been distorted since then.

But I have this question about deity. Christ is supposed to have said that we are "Gods and sons of Gods..." So I figure he's referring to the existence of God in me or me as a part of the overall energy or spirit. Maybe. My Sensei takes it a bit further. He believes we are gods in a more literal sense, and we must rise above this place, these circumstances, and emotions and all that would entrap us and keep us from our full potential, not just on earth but forever. This also makes sense to me.

But am I to <u>worship</u> the all seeing, all knowing One? Something inside me tells me that this is not required (maybe pride?). Let me put it this way. I AM. God said the same to Moses. I AM. We are. Therefore, I am, Christ was and is, God is, and we are. See what I mean? I AM me, Christ, God, you and everyone else. I really felt that this could be what the Masters meant when they spoke of God-realization, but now I'm not sure.

My disagreement with my Sensei's teaching stems from the fact that when I think of Christ and what he did or tried to do on Earth in relation to my own life, I get this feeling in my chest, an excitement that electrifies my whole body. I have an extremely strong sense of destiny, a higher cause that I am a part of here on earth. Not an idea, but a knowledge as though I had scientific proof. But I have none.

I have felt this since I was a young child. I was about eight years old when I first recognized this and at the time I believed I was called to preach the Bible. But now that I'm older, I simply cannot accept all that the Bible teaches. Yet I still feel the same.

Many times I've had people who don't know me tell me that I am a leader, and am going to accomplish something great. Am I suffering from delusions of grandeur? I know that whatever it is I am to do, it is of no credit to me for I myself am nothing. Damn, I don't think I'm making any sense. I hope this conveys what I'm trying to say. I have a minimum of 40 years to serve with good time. But I somehow know that this is not what lies in my future.

I don't know, man. I think I sound like I'm on medication. Do you have any advice to share? It would truly be appreciated.

Incidentally, I know I'm not ready to get out, despite my growth over the past three years. I've much to learn and if I do have to spend my life in prison, I have fully accepted that. I know I can be content and grow no matter what my surroundings are.

Your story about the preacher, "A Matter of Choice," man, that stirred something on the inside of me. I don't know how to explain it. I guess I've rambled on enough for now.

Take care, R

Dear R,

Well, that was about the most impressive letter I've ever received from a nineteen- year-old. Yes, you do have a lot of understanding and insights which can make your life a spiritual success even if you have to do your forty years day for day. You've had an unusually hard beginning, but you're doing a great job of turning it around. It's like you had a load of shit dumped on you, then you rolled around in it for awhile because you didn't know any better, and now you've cleaned yourself off and are ready to make great fertilizer out of it. I'm glad to know you.

But as far as providing answers to your questions about the "I AM" and so forth, I'm reminded of the time somebody asked the great sage Ramana Maharshi, "Will meditation answer all my questions?" And the sage replied, "No, but it will destroy the questioner."

For the state of realization, or freedom, that you and I want, the conceptual questions you're wrestling with are off the mark. A certain degree of spiritual understanding may be important to get us pointed inward, but you're way past that stage. Now it's a matter of letting go of such abstract and complicated ideas, and paying more attention to the roach crawling across your floor, or how the sky looks today, or whether you have kindness in your heart for the snitches in p.c.

What you and I both want is not to become spiritual scholars, but to slowly surrender into an *experience* of freedom which can only come when we have let go of *all* concepts. It's hard to reach not because it's so complicated; it's hard to reach because it's so profoundly simple -- experiencing bare reality, without putting on it any of our emotional, psychological, or intellectual overlays.

So if you're asking for a teaching, the one I'm giving you is this: Conscientiously let go of those biggest ideas every time they come into your head, and return your attention to the present moment. Someday you'll begin experiencing the present moment as much bigger than you had ever imagined, containing all the high states of realization and consciousness you wondered about.

When you're deeply affected by something like my short story, don't "think" about what it means to you, but *feel* it instead. Don't try to understand it, but rather let the feeling sink deeper and deeper into your heart in a quiet and patient way. Let it affect your life instead of your mind. Just watch yourself changing in the ways you think, feel, and act in your everyday life.

That's when all the biblical promises come true, like "when the two shall become one," and "when the inside becomes like the outside and the outside like the inside," and "Know the truth, and the truth shall set you free," and "when thine eye be single, thy body will be full of light" and so forth. Not from understanding *more*, but from giving up all understandings and offering ourselves so fully to this one present moment of life, that we are no longer separate from the I AM we were looking for.

I love you, little brother. Be patient and grow into a mighty eagle.

Bo

• • •

Dear Bo,

I'm a minister's wife, almost 78, but feel like sixteen. Just finished reading your impressive book, We're All Doing Time *and must write to you. Have done some yoga and meditation and have a mantra that always calms me, so I know how effective these practices can be. You have contributed much to many lives!*

Your book made me laugh, cry and feel rage. Years ago, the first time I saw a walled, barbed-wired prison I felt overwhelmed, and thought we are ALL guilty of whatever anyone in there has done. I still believe that prisons are monuments to injustice. When everyone has a fair start in life there will be no need for prisons. It is our job to work for justice (and peace is a part of justice). You and Sita are doing your share, and I believe I am doing mine. I work for and contribute to over a hundred organizations whose goals are peace and justice for all -- including our fellow creatures, whom we call "animals." (As if WE are not animals!)

When I read about your escape from the shark, I thought, "Well, Bo plans to do to the fish what the shark planned to do to him!" Only the shark's behavior is instinctual, while we are capable of reason and compassion. That is part of the reason why I eat no animals or use no animal products. We do not need the flesh of our fellow creatures. In fact, we are healthier on our natural diet of fruits, vegetables, grains, nuts and seeds.

The deforestation and pollution involved in animal agriculture are other reasons for being a vegetarian. And many more people can be adequately fed on vegetarian food than on meat, using the same amount of land.

Your comments about sex interested me. I did feel some relief a number of years ago to be released from the slavery of wild sex urges, but now I enjoy sex more fully, though less frequently.

Well, Bo, I feel like you and Sita are long time friends, so I have spoken intimately and openly. I send my love.

I'm so happy we met! M

Dear M,

Nice to meet you, too. To respond to your observation about my shark story, I agree with you that the shark was just trying to do to me what I was doing to the fish; nothing wrong was going on at all, including my efforts to escape being eaten. Sita and I lived very simply on the boat for nearly a year, and hunting and eating fish was a basic part of the harmony we experienced. I wish life's deepest principles were as simple as "such-and-such is always right," and "such-and-such is always wrong," but that's not the case.

I agree with points you made -- and which John Robbins makes in his excellent book -- about vegetarianism being more ecological, and compassion being so important. For many years my family has used no factory-farmed meats or eggs, and no household products which involve any sort of animal testing or research.

On the other hand, we had a milk cow for five years and we know many wonderful, compassionate farmers, which leads us to a different overall view as to whether eating meat or using animal products is ever "right". The native Americans were probably more in harmony with Mother Earth than any other people in history, and they regarded buffalo, deer, rabbits and so forth as their brothers as well as their food. Jesus ate fish. Ram and Krishna ate forest animals such as deer. We loved our dear Jersey cow as a member of our family, and she fed us milk, butter, cheese, yogurt, and ice cream filled with love.

I'm not trying to convince you to change your vegetarian lifestyle. I'm merely pointing out that an absolute perspective on this subject may be inappropriate. Our fundamental connection with the animal and vegetable kingdoms is not a simple matter; the roots extend all the way down to our connection with each other and with God.

I think we can *all* agree that cruelty in any form should not be supported. But whether all meat-eating or animal husbandry is cruelty -- that's different. My experience prevents me from accepting that conclusion. My family has a near-vegetarian diet simply because most animal products arise from cruel surroundings, not because we feel morally opposed to eating flesh or drinking milk. And in a situation like living aboard the sailboat, I think a vegetarian diet on our part would have been unnatural, like a prideful stubbornness against God's bounteous ocean.

Again, it's nice to meet you and thanks for your friendship.

Love, Bo

● ● ●

Dear Bo,

I hope this letter finds you in the best of health and spirits, and your beautiful wife also. I am doing time in a prison in which I am the only Native American, and I adhere to the tenets of the traditional religion of my people. I've been in prison now for nine years and have spent my time advocating human rights and political rights of aboriginal peoples by publicizing various issues with regard to governments and multinational corporations' violations against the people.

I have some influence on my people because of my dedication to their welfare. My problem is, my involvement in the struggles of my people has caused a bitterness to grow within my heart that is so intense and huge, it scares me. I will be going to the free world in a couple of years, and being the Indian-rights activist I am, I want to do what is best for my people -- with always the future generations in mind.

The elders are wise, and I know they are right when they advocate peace, but I feel that peaceful tactics on our part over the years have only caused the suffering of my people, because the white governments have no morals or ethics or respect for human life, much less all the rest of the Great Spirit's creations, and the only basis for their unilateral abrogation of treaties is "might makes right." Their continual and complete disregard for human rights, inherent rights, international law, and even their own laws, in their policies concerning Indian people, is repugnant to any sense of human dignity and respect.

Could you please give me some guidance in the matter of my bitterness and hatred, perhaps share with me your wisdom so that I may learn a stronger control over my bitterness? I am sure that I will never go against the wishes of the traditional elders when I fight for any particular cause, because they represent all that I live for. But I have no inner peace, because of this bitterness and pain I live with as I watch my people die.

May the music of the meadow with its songs of silver streams bring sunlight to the paths you walk and magic to your dreams.....

L R

Dear Brother L R,

Your bitterness and hatred may *seem* to you to be the result of what the government and corporations have done to your people, but that's not really the way it is. It's the white man's separateness and fear which has allowed him to continually destroy the native people. It's your *own* separateness and fear which react with bitterness and hatred.

It's not that you're terrible or immoral for being bitter, but you are being fooled by faulty spiritual vision. You have every "right" to hate the forces which have oppressed your people, but spirituality isn't about "rights". It's about seeing the way things really are, the deeper meanings, the connections between all of us.

What you want for your people must be what you want for yourself: To struggle however you must for a decent outer life, and at the same time not allow your inner life to fall prey to hatred, anger, and rage. The outer life is over in an instant, and there are many conditions and events we can never control. But the Great Mystery which lies behind it -- that's what you're missing while you're blinded by bitterness.

Look around this culture. Millions of people have all the rights and opportunities you're fighting for, and yet their lives are empty, confused, frightened and lonely.

Your own heart has to be the most powerful medicine for healing the wounds inflicted on your people. Your brothers and sisters must be able to feel the power of your happiness, of your vision; not of your righteous rage. You mentioned that the peaceful way of the elders hasn't worked so well. But has a more violent way worked any better?

Besides, maybe the peaceful way has worked better than you think. The elders aren't fools. They've kept the peaceful native heart alive through 200 years of unbelievable cruelty and slaughter. I'd say their way has worked very well. Death and oppression aren't failures, brother; they're just tragic cycles of human history. Hopelessness, anger, and bitterness are the real failures. And the elders have kept a large portion of native populations from falling prey to those demons.

Take time while you're inside to regain your inner balance. From a strong and clear heart comes much more powerful outer action than ever before.

With great Love and respect for your struggles, Bo

Dear Bo & Sita,

Howdy Do! I see that you were presented with the Quetzal-coatl Award by XAT Medicine Society. This makes me glad -- you are certainly worthy of it. I know that your letter to me early last year has brought Light, Love, and Wisdom not only to me, but to the hearts and minds of many of my brothers and sisters. I re-read it often and learn more about myself each time.

There is something I would like to share with you now. When I got out of the hospital last year, and then finished solitary confinement for my protests to have access to the sacred pipe and other sacred traditions, I saw that a couple of my native brothers had come to this prison. We got together and seeked for prisoners with Indian blood and began teaching them of their Indian heritage, and we started a Native American Brotherhood.

One day, a non-Indian sent a kite to the chaplain asking for a pass to our next meeting. A few of the brothers were uncomfortable with his presence because he was not Indian. They felt he did not belong there because of the color of his skin. In the world today we find a lot of racism and prejudice, especially in prisons it seems.

But there can be no prejudice in our Indian way of life. When we place the tobacco in the sacred pipe, each tiny grain represents some aspect of Creation. There is a grain in there for our Mother, the Earth, and for all that grows upon our Mother. There is a grain for the rocks, the waters, the air and clouds and trees. There are grains that represent all the four-legged brothers, and six-leggeds, and the fish and others who live in the waters, and the winged ones. There are grains that represent the red race, the white race, the black race and the yellow race -- these are also the colors of the four directions.

All of the tobacco that is placed in the pipe represents everything that was created by the Creator. Through the Creator we are all connected. If a brother comes to us with a true heart, we cannot turn him away based on the color of his skin, for in doing so we would be telling our Creator that He has made a mistake. And if our Creator has made a mistake, who's to say <u>we're</u> not the mistake He made?

At any rate, it's a point to ponder! And it is a principle that has opened the eyes of the administration here as well as the brothers who were uncomfortable when the Non-Indian first came to our brotherhood. Ho!

We have a prayer. It is, "Mitakuye Oyasin." It means "all my relations." When we say this, it is a prayer for the well-being and peace and harmony of all that is placed in the pipe. So with this, I will close. Stay well, and may peace be with you, kolas.

Mitakuye Oyasin, L R

● ● ●

Dear Bo and Sita,

You did it again: yes, you made me flip the coin of bitterness and hatred to the coin side of human kindness: After reading our newsletter about my native Indian brother, L.R., I took off my warrior's mask (anger against oppression upon minority people).

Bo, what you told L.R., shook my bones down to the marrow depths of sensitivity. Your "truths" can not be disputed by the man with common sense or even no sense at all. You Bo, surely put my ignorance in check. You let "a spiritual attitude" and a new "outlook" blossom before my eyes. Just like the magic in a bee and its honey and flower. You made me think "sweeter" than I did yesterday. (Smiling) Your one "spiritual truth"...(quote)

"Your own heart has to be the most powerful medicine for healing the wounds inflicted on your people. Your brothers and sisters must be able to feel the power of your happiness, of your vision; not of your righteous rage." *(unquote)*

Bo, again -- these "truths" surely "raised" my "consciousness" from my "overdue" historical ignorance, lies, manipulations, guilt, shame, and wicked outlooks on American men who oppress the righteous native Indians. Yes, my family roots are in the Blackfoot Tribe of Native American Indians.

Just recently, my child landed in prison. And yes, I was outraged. But, I do believe that I can still comfort my child without "rage." Like I said to Sita, long ago: there are two types of people in the world today: those who know and those who do not know -- (how to foster greater human kindness throughout society) (smile). Yes, I was one of those who didn't know. I could pretend to others that I did know, but "truthfully" I did not know about (quote) "...You have every "right" to hate the forces which have oppressed your people, but spirituality isn't really about "rights". It's about enlightenment. It's about seeing the way things really are, the deeper meanings, the connections between all of us." *(unquote)*

And now I can consciously say and believe...I am one of those people "who are in the know." Yes, thanks to Bo and Sita; and all praises and glory goes to our One God (Cosmic Universe; Universal Mind).

"As above, so below" "As within, so without," B

● ● ●

Dear Family,

Has been a while since I wrote ya'll and just figured it's time to tell you that my copy of We're All Doing Time *is still the everyday reason for this happiness I feel and experience.*

Now I want ya'll to know I believe in Jesus without a doubt but just never really knew how to see him until your book got my eyes open a bit. It has taken the place of the Bible for me in a lot of ways. How do you feel about that statement, Bo? I'm serious. It doesn't make me have any less respect for the Bible, I just see your book as more meaningful to me.

Do you & Sita read the Bible, Torah or what? I'm interested in knowing more about ya'lls beliefs and where they came from.

I will go for now. Just knowing everything is really all right no matter what the case may be helps me so much and knowing that is one of the many gifts that are priceless that ya'll have given me.

Love, M.

Dear M,

You asked how I feel about the fact that my book has taken the place of The Bible for you. I feel fine. A lot of people these days are calling *We're All Doing Time* "The Convict's Bible," and I don't think Jesus or Moses or Buddha are sitting around Heaven getting jealous about that.

All genuine spiritual teachers have the same goal in mind. The power in my book is the same power as in The Bible, because there's only one real power, and that's the Holy Spirit.

As for what Sita and I read -- very little, actually. We've read the Bible and bits of the *Koran* and *Guru Granth Sahib* (the Muslim and Sikh Bibles, respectively), and for the past twelve or thirteen years we've had daily readings from the *Ramayana* or the *Mahabharata* (Hindu Bibles). We've read a small number of more modern spiritual books, including *Seven Arrows* (Native American), *Jonathan Livingston Seagull* and several Buddhist books.

To us, they're all the same. The One Holy Spirit moves through them all.

Keep on truckin', Bo

• • •

TWELVE STEPS AND
AN OCCASIONAL STUMBLE

Dear Bo:

I enjoyed your Summer 1990 newsletter, but I do disagree with some of what you said. But I want you to know that even though I disagree with you I appreciate your comments. I think it's important that we in AA stay open to constructive criticism. Dogmatism and narrow-mindedness seem to be an almost inevitable problem in spiritual groups, and AA is no exception.

I am forty years old. I have been meditating for twenty years, have done long meditation retreats, lived in spiritual communities, lived in India for a year, and so on. Also I have had trouble controlling my use of drugs and alcohol since I first got high at eighteen, have been in and out of AA for ten years, and have not had a drink in two years, nine months. I meditate almost every day and I go to an AA meeting almost every day. I have thought a lot about the relationship of alcoholism to the spiritual path.

A person can do a lot of meditation and still not be able to handle alcohol. Vajradatu, Chogyam Trungpa's organization, has a Buddhist Alcohol study group, patterned along the lines of AA. Many of the members have been meditating ten to twenty years. They still can not drink without hurting themselves, and need group support to remind them of this.

Maezumi-roshi, Zen Master at the Zen Center of Los Angeles, was treated for alcoholism. I mention his case because it was published and verifiable, but he is only one of many famous meditation teachers who have had problems with alcohol.

After a year and eight months sober in AA, during which time I was meditating almost every day, I tried drinking in moderation, and ended up staying drunk for four days. A few years later, I was at a month long intensive meditation retreat which involved sixteen hours a day of sitting and walking meditation. There was a one-day break in the middle, when we could relax and do whatever we wanted. I thought it would be a good time to try controlled drinking. I ended up getting real drunk. I had no control.

One of my good friends, who had a daily meditation practice for years, had lived in a meditation community and done several meditation retreats of a month or longer, recently had to be checked into an alcohol detox center. His case is not all that rare.

The point I am making is that meditation for many people is not an effective treatment for alcoholism, while AA is. I don't understand what causes alcoholism. I don't understand the relationship between whatever it is that meditation does and whatever it is that causes alcoholism. It is easy to theorize about these things and say all sorts of stuff that seems to make sense, but let's look at the actual facts. Meditation alone usually does not clear up alcoholism, although there may be some rare exceptions.

You say lifetime identification with AA is a crutch. I disagree for several reasons. Alcoholism seems to be a permanent condition for most people whether they are drinking or not, and part of the nature of alcoholism is the recurring delusion that somehow things have changed, and that the alcoholic can drink without all the problems previously connected with drinking. After struggling all my life with obsessive-compulsive destructive patterns with drugs and alcohol, and after finally having managed to stay sober for almost three years, there is still a part of me telling me that I should go out and have a drink. This is not a logical part of my mind, but it is very strong. It may be there all my life.

I know people who have been through much worse than I, and have been sober much longer than I, who still have that crazy voice in their head telling them to drink. The thing that keeps many of us sober is going to meetings. They serve as a continuous reminder, and offer continuous group support. For many people, thinking of themselves as alcoholics for a lifetime is just good common sense, just as a diabetic should think of themselves as a diabetic for a lifetime. I do agree with you that a person can become overly identified with AA. I'll talk more about that later.

Aside from the issue of AA as a solution for alcoholism, AA is also a really beautiful spiritual path. Would you say that meditating or going to church for the rest of a person's life is a crutch? AA is very powerful and it seems to generate a certain amount of animosity. I constantly hear people say "Why do you go to all those meetings?" An AA meeting lasts an hour. If I spent an hour a day watching TV, reading murder mysteries or talking to friends, no one would think anything of it. But if I spend that hour in a meeting where I am talking to people in a more structured manner that leads to better communication, it is seen as odd.

I think in some ways AA is the most wonderful and powerful spiritual organization on the planet. For example: I think the democratic structure of AA is superior to the hierarchical structure of most spiritual groups. I think the fact that when we come in to the program we admit something very embarrassing about ourselves leads to a greater honesty than in other spiritual groups I have been connected with. I think the 12 steps map out a basic spiritual path that is as good as any I know.

I think the fact that there is a stigma to being an alcoholic keeps us from being puffed up and overly proud, a common pitfall on the spiritual path. For example, I remember when I first got into Zen I felt very hip, cool and wise. Other spiritual paths have made me feel self-righteous. However when I was exposed to the same spiritual teachings in an AA meeting, I was more likely to absorb the real spirit of the teachings, rather than use the outer form of the teachings to adorn my ego, because there is nothing much about being an alcoholic to adorn my ego with.

AA brings together people with a wide variety of different spiritual beliefs; Christians, Buddhists, Jews, New Agers, Atheists, Agnostics, etc., and gets them to communicate and find mutual understanding. This is rare in spiritual organizations.

Most people go through Hell before they come into AA. They are completely beaten. There is a sort of collapse of the ego and they reach out in agony and say "please help me" and then things get better. There is surrender and letting go. I think this process serves the purpose that initiations have traditionally served in spiritual paths, but it is one of the most fiery and intense of initiations, and it creates a bond. The Tibetan Buddhists have to do 100,000 prostrations, and the Zen Buddhists have to sit still at the monastery gate for a few days, but none of this compares to what you have to go through to get into AA.

Sometimes people compare AA to group therapy, and in some ways it is similar, but I think the format of an AA meeting is closer to the format of a Quaker meeting than anything else. Sitting quietly in an AA meeting, watching my mind, listening to others talk, and talking myself when the spirit moves me, can be a powerful sort of group meditation. I have had mind blowing, heart opening experiences in AA meetings that compare with anything else I have experienced in any other spiritual practice.

I have done more good in AA than I could have done in any other spiritual organization. I have dealt with people who were really suffering, and I could share my actual experience of how I suffered in pretty much the same way and how I got free.

I agree with some of what you said. I think support groups such as AA can serve as hiding places and create artificial divisions among people, but that seems to be a problem with spiritual groups in general, not just support groups. The groups are still valuable, we just have to be aware of some of the problems that seem to always crop up when people form groups of any kind.

I used to be in a meditation group that met across the street from a church. I remember on Sunday morning the negative comments and general air of superiority that we had about the people going to church. Still the meditation group was a good place for me to be. If I become egotistical and feel superior to others because I am meditating and they are not, it does not mean that I should stop meditating, but that I should become aware of my arrogance. The same holds true for AA. We need to be aware of and work on our problems, but not reject the whole thing just because it isn't perfect.

When Ram Dass was in Atlanta he did a mild put down of the support group phenomenon. Your newsletter was a mild put down. As I said before I think open discussion is important, and I am glad both of you expressed yourselves honestly, but I disagree with you, and since you are both so influential I feel a need to communicate my disagreement.

Bo, I think you must have a real big influence on lots of people in prison who are spiritually inclined. I guess you know the statistic about what a large percent of people in prison are there because of things they did while under the influence of drugs and alcohol. I think for many of these people AA would be a very appropriate spiritual path, and I would like to help you understand it better so you can help them understand it better.

I don't know what your experience is in visiting 12 step group meetings, but I want you to know that they vary tremendously. One or two meetings are not a representative sample. Also remember that in any group the biggest fools are often the biggest talkers. Look for the good and don't throw the baby out with the bathwater.

Thanks for the newsletter and all the good work you are doing.

Thanks, T

Dear T,

Thanks for your honest and open letter. It's a funny thing though -- you wrote "I appreciate your comments" and "it's important that we in AA stay open to constructive criticism," yet I've never yet made a comment or criticism which you or any other AA member has agreed with. So what exactly is "staying open?" Does it mean merely that you're willing to hear it, and then automatically defend AA in response?

Besides, the great majority of your letter is a response to presumptions on *your* part, not to what I actually wrote. I said only two things about AA -- one praising and one critical. I said AA does a *wonderful* job of beginning to help somebody who's dependent on alcohol, and I said that most members tend to grab on to that identity for a lifetime. I stand by both those statements, and I wonder who it was that you wrote four pages in response to? Certainly not me.

Your defensiveness and projections are what's wrong with AA. There seems to be an almost fascistic need to "defend the faith." I haven't only been to "one or two" AA meetings (another presumption on your part); I've been to many meetings, over many years, as far apart as North Carolina and Hawaii. And my sister was an alcoholic who tried AA unsuccessfully for several years.

By the way, yes I *would* say, and often do, that going to church or meditating all one's life can be a crutch! Again, your presumption led you to a response which didn't fit what I feel. *Any* group, method, or identity can become a crutch, an empty facsimile of what it once meant to us. A healthy, good-humored caution of that possibility is essential to anyone in any group or organization.

You say "I think in some ways AA is the most wonderful and powerful spiritual organization on the planet," and then you say, "there's nothing much about being an alcoholic to adorn [your] ego with." Don't you think it's a tad egoic to claim *your* path as "the most wonderful and powerful" in the world?

You also claim AA's superiority in being "democratic," as if a democratic organization is higher than others. Should Jesus have come off his power trip with his disciples? Should Buddha have stopped being at the center of his meetings? Although abuses and frauds abound, sometimes a "hierarchical" structure exists because there are indeed wise, compassionate beings who have things to teach! Thank God!

But again, I didn't say all those things against AA, you just inferred them. I praised AA and expressed a caution about people identifying with *any* label for their whole lives. By the way, you seem to have been a member of a lot of off-the-track meditation groups; please don't assume there's no such thing as a clear, pure, unprideful, unself-righteous meditation group. There are a lot of quiet, powerful scenes going on without members making fun of churchgoers. I know there are a lot of quiet, powerful things going on among AA groups and members too; I never doubted that.

But as Krishnamurti spent a lifetime pointing out, groups and organizations tend to become more exalted than their individual members, and that's when problems arise.

The inner journey remains an *inner* journey, the mystery remains mysterious, the transcendent remains transcendental. It's wonderful and important to straighten out our worldly problems and to recover from addictions and so forth. But that isn't the whole thing, ever.

AA may be the best practical support group in the universe, but frankly, it's not profound enough to be a religion. And you and too many others seem to cleave to it as a religion. One woman in an AA meeting years ago stood up and screamed at me, "Listen, I don't give a damn about any of this 'inner' stuff, my only goal is to stay **sober**!" Well, that's not a very comprehensive goal, as far as I'm concerned.

I've met too many AA members who have been sober for many years, yet keep themselves on a suffocating leash which doesn't allow much joy or sense of humor in their lives. And I've been to too many AA meetings where uptight people are chain-smoking cigarettes and guzzling coffee -- nicotine and caffeine being two of the most addictive substances on Earth!

One of the reasons this occurs is that AA's "disease model" of alcoholism makes it easy for people to separate their alcohol problems from everything else, as if their inborn "allergy" to booze is totally different from their other behavior patterns; as if it's just an unfortunate accident of birth.

So, like any other path, AA has strengths and weaknesses and pitfalls to watch out for. That's the nature of paths. That's what ultimately keeps turning us inward instead of outward. If I said AA hurt my sister, you would claim that meetings and groups are all different. But if I said AA *helped* her, you'd say "Yep, that's AA." Can't you see a problem in that?

When Ram Dass or I or other teachers offer a loving criticism of AA, maybe it's because we're being *friends* of AA, not blasphemers. You said both Ram Dass and I offered "a mild put down." But those are *your* words. I distinctly remember using the word "wonderful" in one of the two sentences I wrote about AA.

By the way, *any* group that met every night would have a powerful supportive effect on its members; don't confuse format with ideology. The AA nightly format is a great opportunity for people who need reinforcement. That doesn't mean everything done in that format is perfect.

You mention that in other spiritual groups and traditions you've gotten into, you had a tendency to feel "hip, cool, wise, self-righteous, egotistical, superior to others," etc. I ask you to consider that maybe you still have a tendency to do that, because now you feel that AA is the very best. Think about it.

With Love, Bo

Dear Bo,

Thanks for your response to my letter on AA. I reacted defensively when I first read it. On re-reading it I think you make some very good points. I really do appreciate your newsletter, and other similar publications, that are willing to take a good honest look at spiritual life in America today and point out the problems.

You said that you had never made a comment or criticism that any AA member has agreed with. I know that is a big problem within the fellowship. I for one agree with much of what you say. I definitely agree there is a fascistic need to defend the faith within AA, and it is important that I be aware of that tendency in myself. Within AA I am fairly critical of the fellowship's problems, but I may be overly defensive when non-members mention the same problems.

I agree with what you say about the problem with nicotine and caffeine addiction within AA. I am addicted to caffeine. Maybe that's one of the reasons my letters get so long.

I agree that AA does not work for lots of people and that we take credit for our successes but often ignore the people who are not helped -- or even injured -- by AA.

Really your letter was full of good points, and I don't need to list them here. You do have more experience with AA and have thought more about it than I assumed when I first wrote you. I mentioned some of this in several meetings and to a few friends. One woman said it might be a good idea to have regular meetings in which we discussed AA's problems and shortcomings.

As I wrote the last paragraph I realized part of what would cause you and me to see things differently, and maybe in some ways your view might be a more realistic view of AA as a whole. Over the years I have gone to so many meetings and met so many people in AA, and from that huge pool of people and meetings I have selected a small group of people and meetings that I like, associate with, and think of as AA. I know, in many meetings, if I mentioned AA's shortcomings I would get a very negative, defensive response. Like you, I have had people shout me down in meetings, and it was really a drag. Now I just don't go to meetings where there are people likely to do that. I have put that side of AA out of my mind, but I know it is out there.

I do have some areas of disagreement with you, concerning the disease model of alcoholism, the value of democratic structure in a spiritual organization, the profound nature of AA, and a few other things, but I will not get into all that now. Also, I could tell you several of AA's problems you didn't even mention, but won't get into that now either.

My last letter was mainly a response to your statement, "the vast majority of AA members latch on to that identity for a lifetime; yet spiritual work is gradually giving up all identities." The point I was trying to make by sharing my experience of not being able to control my drinking even after lots of meditation, and giving examples of friends and spiritual teachers who also had drinking problems after lots of meditation, is that in many cases meditation does not clear up alcoholism, any more than it clears up diabetes, and it is a good idea that a person think of them-

selves as an alcoholic for a lifetime, no matter what spiritual practice they are involved in.

I say it is often naïve and destructive for a person involved in spiritual work to give up their identity as an alcoholic and a member of AA. That sums up my basic disagreement with what you wrote. I arrived at this conclusion after years of painful experience as a drinking alcoholic practicing meditation.

Thanks, T

Dear T,

We do still have some basic disagreements, and that may always be so. But now I can never again say that no AA member has accepted a criticism from me. You've spoiled a perfect record and humbled me in the process.

The only point I want to address that I think is unclear between us is what I meant about a "lifetime identity." I surely don't mean that anyone should use meditation as a panacea or as an excuse to abandon other important work on themselves. I've referred a lot of people to AA and NA. Spiritual work is indeed about gradually giving up all identities, but the key word there is "gradually." Gradually may mean thirty or forty years, but it is true that the spiritual seeker slowly abandons every identity.

Our genuine difference of opinion is that you equate alcoholism with diabetes and I don't. Diabetes is organic and alcoholism is behavioral. And even organic conditions undergo mysterious transformations over a long period of spiritual work. I don't think you quite understand what I mean by "spiritual work," especially as you seem to have inferred it simply as the practice of meditation. I'm talking about something far more profound.

There is a mysterious process through which we each become what Jesus and Buddha became. It's not just a matter of resolving our addictions and problems and being a good person. There's really a death and rebirth which takes place, and that doesn't happen so long as we cling to identities; so long as we think we know who we are, what we need, and so forth. My life is involved solely with that end of the spectrum -- way, way out there. That's where my comments about AA or anything else come from.

Love, Bo

● ● ●

Dear Bo and Sita,

You mentioned in the summer quarterly that "I'll probably get in trouble for saying this," referring to AA. Well, I'm an AA member that completely agrees with you. I have gotten in shouting matches over this very issue on many occasions. The Big Book of AA uses the word <u>recovery</u> over and over and so many have failed to notice it. As a matter of fact, drinking or drug use is only a symptom of what is really going on. When one gets deep into the program they begin to see that <u>self</u> <u>will</u> is the problem. Only then is recovery on its way.

On page 77 of the Big Book of AA it tells us what our Real Purpose is. It says "*Our real purpose is to fit ourselves to be of maximum service to God and the people about us.*" And on page 128 it says, "*Giving rather than getting will become the guiding principle.*" And on page 130 it says this, "*Those of us who have spent much time in the world of spiritual make-believe have eventually seen the childishness of it. This dream world has been replaced by a great sense of purpose, accompanied by a growing consciousness of the power of God in our lives. We have come to believe He would like us to keep our heads in the clouds with Him, but that our feet ought to be firmly planted on earth. That is where our fellow travelers are, and that is where our work must be done. These are the realities for us. We have found nothing incompatible between a powerful spiritual experience and a life of sane and happy usefulness.*"

Notice that on page 77 when it refers to service to people about us it doesn't say "<u>alcoholics</u> about us," it says <u>people</u> about us. Notice on page 130 when the words "fellow travelers" is used it doesn't say fellow <u>alcoholics</u>.

I know Bo that you have realized when a spiritual leader shows up usually those that follow end up perverting the message, and worship the messenger and not really understand the message.

The word <u>recovered</u> appears hundreds of times and like you said, the majority haven't noticed it. In the beginning of the book on page xiii people didn't introduce themselves as alcoholics, they introduced themselves as <u>members</u> of Alcoholics Anonymous. Not an alcoholic in and of itself. I don't know how it all got twisted, it just did.

In the book Twelve Steps and Twelve Traditions, *on page 92 paragraph 2 it says "Finally we begin to see that all people, including* ourselves, are to some extent emotionally ill as well as frequently wrong, and then we approach true tolerance and see what real love for our fellows actually means. It will become more and more evident as we go forward that it is pointless to become angry, or to get hurt by people who, like us, are suffering from the pains of growing up."

Here Bo, it can be seen clearly that the problems that confront AA people aren't any different than the problems of any <u>Fellow Travelers</u>.

Thank you for saying what I've been saying all along but can't seem to get but a small few to see. Ears that don't hear and eyes that don't see.

Love, D

● ● ●

> We always did feel
> the same, we just
> saw it from a different
> point of view;
> Tangled up in blue.
>
> — Bob Dylan

TANGLED UP IN BLUE

Dear Bo and Sita:

I learned about you from a friend of mine upon telling her I have fallen in love with a prisoner. She (my friend) and I are both social workers and psychotherapists, and also both interested and involved, clinically and personally, in the so-called spiritual path.

I met V a few months ago when he answered a personal ad I had run in the Village Voice. I am 37 years old, never married, though I've had several relationships, and feel myself at this time to be ready for true love and intimacy. Well, V's letter was intriguing: intelligent, literate, friendly, charming, and I decided to answer it. Our first few letters were him writing to a box #. When that expired I realized I'd have to take responsibility for this correspondence and either get another box, give him my address, or end it. I gave him my phone # so I could hear him, as of course I was wary about giving my name and address to this man who'd been in prison for all of his adult life (he went in at 20; he is now 36).

Well, he called and he sounded as wonderful as he did in writing. Then I went to visit him. That was two months ago, and I've been going up every week since and spent my vacation up there, visiting him every day.

It's an unbelievable experience -- like one day I said to him with a somewhat sardonic laugh -- it's as if God, or the Universe, or whom- or whatever makes karma, said "OK, now we'll send D someone to fall in love with -- but we'll have him be in prison." It's incredible -- astrologically I knew I was going to be meeting "the love of my life" and here he is -- but I can't "have" him. At least, not yet. This is in part, I guess, why I'm writing to you. I have so many questions and doubts that I thought with all your wisdom you might be able to shed some light.

The thing is -- V is enlightened. He is very aware and conscious. He is warm and loving and giving -- not only to me but to everyone around him. He will be applying to the governor once again for clemency and he has a pile of letters and attestations to how wonderful he is, three inches thick. If he is not given clemency, he will be eligible for parole in four years.

First of all, I can hardly believe he's as "good" as he is, i.e., he seems too good to be true. (Though this may have to do with my own issues, being an adult child of alcoholics so I have my own negative shit I've been trying to eradicate for years.)

But secondly, I can't stop myself from thinking: will he be the same when he gets out? So when I say this to him he says things like "D, there are never any guarantees," which of course is true. But since I have a biological clock ticking away, I feel a sense of urgency and like I don't have time to waste.

The amazing thing is I trust him and have more faith in him than any man I've been involved with. At the same time I can't help but wonder, and think, I can't afford to "waste" four years (assuming he doesn't get clemency).

Then there's the small matter of waiting four years, and waiting means postponing actively sharing our lives on a daily basis, not to mention sleeping together. As it is I feel that I am bursting. Here I have all this love and happiness for and by and about this man, yet I must contain it. It does, of course, come out in the ways that it can, i.e. my dealings with friends and clients, and in my limited contact with V. But it's a special sort of patience I must cultivate and an even greater challenge to "being here now."

Any words of wisdom -- or any type of words to share?

I've been greatly enjoying your book and feel it's wonderful work that the two of you have been doing with prisoners. The title We're All Doing Time *is so appropriate and true, though so many people will think of it in only a literal and/or negative sense.*

I feel that V and I are on similar paths. (I was "wild" too in 1970; I just didn't get locked up.) I guess I'm having a hard time dealing with doubt and with frustration.

Thanks for your time, and your love.

D

Dear D,

Not knowing you or V personally, I hope you understand that anything I could write you is just an intuitive response to your letter, and might have little or no value for the tough issues you're wrestling with. I mean, there are women in your position who have made the choice to wait, and some found happiness and others misery. And there are women who decided not to wait, and some found happiness and some found misery.

There's one other important perspective to consider. You're basing nearly all of your feelings on the future; on the assumption that V will be out either any day or in four years. But it seems to me that your relationship needs to be satisfying to you right now, as if one of you were to die tomorrow. Does he so fill your life that you can sacrifice the physical intimacy you could have with someone else? Or do you just *wish* he did? Because if you remain in love for the next four years, and then he gets out and you two split up, you shouldn't feel that you "wasted" anything. These four years have to be sufficient unto themselves. If they're not, you have to consider what your needs are, and act on them.

It makes me very uncomfortable to read "The thing is -- V is enlightened." Because the thing is, he's almost certainly not. There may be a handful of enlightened beings in the world at any one time. And while you may argue theoretically that he could be one of those few, practically speaking, my gut tells me he's probably a really nice guy with very spiritual attitudes. For you and/or him to consider him enlightened (with the assumption that you're not) creates a dimension of your relationship which will doom it in time. Please don't pass this off too lightly. There are a lot of women who for one reason or another want to see their men as perfect, and a lot of men who can't resist that opportunity to play the part. It's no good.

A relationship between you and V has to be a lot more equal than that. If you see no imperfections, then maybe he's not sharing enough of himself with you. Maybe you're setting the stage and he's acting on it. Lots of couples go for years in that groove, but according to your letter, you'd rather not waste time if you can help it.

You're right about not being able to predict what V will be like in the outside world. Sita and I don't even try to predict anymore. We respect that longtimers like V have a tremendous amount of adjusting and exploring to do, and it's not all going to be easy. It's like going from 5th century BC to 20th century AD. He would need a lot of support, patience, and commitment from you if he paroled into a marriage.

The way you ended your letter ("I guess I'm having a hard time dealing with doubt and frustration") sounds to me like you're hoping my response will reassure you to stay with V and take your chances. It sounds like that's what you want to be convinced of.

Of course, I can't do that. This decision has to be yours and yours alone. Maybe V is really the love of your life, or maybe he's just the first man you've been able to love as courageously and joyfully as you have. Maybe his incarceration is simply "ironic," as you noted, or maybe your own psychology perceives safety -- although bittersweet -- in loving a guy who's locked up. Only your own quietest mind knows which "maybes" are true.

Whatever the case, I hope even in the depths of your struggles you can see that this situation is an integral step along yours and V's spiritual paths. The love you feel between you is the very same love we'll all eventually feel toward ourselves and toward life itself. You've already helped each other enormously by opening into that love. I hope you can respect whatever the future holds for you, and appreciate that any decision you make will bring both joy and sorrow. That's the way of Life for all of us.

Love, Bo

Dear Bo,

Thank you for taking the time to answer my letter. I appreciate your "intuitive response" and speaking to me like a brother. It is just what I needed. Your letter was supportive and comforting to me. I realized that when I said "V is enlightened," I was using the term loosely and didn't mean it·in the strict sense of the word. But your comments regarding my not seeing a man as perfect and putting him on a pedestal were well taken, as was your discussion of needing to have the relationship be rewarding, etc. in the present. In fact when I first met V and he started talking about the future, I had trouble (still do). I said, here I've spent all these years, saying "Be Here Now" and meditating so as to be in the present, and here's someone talking about the future. I guess the challenge is being in the present, understanding that thinking about the future is a present activity, and allowing for both.

Thanks again!, D

• • •

Dear Bo,

Can't you somehow find the time to write a book on raising our children Spiritually? How to teach them meditation, how to be non-violent at the violent playground, how to build up the ego's self-esteem yet lead them further into the heart chakra? Bible stories just don't hack it, and neither does the Ramayana! So much violence and battles.

Love, K

Dear K,

I couldn't write a book on child-raising because it would only be about a page long. I don't think we have to learn strategies, methods or subtle tricks to lead our children toward the Light. To whatever degree our daily lives are truly about Spirituality, then exactly to that degree our kids will experience it from us.

The instant we separate parenting from our own work on ourselves, it becomes manipulative and hypocritical, no matter how sweet the motivation.

My best advice on childraising is almost no advice at all: just do your own work in every part of your life, including being a parent. It's not important to create an artificial peaceful environment; just an honest Spiritual one, which comes naturally from seeking the truth about yourself.

Our desires to get children into meditation or yoga arise mainly from fear, and fear isn't a good basis for anything. When we truly understand that the whole world is our church, that all are our family, and that every single experience is our Spiritual practice, we can be fearless enough to allow our children to find their own path. When we see who they and we truly are, we can laugh hysterically at how worried we once were about a petty thing like whether or not they would meditate.

This may upset you, but the same holds true for competitiveness and violence. Life is competitive and violent every time we breathe or take a single step. Our work is to poke through the mysteries, not to cling superficially to nonviolence and cooperativeness in order to avoid reality. The Bible and Ramayana are profound; don't sell them short. And don't sell your kids short on their abilities to see through the battle scenes to the heart of the matter.

Many kids whose parents deny them toy guns simply pretend with sticks when their uptight parents aren't looking. They get the clear message toy guns are "wrong" and yet they feel no evil or harmfulness in their hearts. That can confuse them away from their inner guidance.

The Spiritual seeker can live a life of fearlessness, joy and a great sense of humor once he or she stops trying to make life into a Sunday school class. Spirituality should make us broader, not narrower; able to better handle any situation anywhere, because we embrace and accept the entire world as it is, warts and all.

And children are a great way of showing us we can't rely on our expectations and plans. Instead of giving our children heavy philosophies, we can show them a lightness and dignity of Spirit which can carry them through anything they ever have to face. If we're a walking example of self-honesty, courage, kindness, humor and wonder, what preaching do we need to do at all?

Love, Bo

Dear Bo and Sita,

It was quite a surprise to shuffle through my pile of charts, lab reports, and medical journals at work to find your letter! It caught me unawares, first of all that you had the time and interest to write, and secondly to find such precious words of guidance in the middle of my routine work mail. It was unexpected and sort of undeserved, like the grace of God. If I feel like this, I can imagine how a prisoner feels upon receiving a letter! I'm not trying to stroke your ego, Bo; I'm a doctor who tries to do a good job and I'm often thanked; you're a good teacher and I'm thanking you.

I shall take to heart your opinions on child raising and on being free vs. "nicey-nicey." The way I was raised, "nice" was the ultimate good and a swear word the ultimate bad. It's easy to unconsciously pass that on to your children. Now when I feel fear for my childrens' future (and whether I was a "good mother") and the need to control their behavior, I remember your essay -- that we need to remember 2 things: 1) that we (and our children) will die, so much of what we think is important is petty; 2) that we are saved and don't have to worry and are free; that we don't work so hard at our spiritual practices and pursuits in order to reach God, because in fact He is already here -- we work hard to open up to know that He is here. Thanks for the essay.

I feel very fortunate in being a doctor for I can't possibly deny the darker side of life. I must acknowledge pain, undignified deaths, seemingly unfair tragedies, people refusing to acknowledge that they are reaping what they have sown, and the stupid barriers families create between themselves. I've always thought that my Mother wouldn't be so glib about life and brotherly love if she'd had to wash the maggots out of an alcoholic's frozen toes. This profession tends to keep one real.

And the little beauties I see can make you cry -- an older couple caring for each other, a cataract patient discovering color again after surgery, a lifted depression . . . .

But -- Oh, Bo, don't you think there is something real about this longing for niceness, this yearning for ecstasy, this desire to be bathed in the light of God's presence? Not all "niceness" is out of fear. God put this craving in me! Alternately I'm at peace - or - unsettled with a longing for growth to a higher or deeper spiritual plateau. I do unrealistically impose this desire for perfection on myself and others, but mustn't it in part be based on a knowledge of God's perfection?

Thanks again for your guidance; it's precious to me and thousands of others. Don't give up; just keep on pounding those same words into our heads until they become our experience.

I think of you, your prisoners, and other seekers each Monday night during yoga class by the river. As we open our eyes after meditation the room has become dark and the images of pillars, walls, and seated figures are timeless in their silence -- they could just as easily have been in Tibet 2,000 years ago. What a fellowship!

Love, K

● ● ●

Hi Bo,

Bo, at our last meditation workshop, I said I would write to ask you some important questions. Now, I will give you some background on myself. Bo, I'm a transsexual. Verbally speaking that is simply to say, that my mental plane is that of the feminine state, and also, the fact is, medically speaking I do have and have had a hormonal imbalance. This was first discovered after several tests were done on me at age 14...

Upon discovery of the hormonal imbalance, I could have taken testosterone, a male hormone. But the doctors said such medications would increase the risk of getting cancer by the age of 25 -- a 90% chance. Well, of course my parents and grand-mother wouldn't permit it, so I was left alone in my behavior patterns which were based in the feminine state of mind. Well, al-most left alone. I still had to prove to my brothers that I was just as good as them. I did. It didn't help me in becoming "a man."

In my early 20's, I decided I would have the sex change. I un-derwent castration and hormonal therapy (female). Oh, I was told that taking female hormones was only a 20% risk of cancer, and with castration, practically none. My conclusion in it all was to say that since I was not going to live forever in this body, I may as well die as the person I felt myself to be: A woman. A woman at least mentally, and constructed surgically to fit the cause.

The hormonal and castration were 2 parts of a 3-part ordeal. Simply defined as phase 1-2-3. In completing the 3rd phase, I would have to undergo the construction of the vagina. I didn't. Bo, the operation was so shaky and the success rate so low -- I did not complete it.

Now, I come to the questions. My family was and is Christian. I mean the whole Holy Roly bit. To the point where being born was a sin. Really, Bo. How my parents continued to love me with that belief (unshakeable) I'll never know. To me, at that time, I felt as though they were defying God. So, as you can gather, I grew up with all the Sodom and Gomorrah stories and the Abominable Sin of being with the same sex.

This, I realize now did cause me a great deal of anguish. I mean, I could pretend I was a man, but in my heart I knew different. So where was the saving the sinner located in that? To me, it would appear and actually be being what people wanted

*me to be and not who I was. But I defied that. With my relatives'
love and care -- I said screw the people, I know someone does
love me. I'll face God when the time comes.*

*Now, I will ask you about those verses in Genesis and Leviticus, about being with the same sex: Just what does the Bible
mean by it, and why would a God create someone like myself only
to suffer such hate from people? Bo, I await your answer....*

Love, C

Dear C,

As for the Bible verses, remember the old saying, "Even the
Devil can quote scripture;" which means that you could find a
verse in the Bible to support or condemn just about anything.

Why not keep it simple? Jesus said, "I give you one
commandment: That you love one another, as I have loved you."
How can Christians hate you by quoting Leviticus & Genesis, yet
ignore what Jesus Himself commanded? People who want to hate
you will find an excuse, and people who want to love you will find
a way. The whole purpose of the Bible being full of contradictions
is so that each of us must wrestle with our hearts and minds and
make our truth a living truth instead of a dead set of rules.

Why God created you is no different from why God created
anyone else. We all have certain qualities and conditions to learn
from. Every single condition -- including transsexuality -- is either
a blessing or a curse, depending on whether we use it or not spiritually. It can be a blessing if you use it to develop humility, compassion, patience, empathy, etc.; and a curse if you use it to feel
lost, alienated, depressed, punished, etc. Those choices are up to
you; the condition itself comes neutral from the factory.

Some conditions are more difficult to bear than others, and I
know transsexuality must be really tough. I guess you must be an
"A-student", because the Teacher gives the toughest assignments
to the best students. You can handle it. I know you can. You have
grace and presence and an inner glow.

Sexuality fades for us all as the years roll by, but those other
qualities grow stronger. Put your attention on what lasts.

Beyond brother or sister, Bo

● ● ●

Dear Bo,

I've got 18 months to do, day for day; three 6-month sentences for assault, all for dealing with my wife! Anyway, her and I try to make things right again, but it just won't work. She's out there whoring around, my oldest daughter, 14, is on crack, my oldest son, 12, is selling drugs and stealing. All of the above and my surroundings is driving me MAD!

I read your book from front to back six times, but yet still all I can think about is how my family is falling apart and how my children need me and how I must do 10 long lonely months before I can rise up from here. And the growing hatred I've got for my wife now (not for me being in here, but for the lack of concern for our children), and all she worries about is her men-friends. Bo I hate to think what I might do to her once I'm released if something happens to any one of my six children.

Bo, I still love my wife even though she's a whore now, but my hatred is starting to take me over once again, and I'm looking forward to getting out for all the wrong reasons. I know it's wrong. Mentally I feel I'm getting weak, I'm so far away from home now, and nobody to share or kick my thoughts around to. I feel I must get it out to someone before I slam the fuck out of my mind.

Look forward to hearing from you, R

Dear R,

I feel bad that you're suffering so much, but I don't know what I can say to make things any better. You said you read my book six times, cover to cover. Well, reading it isn't enough. You have to be tired enough of feeling all this hatred and bitterness, that you decide to start doing some of the techniques every day. Techniques like meditation, breathing exercises, etc.

I'm your brother in this struggle, but I can't hold your hand -- and it wouldn't do any good if I could. Every one of us has hard times, and we have to figure out how to keep going without getting so lost in bitterness and self-pity. Look around you. Every guy you see has had a lot of bad shit happen to him. Your wife has had a lot of bad shit happen to her, too. I don't know whether you're going to be able to help her or change her, but I do know there's no chance at all if you don't find your own faith and strength. You ain't gonna help her through your anger, violence, or self-pity. And you ain't gonna help your kids, either.

There was no inner strength at all in the letter you wrote me; no faith that there's a purpose to life, even though it moves in strange ways; no sense of responsibility -- your own responsibility for what your wife and kids are going through. Don't forget why you're locked up in the first place! All there was, was anger and self-pity. That's not going to help anyone at all, including you.

My very best advice is still to do some stuff to work on your head and heart every single day. Pray for help. Become more honest with yourself about your own faults instead of concentrating on everyone else's. There's just nothing else I can offer you, brother.

Love, Bo

Dear Bo,

You're right! I received your thoughts today, and just like your book, you hit a home run. Damn. Words alone can't express what I want to say to you my brother, but I'm damn sure glad and proud to be on your team.

I'm going to re-read your book, but this time with a open and clear mind and heart. I feel now that even though I read it, all my hatred and bitterness didn't really allow me to understand what I should have.

I heard from my wife yesterday and like always, she wants us to try again. Still telling me a bunch of shit and lies, and like always I'll try again. But Bo, I'm really scared, see I know once I'm released in ten months, the truth will come to light as far as her whoring around and shit, and I'm really scared that the pain, shame and grief might be too much for me to handle at that moment and I could go slam the fuck off, and this time instead of doing 18 months I'll be on death row! This is what scares me; I've dreamed 1,000 times of just that.

My mind is telling me to leave her totally alone, but my heart won't let me. And after these 18 months, God knows I won't put up with no bullshit, and damn sure don't have the time for it. Bo, I know how she's being and continues to. It seems like every time I feel myself getting strong mentally to deal or not deal with her, I get one of those bullshit letters telling me she loves me and hasn't been screwing anyone. I'm not upset or mad with her because of the affairs, but the lies just tear me up.

But anyway, I'm going to pray a lot and my faith will grow and things will be as they should be. Take care,

Love and peace, R

Dear R,

You've got ten months. You've got the choice to use it to save several lives, including your own. I suggest you get down to it, using every inner and outer means you can find. You talk about your wife's lies but say nothing about your own lies to yourself. No outside situation ever forces you to "go slam the fuck off." The truth is, you have a terrible temper and almost no sense of control or responsibility. Look at these things.

You're not a bad person in your heart, but your heart is buried right now under about a hundred tons of ego, pride, and selfishness. Even your concern about killing your wife is based around you, not her (you winding up on death row). That's very distorted, brother. Use your time as well as you possibly can. Meditate. Pray. Write your feelings down. Talk with counselors or caseworkers. Ten months can bring a lot of change if you're using it right.

Go for it, Bo

● ● ●

Freedom is what you do with what's been done to you.

-- Jean-Paul Sartre

Dear Bo and Sita,

I'm still here at S prison, doing great, growing and learning spiritually. Even though I didn't commit the crime I'm in here for, it's much easier showing love rather than hate. The hard part was opening up and accepting people for who they are. I still stumble but God always seems to allow me an escape before it gets too damaging! I'm really thankful for that.

I'm mainly writing to share a "lesson in love" I have recently been fortunate enough to experience. As you know, my wife and I lost our son and shortly thereafter my wife went her way. Since then, we have communicated through writing every so often.

I've tried numerous times to patch our marriage back together and prove my love is unconditional for her. And as of a few months ago I've been trying to get her involved in her "spiritual journey" using the Holy Bible *and* We're All Doing Time. *I think a seed has been planted.*

Well, I had written her telling her that I love her and still want her as my wife and I know she has needs and desires and to take care of them, that I understand and wouldn't love her any less. (I told her this before but asked her to at least be there for me when I need her.) But this time, this time I told her I would be here for her and would help her in any way I could. When I said that I opened myself up for something I wasn't expecting.

I got a letter from her asking me, her husband, for advice on a relationship with another man. It kind of blew me away at first and then I said "Well you asked for it D., so now what are ya gonna do?" I thought "Well if I really mean what I said about unconditional love I have to feel what I feel (anger, pain, etc.), and let it pass on by and put myself aside and <u>help my wife</u>."

I then took time to feel my emotions and breathed in love and breathed out love about 5 times and proceeded to give her good clean honest advice and wished her happiness and the best in her life. Well, a week or so later I get a letter from her saying she sincerely wants to work our marriage out and how unhappy and confused she is at this point in time in her life.

I have really been through a lot of shit with T. Man after man after man, I have truly forgiven her and want to honestly work our marriage out. I run into a "little green monster" called "fear" and it's really funny all the shit he will come up with to throw me off balance. I just let it pass. I have faith that if I approach anything with my heart open and love flowing with all sincerity I could never be scared or regret whatever the outcome may be.

My marriage is spit in the wind compared to my and her Spiritual Freedom and that's the way I'm approaching this situation. Regardless if we get back together or not, I must try to help her get started on her Journey! I definitely want her to feel inside the same uncomprehending love I feel. Cause I can't explain it in words but it's damn sure the best feeling I've ever felt.

I know I have a long way to go and getting through the block of love has helped a lot. I don't want to ever lose this feeling and therefore I gladly keep struggling on. "Bad times are Good times with love to light the way." Pray for me.

Love ya forever, happy as can be, D

Dear D,

I'm happy to see you're going through so much growth and challenge. The situation with your wife is a unique, <u>powerful</u> lesson in unconditional love. I hope you continue to see it so clearly. God sure works in strange ways. At least it's not boring!

Keep the Faith, Bo

Dear Bo,

Bo, your letter said so much and opened channels I wasn't aware of, to be so short! "God works in strange ways." You said that right!

Bo, let me tell ya what your letter did to me before I even opened it. Ha, ha. The guard slid it under my door and when I seen who it was from, this huge smile appeared on my face and a warmth filled my whole being. Your love my friend is pure and great to feel, better than any drug and lasts way longer in fact never goes away!

I feel your love every time I meditate and send mine to y'all in return! Thanks for your love and wisdom. May we all grow toward God and shine brighter as every day passes.

Love and Peace, D.

● ● ●

Dear Bo,

Things for me have gone from bad to worse and worse still. Right now, I feel lost. The still small voice seems to be over talking to someone else, not me.

I was in an abusive marriage for 22 years. Being a survivor and intelligent, I tried to "fix" me or my situation. I covered pretty well, but I didn't notice this last slide down until I'd gained 45 pounds (I lost 35 recently -- Thank God!). But, while I was busy with my business and kids and tried not to let myself see who and what my husband is -- my "higher self" (or whatever someone calls the part of a person that slaps you upside the head from time to time to wake you up...) helped set me up to see.

I'd read a lot and knew a lot of metaphysical and spiritual ideas and I was busy working and feeling these -- but every time I SAW my relationship with my husband, I only saw a little of what was there. Whoa, talk about denial!

I've also been trained as a counselor so it was very natural for me to help and counsel and become good friends with 2 prisoners who sold me artwork for my shop. I developed good friendships with these two men. One has been "in" for about 29 years, the other for about 14 years. These men shared themselves with me -- honest and open, just us. I did in return, even when I'd have problems and they were very supportive.

I learned about TRUE friendship and caring and after writing one for 4 years and the other 2 years, I <u>SAW</u> that I was lacking love and friendship from my spouse -- and I had other people gently show me that I have lacked even the simplest kindness from this man. Boy was I into the sand -- didn't see it was killing me and my children.

I've been beat, strangled, bloodied, sexually abused, emotionally abused, isolated, left without money and transportation, etc. I filed for divorce -- I have no car. My car is disabled and I can't use his. He won't give me money that the courts ordered.

Before the car went, my youngest son and I gleaned a neighbor's field for onions and sold a few -- we made 30 bucks! I've been beat up twice in the last month. Sheriff won't do anything, though I have a (ha, ha) restraining order. He's stolen my mail and voucher for food stamps -- he can't cash them in and "they" will *not* reissue a voucher.

My eldest son is on medication and can't handle stress. He has since my last spousal beating decided "this is what dad does so I should" and he and I argued, he kicked me and knocked me down. He is 17 and 220 pounds! I took him to a psychiatrist in Augusta (a girlfriend flew out to help and rented a car, but she's leaving in 2 days and I think I'll lose my mind!). The doctor said my son has grown up in a dysfunctional family and will always be screwed up by it.

Three weeks ago my father died. My youngest son is in Atlanta with friends. My mom lives in Idaho and I am basically ALONE here (9 miles from town). Oh, my 17 year old can drive his dad's car. I have no phone and there is not an abused woman's shelter.

Other than that, I'm fine. I still believe in what you do.

M

Dear M,

I'm *so* sorry to hear of the time you're having. I don't want to lay platitudes on you at a time you're suffering, my dear sister, so let me just comment on one thing you said in your letter. About the still small voice "talking to someone else, not me" -- M, this is *exactly* the time you need to know that you are smack dab in the center of your spiritual journey. None of this mess is an accident, an interruption, a detour, a hindrance; none of it. It's very painful, and scary, and very very tough, I know. But *please* remember that you are still on course.

You're being given a trial by fire, and you're being required to be heroic, courageous, self-honest and even to keep your sense of humor about life. I'm not asking you to be "thankful" or any nonsense like "I'm in a period of great opportunity." It's terrible, right; but it is definitely on your path, and you do have the power to come through it more alive and illuminated than ever before.

My Guru used to say "Do whatever you must with people, but never shut anyone out of your heart." Try to see your husband and son as confused children of God, but also never let either of those brutes lay a hand on you again. There's no conflict between being spiritual and locking their asses up in jail.

There also may be no reason for you to stay in a situation like that. Maybe you need to go stay with your mom or other out-of-town friends until you gain some equilibrium about this thing.

One thing is for sure: This whole deal exists for you to react to it in the clearest, strongest way you can. If you don't, you're wasting a lot of pain. React. Think big. Don't be limited by fear or assumptions.

Please, please, please do something for yourself. Don't just wait it out. The still small voice is shouting for you to act. It's shouting so loud you've forgotten what it is.

All our love and prayers, Bo

• • •

Hello Bo and Sita,

How are you all? As for myself, I am blessed with health and understanding. I am doing time at the Reformatory for Women.

I will not elaborate on my crimes at this time, though I will say that they were ignited by foolish pride, showing everyone I could take care of my family on my own, no matter what! Now those beautiful babies are without their mother. Kind of defeated my own purpose, wouldn't you say? Thank God, they are all together and safe with grandma!

I have not seen my children in years. I am divorced. My mother is arthritic and it is a six-hour trip both ways. She can hardly walk, her feet are so bad. Driving is out. Which I have accepted, it has been so long now, that it would be too traumatic for them. I could not touch them anyway. I am in A-C (Administrative Control-Isolation).

I have been back here in A-C eight months now. Another woman and myself just got tired and decided to plan an escape. Obviously, it didn't go through!

Bo and Sita, the time I have spent back here has been the most productive, growth period of my life. I won't go into my rotten past, but I have come to terms with everything, especially myself. This is the first time ever that I have spent with me -- only me -- talking, learning, laughing, crying, learn, learn, learn and grow, grow, grow. I found that I am not so bad -- I even love me! I can look in the mirror each morning and smile as I renew my love daily for God, me, and all creations. This is true peace!

Some consider this little room real suffocating, not me. I will never forget what freedom I finally found in this little dwelling. I love this little room for giving me time with me. It was a blessing in disguise.

I was the bad, black sheep, evil, disruptive, no good kid, who never graduated and wanted to explore life independently (at 12) through drugs or whatever came my way, a rebel without a cause. This is my family's view. I have learned now that I was a lonely, mixed up adventurer willing to try just about anything.

You're going to love the punch line -- I now have a G.E.D., I'm a certified nurses aide, and am about 1/3 of the way to my teaching degree. My self-esteem has catapulted with these accomplishments! Yes sir -- the fucked up kid, always running, has gone this far -- so far! I am not running any more and am finally going somewhere!

In January, I started meditating, finding the real freedom of love I had been seeking all my life. My parents' point of view (step-father's) has been that my whole life and me have always been a screw-up. My mother is trapped by him and shares these views. She is a real gem, though. God bless her.

I did experiment a lot with everything, drugs, religion, men, anything new. I did have a bad marriage but that doesn't make for a screwed up life. I have 4 of the most lovely children (totally unbiased opinion, of course) and that is nowhere near a screw up!

All of these good things have been happening once I saw my pride, anger, fears and doubts as unreal. I learned from them, and found a source of love in me. After my divorce I was untouchable -- I thought I could take on the world and raise my family and refused help! I was no charity case -- I was a sad case, really lost and scared! I needed no man ever!!

One month after my awakening, I needed legal help. I was ignorant of the law but just knew I was being railroaded. Anyway I wrote and received a response from the most honest and caring man I ever met. Now I was overwhelmed. Well, we have never met in the physical sense, but we know each other's hearts and minds, and I have plenty of pictures and hundreds of pages of thoughts. He has been on his grand journey for 4 years now. He has so much spiritual love and strength, he overflows. He is a gift from heaven to me, and says I am a miracle in his life.

I was traveling slow and sure at first, he has given me the reassurance to go forward with all I feel. My realizations weren't crazy to him, he would thank me for sharing my experiences. He has been a teacher to me in legal work and school. He has been a help in my spiritual growth. Not pushing me, but lets me see things for myself, make my own realizations, then sends Tao chapters to tell me what it was I just did!

He is founder, and this year, incorporator of his dream project to help kids! He wants to take on the responsibility of me and my ready-made family. He has most graciously offered me a job. I would love to teach, help and love abused, addicted or confused kids! To give them, or more importantly, show them the love they deserve. Tomorrow's future are the children of today!

Sounds great, right? Now here's the punch line -- He has accomplished all of this and more behind prison walls -- and is doing natural life! It doesn't bother me one iota, I will work by his side and help him work every legal avenue to gain physical freedom -- Amen. He is setting up a place for my family now.

The punch line is (thank goodness for my sense of humor) my poor mom is going to freak! I can hear it now -- is this going to be the ultimate screw up in their lives! Poor ma! I have to laugh because this is the first time I am doing something right and for all the right reasons. Do I have you convinced yet, Bo? (snicker) I am practicing on you two! When the big play opens I will most definitely let you know the final scene of my scenario!

"Hey ma -- I am free and going to marry a murderer and save kids' lives!" Oh, boy -- give me strength for this one! Put like this, it sounds crazy even to me. But I feel this is the most sane thing I've ever done!

After our correspondence and then last month's proposal, I pondered in my mind until now. It was a small battle in my head, all logic and rationality just doesn't hold up. My self made arguments were to no avail. A battle that never should have occurred, my feelings and love prevail! That's what's real. So for Father's Day I accepted this most beautiful proposal!

We have such an open, honest, free love that neither of us has ever had before. We call it our "virgin concept" since we both are in this. Bo and Sita, I just had to tell someone, so I decided on you two. I couldn't see telling Mom in a letter. I can't believe I even considered marriage again. But it feels so natural, all of it -- God knows what he's doing. My board date is now February '89 -- only months away!

My friends, you are both busy people and I thank you for your time. Keep up the good -- great work you're both doing. You are truly blessed spirits. My prayers are with you!

Love you all, C

Dear C,

What a beautiful, sharing letter! We felt like we were holding hands with you as we read it.

All any of us can do is to follow our Great Adventures with courage and honor. If your next chapter is to marry your loved one, then your mother's next chapter is to deal with that. However, one thing you may want to think about is this: Maybe your marriage is the chapter _after_ next. Since February is so close, maybe you should be getting reunited with your children first. That's a pretty full adventure on its own!

You should do whatever you honestly feel is best, but I'm just bringing this idea up for you to think about.

If I were in your position as a mother, I might want to make the reunion period as uncomplicated as possible. February is right around the corner, and your boyfriend isn't going anywhere. When your relationship with your kids is pretty solid again, then they'll be able to handle your marriage with more understanding.

And your mother, too -- after she's had a chance to see all the positive change in you, she won't be so quick to think you're doing the wrong thing. You might even have her blessings to do everything you plan.

As I said, you have to do what your heart tells you is right, but I wanted to share those thoughts as your brother. You certainly have our blessings and best wishes whatever you decide. We love you very much.

All the best, Bo

● ● ●

And someday there shall be such closeness
that when one cries, the other shall taste salt.

-- Unknown

Dear Bo,

I have a problem and would like some advice. I'm doing life for killing my stepfather. I'm not proud of it, yet at times I find myself wanting to justify it because he was an asshole. At the same time, I was a 16-year-old drug addict. I was confused then.

Now that I accept what's done and use it for a learning experience (4 years later), I want to renew contact with my family and try to make amends with them. I feel like an outsider because I was adopted and don't know my biological parents or family. But I want to be accepted by my family.

I don't know how I should go about contacting my mom. (I'm speaking of my adopted family.) What should I say? It's difficult enough for me to bring up my past, so I can imagine how difficult it would be for her, who'd been married to my dad for 24 years.

A lot of people would be proud of what I did, but I don't see how I could be. I'm not a "weak" person. I'm strong and I survive. But I think it was in a way, "weak" to pull the trigger that ended my dad's life. It's not something I'd do again. That I do know. But I wonder what my family thinks of me now.

Can you give me some advice on how I should go about renewing my relationship with my family? Most feelings I've experienced in the past year or so are new to me. I was once a cold and impersonal person.

You see, my dad was an ex-con. He was also two-faced. For 3 years, he'd condoned and participated · with me in many illegal activities. Yet, when mom would find out or dad got in a weird mood, he'd physically assault me for doing exactly what he was condoning and doing along with me. This became very confusing for me. I eventually felt very stressed and wanted out of the "trap" I was in with my dad.

I tried running away. I tried reasoning with my parents to let me go on my own. This did not work, and problems got worse, so I killed him. At the time, I seen no other way out. Now I regret my decision. Please give me some advice.

Sincerely, D

Dear D,

I wish I had some magic to tell you about renewing contact with your family. The first step is obviously just writing to them simply and honestly about what's in your heart. Without getting into too much detail -- and *definitely* no defenses like "he was an asshole," etc. -- just write them that you deeply regret having done what you did, and if you could change it you would.

Tell them you've grown up a lot in the past four years and you realize how important they are to you, and hope they can find it in their hearts to re-establish contact. Just really lay bare your heart and soul to the best of your ability.

Once you write them, then it's mainly up to them. You have to be prepared for the possibility that they don't want anything to do with you. That would be sad, but you still have a life of your own to create. And by living it in a good, kind way, you'll make your "payback" as best you can. Also, time brings many changes, even to what may seem hopeless right now. You may need to be patient with them, and keep sending birthday cards, mother's day cards, Christmas cards, etc. Your loving persistence may soften them after a while.

Love, Bo

● ● ●

Dear Bo and Sita,

Hello, my name is T and I am one of many who ended up in the system. I am a convicted prostitute and drug user. Doing time has not been easy for me and I'm sure it never will be. I have gotten into the drug program here and it has helped bunches. I have made many changes but still have a good ways to go.

I am working my twelve steps and I am kinda stuck on my third step, the willingness to turn my life over to my higher power. I have found God and am willing to turn my life over to Him. What bothers me is, when you're locked up you tend to believe in change and becoming different and you work on it. But when you actually walk out the door it's another story and the change you fought so hard for in there goes to hell.

I am scared of leaving cause I'm afraid of this and I know it can happen, cause I've put in my mind before that I'm gonna do right, but as soon as I was free I did just the opposite.

Coming to prison is really different with a 4-1/2 year sentence hanging over my head. I was due to go home August but now, the system has a new law and it involves all sex-related offenses, including prostitution. Well, what credit I've received to put me home in August will be taken and I will no longer receive it, only getting the 20 days a month gain time so now I'm looking to do about 11 more months on top of the 8 months I've already done and man, is the living hell. I was looking so forward to going home to my 2 year old son who I don't even know and having a chance to be his mommy again before he could know anything.

Now I won't get to do this until he's 3 or 4 and I'm hurting. But for the grace of God I am accepting it and looking at it as if there is a reason and the only reason I can come to terms with is, it's God's way of letting me know I'm just not ready to go. With that attitude I can deal with my anger and just let go and let God.

Well, I thank you for allowing me to get this off my chest and I truly hope in any small way you can give to me an encouraging word or two to keep me headed in the direction I'm going.

T

Dear T,

It sounds like you know what you need to do and how you need to look at it. Maybe the help I can give you is to point out one part of the problem which you may not see too clearly: Fear.

Fear is a destructive problem in itself. You're afraid that when you get out you won't be able to stay straight. You're afraid that while you stay in these extra months, you're missing precious experiences with your family. You're afraid your son may not relate to you in the way you hoped. You're afraid your new attitude might regain some old bitterness. You're afraid that before you know it, you'll be right back in the joint looking back on one more crushing disappointment of your hopes for a better life.

But FEAR is the problem, not any of the things it pretends to be about. Don't let fear or any of its lieutenants -- worry, anxiety, panic, denial -- fool you into giving up the changes you've worked so hard to achieve. You're a much different person now than when you were busted.

You have much more awareness of the effects of drugs and prostitution on your life. You have more awareness of the kind of life you really want. Don't let fear twist your mind into thinking you haven't changed, that you're just playing a game, that you'll be back into all your old shit as soon as you hit some hard times. That's just fear talking, and it's a lie.

In the beginning of your letter you said you were afraid to get out yet, and then you mentioned the new law and how upset you were that you can't get out yet. Well, I think you're right to try to see the new law as being a gift of a little more time to pull your life together. You felt you needed it anyway.

Being a GREAT mother to a three-year-old is better than being a scared, inconsistent mother to a two-year-old. Use your time to keep gaining strength and faith, and to quiet your mind so that you stand up to fear and refuse to be its victim anymore.

Your life is going to be whatever you're willing to make it. Don't let fear make you think you won't "be able" to do what you want to do. Start refusing that kind of crap right now.

Your Loving brother, Bo

● ● ●

Dear Bo,

I called my ex-wife, that I still love very dearly and still consider my wife; anyway I called her the other day and the things that she had to tell me really blew me up.

First she told me that she was getting married with someone that loves her. But Bo, I've known her for twelve years and I know that her love for me is still there, she's just afraid to take the chance with me because she don't believe that I could have changed from the unfaithful, ill emotional, irresponsible, selfish S.O.B. that I once was.

Bo honestly speaking I'm 31 years old now and my eldest child is 10 years old, my baby is 6 years; my life long dream is to raise a family -- my family!

My wife and I separated when I was doing time and I figured that given a little time for her to see that I want the same things in life she wants, we'll get back together and raise our two kids and the one that she had while we were separated. I love her now more than ever. I love her, Bo! There's not a woman in the world to compare to her, Bo. I need help! Please help me!

Want my wife back! M

Dear M,

I can feel how painful this is for you, but what you want, I can't give you. People we love leave us. They even die. Life constantly changes. Some of the changes we like, some we hate, but it keeps changing. Your ex-wife's decisions can never be under your control. What can I do about that?

By your own admission, you were "unfaithful, ill emotional, irresponsible and selfish," so now she has decided she doesn't want to find out whether you've really changed. We don't always get second chances when we blow it, M. I dozed at the wheel for just a second, and my entire life changed forever when I hit a truck. No second chance. That's just the way it goes sometimes.

But M, I'm not a minister or a social worker. What I'm about is much different than that. There's a big secret about life which I try to help people find. That's all. If your ex-wife loved you and decided to stay with you forever, you'd still need to find out that secret at some time. That's the only thing I can help with. That's what my life, my books and all my newsletters are about.

The secret is revealed to you in silence, deep within yourself. And when it is revealed, the situation with your ex-wife looks completely different than it looks now. Everything does. But I can't describe it any better, because it's something you have to find out for yourself.

There is definitely a deep, rich, beautiful journey for you to find out about within yourself. Believe it or not, the pain you're feeling can HELP you find it. Sit perfectly still, and feel ALL THE PAIN without moving. Feel the pain, fear, disappointment, feel your broken heart, in perfect silence and stillness. Then you'll touch the big secret. I can help you find what is real, but I can't help you get what you want. I'm truly sorry.

All my love, Bo

Bo,

You are good people, I mean it from the bottom of my heart. If this world had more Bo's it would be a far greater world, I mean better world to live in. Your last letter to me in response to "wanting my wife back" hurted very much. Yet it made me realize what I must do.

I'll never give up hope that one day she'll return but I don't hurt now as much as I did before reading and rereading your letter over what seemed like a hundred times. (At first, I was plenty mad with you.) But after a many sleepless night of your letter played back in my mind a light began to shine and that light was the reality of what you said was nothing more than the truth.

Bo, I admire you, yet I envy you for being able to deal with the truth so easily and with so many helpless people, such as myself, and you help us see life the way life really is. "How do you manage my friend??" "Wow." You said that you can't help me with what I really want, you've given me that already, the key (TRUTH) that alone brother Bo is the answer.

You and the people that you speak of I've recognized deals only in truth. I Bo want to become part of that chain of friends. Seeing my letter published in your newsletter made me realize that you really do care.

Love you Bo, M

Dear M,

Thanks for brightening our day. I know it must have been hard for you to cop to my letter, and I respect your strength and honesty in being able to do that. Sometimes the Truth hurts (Hell, probably *most* of the time it hurts!), but it's the Truth anyway. It takes a big man to let it shine through his shit like you did.

I hope now you can keep clearing your mind and opening your heart so you don't backslide into the painful confusion you were in before. Keep working on yourself, brother, and have faith that all these difficult lessons have a powerful purpose. You're on your way now. Let yourself feel good about that. At least there's something going on, and you're not stuck in concrete anymore.

Love, Bo

Bo,

I've tried all I could to do the right thing, I've accepted the decision that my wife has made concerning her life. I don't bother her at all. I called to talk to my eldest daughter as I usually call every other week, through a three-way line and my baby just talk without her mother knowing. I don't talk to my youngest girl because she doesn't understand things as my older girl does, she would have told her mother and her mother would have gotten mad with my older girl for talking to me and hiding it from her.

So the other day I decided to talk to my baby because I longed to talk with her after not doing so for so long, but to do so I had to just talk with her mother. Well I did talk to her and she has the understanding of a road or a tree. I've tried with all that I know how. I've written her letters asking her to forgive me for all the hurt and pain that I've caused her and for the sake of the kids we should be friends. She never wrote back.

Now after talking with her the other day not only does she continue to throw the past back in my face but she's also talking about adding to my world of troubles in any way that she can think of, to start off with it will be child support. I don't know how long I'll be locked up but when I get out she'll get her due!

I've had all I can take of this life. When I look at it I don't really have much to live for anyway so why shouldn't I end it my way. My mother was murdered by the hands of my daddy so I'll just follow the set pattern. That was March '65, on November 5,

1986 my eldest brother was murdered by two of my first cousins. They got off scot free, they ambushed him and crushed his skull in with a two-by-four. On April 1987 about the 10th my youngest brother was murdered during a fight with a friend of his. He got off scot free. He was stabbed in the head. On January 10, 1988 my eldest and only son Michael Jr. was murdered by a hit and run driver while walking on the sidewalk with his sister. He was 10 years old. The guy that hit him or better yet murdered my son was run down by a couple of witnesses but he got off scot free also. How much am I to take?

In 14 months my life was totally destroyed. My marriage flopped during the same time all this other shit started happening to me. I've tried to regroup, honestly I have but I quit trying. Now I'll just do what should have been done from the start.

If she thinks that she can torment me and get off because I've let everything else get by, now it's time to pay the piper. This is what she wants, I can feel it in my bones.

Now I must strike back. I won't take crap from no one anymore in here or out; no more trying to reason with these simpleminded idiots. Now I'll exercise what's been locked up in my heart for so long. I must write her a letter of thanks for making me see there's no other way.

On a Mission, M "Too Tough"

Dear M,

If you meant what you wrote me, you wouldn't have sent it to me, because you know the kinds of things I would say. So instead of pretending that I'm laying this advice on you, admit that it's you who doesn't want to follow the terrible cycle of violence you've seen in your family. It's you who wants to figure out a better way of dealing with life than by hurting or killing the people who get in your face. That's the only reason you wrote me, and you know it in your heart.

You're a decent guy, M, and you want some advice so you don't go down the tubes. That's what's really going on, so admit it. The thing is, you already know my advice: Use your time to work on yourself and see the truth about your life and your feelings. Quiet your mind and open your heart before you hit the streets. Pray for guidance. In other words, don't just *think* about all of this stuff; change the thinker instead.

The truth is, we all have pain in our lives and we have the choice of learning from it or resisting it. What your wife is putting you through could make you a kinder, stronger person instead of a raving maniac killer. It's your choice. What did Jesus ever do wrong? Was it "fair" that they whipped Him, imprisoned Him, and crucified Him? Wouldn't he have been "justified" in getting pissed off and bitter and violent?

You can lash out in pain all you want, God will still love you; but you'll miss the whole point of the Mystery. **Nobody's life goes how they want it to go.** Quiet down for a minute and see the Truth. It's entirely up to you to take what's given you and make something out of it, or just to bitch about it and strike back like all the relatives you mentioned who killed and got killed. Did striking back do any of them any good? Is that the path you want to follow?

I'm telling it like it is, brother, I'm talking about reality. Reality is, your wife is doing what she's doing and you need to deal with it in a way that won't destroy her, your kids, or you. Real love requires some huge sacrifices and patience. That much is up to you. You have all my blessings and prayers for your tough work, M. Keep me posted.

I'm pulling for you, Bo

[a few months later:]

Dear Bo,

Thanks to you Bo, I now have a destiny. I would like to help people also. You've shown me so much love and care that I've got to spread it around.

No, I'm not planning on killing my ex-wife anymore, but as to whether I plan on getting back with her, that my friend will be totally up to the good Lord and her. I wrote her a short note awhile ago and explained myself in every detail and that's that. Not with any hope, just to express myself. Now I'll just let nature take its course.

Thanks for being my friend, M

● ● ●

I like your smile and your fingertips;
I like the way that you move your lips;
I like the cool way you look at me.
Everything about you is bringing me misery.

-- "Buckets of Rain," Bob Dylan

> *Art is as mysterious and important as the whisperings of God.*
> *-- Horace Parker*

THE WHISPERINGS OF GOD

Horace Parker

Peace, Bo

July 29, 1976

I have been working on a painting for the past few days. It was a tense, tiring, but exciting struggle. Today the forms and colors seem to have found their proper place, their most interesting interrelationship. It feels right, and as a result. I feel good. This struggle to express a personal interpretation of the nuances of moods, experiences, places, and personalities is not easy when you're trying to be honest, and in my case it is even made more difficult because of my lack of extensive formal training. But it deepens me and gives my life more meaning.

Art is as mysterious and important as the whisperings of God. Perhaps Art is the whispering of God. And all men and woman are artist when they are trying to express the innerspace in which they journey, or when they are truly trying to tenderly touch the substance of someone elses experience.

HORACE PARKER

"Hawk"

Dear Bo,

The world is a ghetto,
a utopia, a war zone,
anything you create it to be....
The world, is a state of mind.

              -- Hawk

Hawk

Dearest Bo and Sita,

A very loving friend of mine
gave you my name and address,
thinking it would be the right thing
for her to do, since she didn't know how
else to save me from myself at that
time. And of course, it was a great deed
on her part, because I had no idea of the
Ashram Project at all. *We're All Doing Time* is a fine piece of
work, and I now refer to it often, even though I've read it
through. Thank you.

I know that I don't have to tell you about Texas prisons, not
to mention the goings-on here, so I'll just say that I'm serving a
25-year sentence for aggravated robbery. I've been here for four
years, with four more to complete before I come up for parole.
I'm a Black American. Everybody calls me "Hawk" and I prefer
that to my slave name. I am a criminal, but more than that I am
an artist, and as you can see, a writer.

As with my contemporaries, my story is long and extremely
confusing, filled with unhappy realizations, and very painful
endurances. But despite, regardless, and nevertheless, I'm going
through my experience with keen awareness.

I want to thank you both for your contribution to my personal *well-being, because I had indeed jumped into the mix, lost my identity, and gave up on my own life. You reminded me of who I am, and of my purpose upon the face of this earth.*

I was introduced to Zen over ten years ago by a Viet Nam veteran who served in Special Forces (Seals). Along with meditation, he taught me martial arts and yoga. But afterwards, I was deeply wounded by my life experience, and out of bitterness and the ignorance of youth, I began using my powers for wrong and self-destructive uses.

I lost my identity for a long period of time, and fell so deep into the mix that it was very difficult for me to climb back out, working myself deeper and deeper. I disobeyed my teacher, and ignored my Karma. I executed somewhat of a Robin Hood format, calling myself "balancing out the wrongs." My conscience is terrible. I became so good at what I was doing, that out of all 46 robberies I never physically hurt even one person. I don't use drugs, and it wasn't for the money; my prime motive seems to have been to destroy my own life, indirectly.

It has taken me all this time to accept myself and my life. My present state is a far cry from how it was four years ago, and your help has made that possible. I've still got some heavy details to iron out in my life, but my optimism is fresh and healthy enough to sustain me through the rest of this experience.

Sita, Bo, to show my appreciation, I lend my talented hand to the Project in the form of this artwork, and hope that you will accept. It is probably the only real accomplishment I will have time to perfect, "in this time around."

With this said, I end this letter, but not my love and sincere friendship. Be cool, and tell Josh he's with me too. I'm just beginning to enjoy my journey.

Love always, Hawk

Self Portrait
age 35

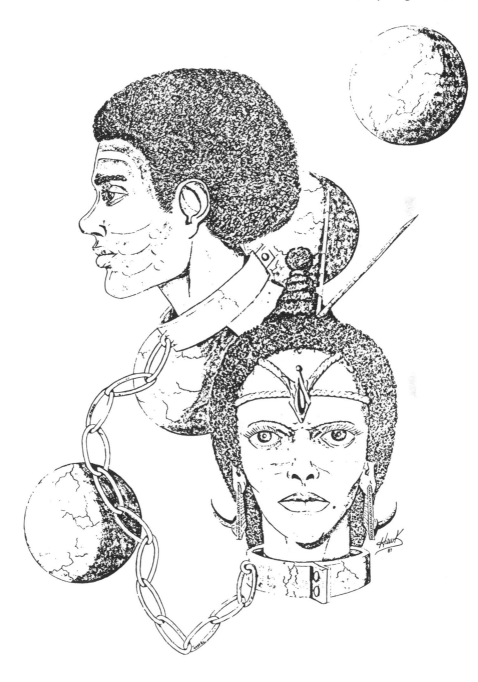

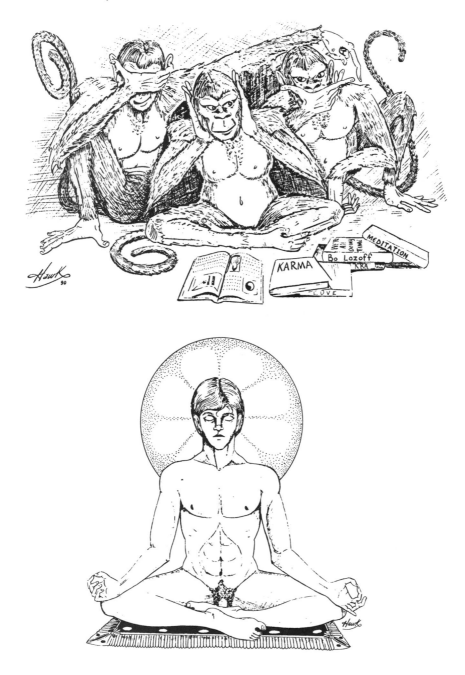

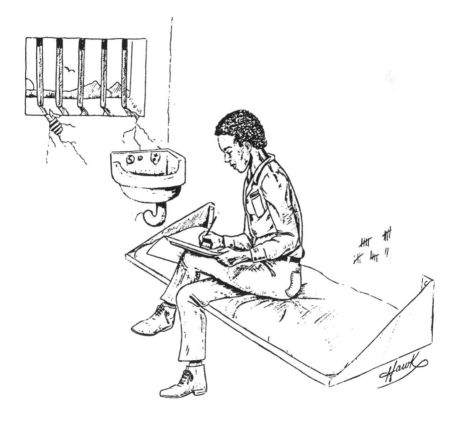

Arthur Goodwin

Tim Prock

Self-Portrait

AIDS Plays The Blues

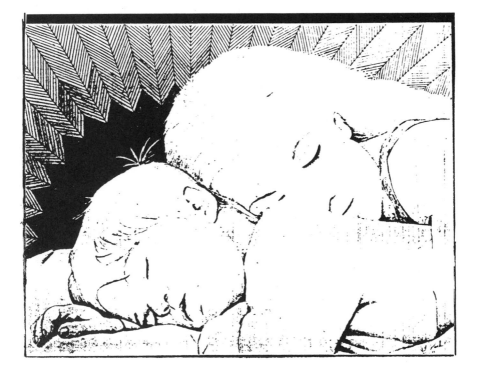

Love Lies Sleeping

WANTED

THE ESCAPE ARTIST

The Escape Artist
"Self-Portrait"

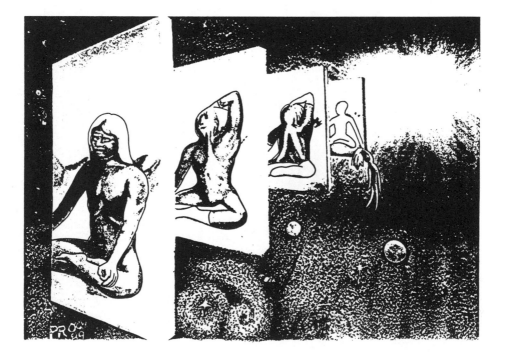

Going Home

John Williams

JUD NELSON, BLACK SMITH , SUGAR VALLEY, GA. 1988
15/90

JOHN WILLIAMS 1988

Jud Nelson, Blacksmith

"Bullett" Bouldin

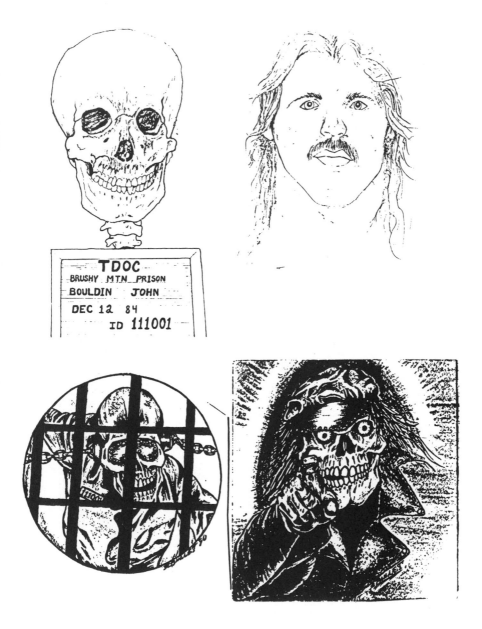

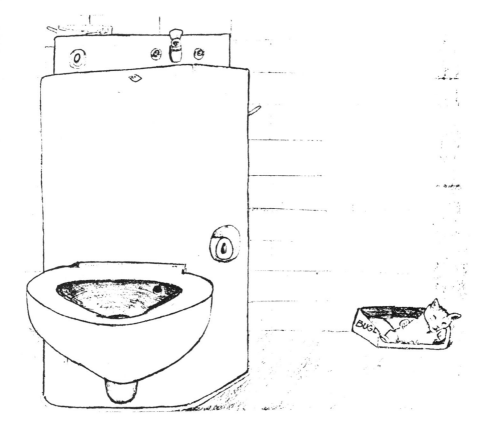

John Mullis

HOLDING ON

Well I asked for help, and it don't seem to come;
Yeah, and I prayed for help, and it don't seem to come;
Sometimes I beg for help, and it don't seem to come;
Ah, but I'm holding on, yeah, I'm holding on.

They say ask, and you'll be answered;
They tell me seek, and you will find.
They say knock, knock, knock and the door will open;
Well, I've been knocking now, such a long long time,
And I'm barely holding on; but I'm holding on. I'm holding on.

They say every prayer gets answered;
And in this, you must just believe.
'Cause it may not come as you expected;
No no, not what you wanted, no, but what you need,
So you got to keep holding on, yeah, 'n I'm holding on.

And when my time is ended, and I see Him on His throne;
And I say "Lord I prayed, but where were you?"
He'll say "How do you think you kept holding on? I kept you
holding on! Yeah, holding on.
Yeah, I kept you holding on, holding on."

Sid Tyler 1987

GOT TO KEEP HOLDING ON

Dear Bo,

I was recently sentenced to death and currently live on death row. I am a male-to-female transexual but have not had the surgery and it doesn't look like that's going to be possible now due to my death sentence.

I was taking female hormones for a couple of years under a doctor's care in preparation for reassignment surgery. Since I arrived here the medical staff has refused to continue my estrogen therapy. It is absolutely vital to my psychological well-being to continue this treatment, and even the doctors I have seen here in prison agree to that fact. But I have run into an ultra-conservative political wall and getting the treatment looks grim at this point.

The other problem is that I've been infected with the HIV virus. I don't have full-blown AIDS yet but the doctors give me the prognosis, due to the somewhat rapid decline in my t-helper count and the presence of HIV-related symptoms, that I will develop full-blown AIDS in the next 18 months.

The state department of corrections has a unit that provides care for people who are HIV-infected, but due to my condemned status, I can't be transferred there. I am the only person who is permanently assigned to this prison who has HIV-related problems.

I am receiving <u>none</u> of the special care my illness requires. All my attempts to get proper care have failed. This facility just isn't equipped for a condemned transexual with AIDS and I am very concerned at the attitude of indifference to my problems.

I know that these are very unusual problems, and I don't know what you or anyone else can do about them. But please send me your books, and offer any assistance you can.

sincerely, J

Dear J,

Hope you've gotten our package of materials by now and that you find some of the answers you're looking for in them. We have no knowledge or skills to make suggestions about the complex legal issues over your gender treatments and HIV-related stuff, but the blue card enclosed with your books has some helpful addresses on the back which you can try.

I hope my advice doesn't offend you, but here goes: J, you're on death row, you're in a gender Twilight Zone, and diagnosed as HIV-positive. Don't you think maybe it's time for you to focus your remaining energies on your inner work instead of legal/medical issues? I'm not saying you shouldn't try to get better treatment or anything like that; again, the legal resources on our blue card may be able to help.

But I'm talking about *your* energies. At a certain point, life slaps us upside the head hard enough to make us consider the truly profound issues -- which, frankly, have nothing to do with gender, sex, health, race, age, or any of the other "packaging" we find ourselves in.

That's really what my books and this project are all about. This isn't a sweet support group, it's a radical spiritual resource which few people use to its fullest. Given your situation, it seems like if anybody decides to go all the way with us, it should be you.

So when you read the books and newsletters, don't read them as nice liberal affirmation-type spirituality. Let's cut out all the bullshit. Read them openly and try to see that we're talking about truths beyond space and time, beyond life and death, beyond the countless conditions which fill our lives.

We're talking about the Great Mystery. There truly is one. We're talking about a part of you which is free and joyful beyond your wildest dreams. And it is absolutely independent of whether you complete your sex-change, fulfill your death sentence, or contract AIDS.

Again, I don't mean to offend you by all of this. But I do hope it has some spiritual shock value which can jump-start you on a new course of how you decide to spend your time. I wish you all the best of everything in whatever you try to do.

Your Brother, Bo

● ● ●

Bo, Sita,

My problem is this: I am a pedophile. I have never been arrested for it, though it's a miracle I haven't. I got warned by the law twice. To say that this habit has become so ingrained into my soul as to virtually rule my existence would be an understatement. I am sleazy, low-down, used to spend 10, 15, 20 hours a day doing some things so vile and bizarre that I'll not mention them. If you want particulars I can supply them, endlessly.

Suffice it to say that this thing virtually rules my life. I can't seem to get away from it. Even after being down for 3 years, a picture in a magazine, on TV and the most graphic and rancid fantasies kick in. I am constantly paranoid around children. My sister has a kid now and my girlfriend also; so I must do something about this problem. I have tried ignoring it, it only comes back stronger. I have been living this double life since I was maybe 12 (that's 15 years now) and I don't know how it got started. I was not subject to anything unusually sexual as a child and as far as I can recall had a very "normal" upbringing.

The extent to which this is a part of me would boggle your mind. Hell, it boggles my mind. And I must find a way to get rid of it. I have spent thousands of hours thinking about the philosophy of it all and could elaborate at great length. But I shan't. I will seek professional help some day. But when I get out I'm gonna be without many contacts and in situations where children will be very available. What can I do? Can you help? Do you know someone who can?

Thanks. Peace and love, M

Dear M,

First, you have to deeply, deeply get it straight that <u>you are stronger than your fantasies.</u> Obviously the best thing is to get completely "cured" somehow, but even if your mind remains exactly the same as it is now, <u>you don't have to act on those feelings.</u> It's like falling off a wild horse. I used to tell my son, "The horse can't really buck you off if you never let go. The only way you fall is if your fear convinces you to let go." People can say "That horse bucked me," but that's never quite true, just like you can say "I can't fight the urges, they're too strong," but that's not true either. Once you get it all the way through your head that you never have to give in, you'll be halfway home.

Second, you shouldn't wait to get professional help. I'll bet there's <u>one</u> very decent psychologist or counselor in your prison; there usually is. I know it's hard to lay all this out to somebody, but you've got to at some point, and the sooner the better. You don't want to get out and screw up your whole life and the lives of innocent children.

Go to the library and begin reading about pedophilia, start educating yourself about what sort of treatments are going on.

Third, start concentrating on it from the victim's point of view -- not only the child, but the parents and relatives as well. Think about how traumatic it is for their whole lives; think about what kind of karma you create for yourself by being such a bad force in a young person's life. That's not what you want to do. That's not how you want your own life to be remembered.

Fourth, start praying. Pray like hell for help to see this more clearly, and to have the inner strength to do what's right. Then you have to trust that your prayers will be answered. Be open to the help that may come into your life. Be on the lookout for it, and take advantage of it when it comes. Pray every day, several times a day. You say this thing takes up so many hours, well turn all those hours into prayer against it instead.

I could tell in your letter that you haven't fully decided to give up this part of yourself yet. There are various ways you expressed yourself that reveal you're still holding on to the possibility of acting it out. Let it go, M. Let go of the fantasy that somehow, you could do it once or twice and not get caught. Give it up. It will ruin your whole life and damage other people's lives as well.

If you meditate, do yoga & breathing, keep your body in good health, seek professional help, and pray with all your might, you'll beat this thing. But beating it has to become the prime focus of your life. Are you ready to get down to it, or are you just making noises and looking for sympathy?

To quote a line from my favorite holy book, *Make one fast choice now, and no second.*

I'm pulling for you, Bo

[I dropped M a note about a year later, in fall 1990, for a progress report. It wasn't good. His response follows:]

Dear Bo,

Not out yet. Early '91. Have decided it's better to enjoy what I am rather than try to change. It's not really such a big problem, man. It's like much else, parallax. I had myself convinced it was a problem, but from this vantage point, it's really quite beautiful.

Appreciate your note. Please cancel my name from any further newsletters.

Peace and Love, M

Dear M,

I'll take you off our mailing list if you want, but not without trying to talk some sense into you. Your letter is crazy, brother, and you know it. Giving in and being a child molester is not going to create a decent life. And bringing that kind of damage into other people's lives is going to guarantee you worse and worse troubles until you off yourself because you can't bear your misery.

M, I swear to you that you can do what you need to do to have a better life than that. Others have done it. But it takes a tremendous amount of courage and work on your part. You have a clear choice of whether to be the hero or villain in your own life. Only you can make that choice, and right now you seem to be making the wrong one.

Please do the right thing. You're a decent guy; don't deliberately choose to do evil. Re-read my letter to you from last year; pray; talk to someone; get some support. Please. It's still in your hands to write your own future. I can't imagine why you want to create hell on earth instead of being a good guy.

Write back and tell me something good, come on. At least write back and tell me even if you haven't changed your mind, so I can figure out how hard to pray for you.

Love, Bo

Bo,

Have just completed a six-page response to your letter. But decided not to send it because you don't really ask for an explanation.

Answer: Ain't changed my mind, don't think I'm gonna, I'm happy.

Thanks for your sincere letter. And for apparently caring.

Peace and love, M

PS: Don't worry about me ever "offing" myself; ain't got the balls.

Dear M,

Thanks for being man enough to write back. You didn't say whether you still want me to take you off our mailing list or not, so let me know.

M, no way in the world you can convince me you're "happy" planning to get out and be a dangerous, harmful bastard to innocent children. You're not pure evil, bro, you're just stuck in a rough problem, and you need to do something about it before you ruin your own and other's lives.

I don't know whether you noticed, but a few newsletters ago we printed the name of a group set up to help ex-pedophiles stay straight. They know and understand what you're going through, M. Why don't you write them and see what happens? [name & address given]:

Come on, buddy, get back on track. As your friend and as a father, I can't let you go this way without a fight.

Your brother, Bo

[this correspondence is still in progress]

● ● ●

*As far as Buddha Nature is concerned, there is no difference
between sinner and sage...
One enlightened thought and one is a Buddha,
One foolish thought and one is an ordinary man.*

-- Hui Neng

Dear Bo and Sita,

G'day my name is P. I'm a 21-year-old pakeha and at present I'm doing 9 months in prison here in New Zealand, not long to some people but long enough for me. I'm just about finished the book We're All Doing Time *and boy is it good. I came by it in the library here in the prison. I thought when I got it that it was a book just about doing time but when I opened it wow it freaked me out but I read and read until it's just about finished and it's the best book I've read in a long time, straight up too.*

It set me back quite a bit, mostly the letters. Heavy shit, it made me think, man I only ever thought about myself but those letters they blew me away. And I thought I had it hard, no way man, not any more. I started to think about it more and more and I would like to do something. I don't know, anything I suppose. I pray for my brothers at night and have started meditating at night but it's not enough.

I was really touched at the letters of Maury Logue but I was deeply shocked when I read at the end that he had been stabbed to death. Reading his letters and yours also you could feel that he was getting there, slowly at first, but he was getting there. It makes me wonder if it's all worth it sometimes. Even though it's 1987 my heart weeps for Maury even though he's gone.

I really feel sometimes is it all worth it really? They might as well shoot all inmates who go inside. All they do is fuck up your minds, make you paranoid and lock you up for days on end and treat you like garbage. Is it worth the pain, the treatment they give out? Fuck no, it's bullshit. You know if I was doing a long stint in jail, I'd kill myself and start again. It wouldn't be worth the shit to do your time and be treated like animals but you know something, it's just the tough ones who survive and the rest if you can call them that are treated like shit.

If I could have one wish then that would be to shoot or just kill every god dam body in prison. If it happened tomorrow then it wouldn't worry me. I'd be amongst the dead, that way we could be at peace within ourselves, you know what I mean, Bo.

Well, I do want to bring back peace and love to all and get rid of all the hate and fear, it's the only way to do it even if it means getting rid of prisons and the people inside them. You know I feel sick inside but can't get rid of it. Meditation helps some but maybe I need something else. You know I still don't know where I'm going or coming from. I've talked to God, I've opened my heart to Him but nothing happens. Maybe my fate lies in a different direction, I don't know.

I sometimes think I'm a lost soul you know, maybe I am just drifting here and there not too sure where I'm going or what I'm doing. You know it freaks me out quite a bit. I can't seem to be able to do things right. I'm what they would call a fuck up person, really strange, and yet really freaky or weird. I don't know, maybe they will right themselves. I don't know, too far beyond me to understand.

You know, I really love people a lot but I cry in my heart, I cry out for something but I don't know what it is, how can I find it Bo? I'm at the bottom of the tree trying to reach up but there's nothing there, yet I know there is. How do I find that inner peace inside of me? I'm looking but I can't see it.

Please help this lost soul find peace. I hope I haven't bored you good people to death by writing this, so I sign off.

Love and best wishes, P

Dear P,

Thanks for all the kind words about my book. But you know, the whole purpose of my book is to help people answer questions and problems like the ones you wrote about. So if you're still sitting there thinking "All this crap just isn't worth it", then maybe my book's not doing such a great job.

You said you've just started to meditate and talk to God, etc. Well, give it a chance. The first thing you need on this journey is **patience**. We spent a good many years screwing our lives up; it stands to reason that it might take more than a few days to set things right. Meditation is slow, but sure. Prayer is slow, but sure. And my book was not meant to be read one time, but many. Each time through you'll be focusing on different stuff with new meanings as you begin making changes in your life.

You say you're reaching up but there's nothing there. I say, there is definitely something there, just keep reaching and don't be in such a rush. Work with some of the techniques in my book. Real change takes work. Just because you agree with something, that doesn't mean you've taken it all the way into your heart.

One very important thing you're missing when you talk about dying and killing: Death isn't the end, and it's not even a brand-new start. You don't escape problems by dying. The reason you're in prison is to learn something which you really need to learn. You're missing that point. At some time or another, you need to look at your life with a little more wisdom and faith. Don't assume that you understand what's good and bad.

There is a great deal you don't understand about yourself, and about why things are the way they are. So be more humble, more of a student, and stop talking so loosely about dying or killing. Just take what life hands you each day and try your best to learn something from it that helps you become stronger, kinder, and more honest with yourself.

This life is a hard, mysterious journey for all of us, P. Try to quiet down and get a little deeper. Don't be so misled by the surface appearances.

Keep on keeping on, Bo

● ● ●

What doesn't kill me, makes me stronger.

-- Albert Camus

Dear Bo,

It probably doesn't make a big difference to you why I'm in prison, but there's a reason for me to tell you. I understand well the mystery behind the act of forgiveness -- which is to repent. To write it down on paper and send it to someone really impresses the subconscious mind -- if you honestly have regret, which I do. So my friend, here goes:

My father was a drunk. Used to come home and beat on me and my mom for no reason at all. This went on for years before me and my mom finally moved across town to a place of our own.

Because my parents were separated, the army stopped my father's check, so he had no money coming in with which to live on -- so I moved in with him to pay some of the bills. I was living with him for about two months, and one day I got to thinking about what he had done to me and my mom and I just lost control, picked up a high-powered rifle, went into the bedroom (he was sleeping) and shot him twice while he slept -- killing him. I refused to take the stand when I went to court. The judge sentenced me to 30 years, so here I am. I've been in since 1981.

Well, there you have it -- my written confession. This is the first time I've told anyone the truth about why I'm in prison -- but it feels great to be open with someone for a change. This is step one in another of my problems -- dishonesty. I'll record that in my journal for today!

May God richly bless you, J

Dear J,

I'm glad you're able to write about killing your father. Stay open to your feelings during meditation; you may be able to pass through a lot of stuff without moving an inch. I don't think it's up to you or me to "forgive"; that's God's department. Our business is to get completely honest with ourselves and to have the courage to move in the directions our honesty reveals to us as being right.

It sounds to me like you're moving along really beautifully. Just take it one step at a time, slow and gentle. It's a long and mysterious journey.

all the best, Bo

● ● ●

Dear Bo,

I'm not trying to be a pest or anything, I just wanted to thank you for your book and newsletters, and the picture. You have a beautiful family. Thank you for sending it all; it's appreciated.

I've read part of the book, but I have one problem. I don't believe in God. So if " God' is the way to find peace, what does an atheist do?

I have no problem dealing with how my life unfolds, 'cause I don't worry about tomorrow 'til I've made it through today. I guess I just don't give a shit, to be honest. But I do hurt for someone else. I'm in love with a girl on death row. And the tears I shed, I shed for her. It rips me apart inside. She's the only person in this world I can talk to, the only person I care for, and they want to kill her.

How do I deal with that? If you can tell me how to handle that, then I can handle anything. Life is a joke, but that's one punch line I can't laugh at, only cry.

Take care, y'all, B

Dear B,

Got your letter, which was very touching. I can feel your pain, and I can also feel your love behind it.

You say you "don't believe in God, so what's an atheist to do?" Well, I don't know --- in a way, "God" and "atheist" are just two words, and I don't care too much either way about words. What I do know is that there is much more to reality than what we see and hear. There's a profound mystery at work in all of our lives. I know that much beyond any doubt, because many times I've touched that mystery and had my mind blown. So whether you want to call that "God" or just "far out," I don't care; it's real either way. And either way, life never quite makes sense until we open ourselves up to that mystery.

It doesn't make sense that your beloved is on death row. It doesn't make sense that you can't touch each other to express the beauty and purity of your love. It doesn't make sense that we're destroying this beautiful planet which we need to survive. None of it makes sense unless somewhere along the way you tap into the Big Mystery, and suddenly it not only all makes sense, but it's perfect and beautiful -- even the ugliest parts.

But this enlightened attitude isn't something I can convince you of. If you get tired enough of feeling the way you feel, then you can begin to realize there are roadmaps into the mystery, and begin trying them out. And it's not about believing in God or anything else. It's about working with yourself in some very powerful ways to open up your deepest power and wisdom and enlightenment. That's all I can offer you. I can't get your girl off death row or change your life story. But I swear to you, there's a lot more going on than you understand. Go for it, bro.

Love, Bo

Dear Bo,

I hope this finds you and yours steppin' high. Things stink on this end, but who gives a shit?

You know, I'm not writing to fuck with you or anything, but I've waited a long time to speak my peace about what you said in reply to my last letter. I just wonder, if it were Sita sitting on death row, would you find "beauty within the ugliness" then? I don't think so.

So how the hell am I supposed to? You don't have to answer that... you don't even have to answer this letter as far as that goes. I just wanted to say what I wanted to say. I did.

B

Dear B,

Back to the drawing board, brother, because you still don't get it. Yes, if it were Sita on death row, or my mother, or me, or my son, it would still be beautiful amidst the ugliness and pain of it.

This is a lot bigger ball game than you realize, and you have to quiet your mind to understand. I KNOW it hurts; please don't think I'm being casual with you. I'm just trying to point you in a very real direction of ancient truth and other levels of reality. What do you have to lose by looking upward and inward? It's not bullshit, I swear.

Your brother, Bo

● ● ●

IT'S ALL RIGHT HERE, YOU KNOW

Dear Bo and Sita,

<u>Thank you</u>! I feel like I'm on the right path now, you've give me direction and something to strive for. I love you guys and what you're doing!

I'm in the hole right now, which is OK, I have all day to meditate, do my pranayama exercises (I combine the two), pray, do my hatha yoga exercises, and read my Bible.

I know I've still got a long way to go to get in tune with myself but in the short time I've had your book and started the exercises and prayer and meditation, I already feel better both physically and spiritually and finally feel a sense of worth!

I never thought it would be possible to feel good in here, knowing that I'll never get out, and I don't all the time but there are moments when I feel so good I feel like I'm gonna burst. I get waves of a very good feeling in the chest area which is the 4th chakra, the Christ heart.

Anyway, I mainly wanted to thank you, and to let you know how I'm coming along. Everyone I come in contact with here in the hole I try to turn on to what's happening, especially the guys doing a lot of time, I would like to see some peace and understanding and love come into their lives also.

I have my own sign hanging over my bed "It's all right here, you know." Good story, I can relate very much to Monk because I've got natural life too. I want so much to feel like Monk did, all the time, not just part of the time like I do now, but I know that change doesn't happen overnight.

Once again, you guys, <u>THANK YOU</u> for the impact you've made in my life to open my eyes instead of walking around blind. Thank you for what you're doing in others' lives also.

If there is anything I can do to help out in any way, please advise me, I'd be happy to help with anything that is within my limitations here, artwork, correspondence, etc.

I love you guys, from the heart, M

● ● ●

Dear Bo and Sita,

I've spent many happy hours reading through We're All Doing Time. *It never fails to give me a lift and put me back in touch with the Universe whenever I let the magnetism of my lingering negative aspects pull me from the path. Like most folks, a graph of my spiritual progress would resemble a diagram for the world's hairiest roller-coaster-ride. But finally I've gotten to the point of enjoying a lot more peaks than valleys.*

I have intended to write for a long time, and began a couple of letters that rambled on and on and gradually digressed into a bunch of b-u-l-l-s-h-i-t. I'm one of those guys that think nobody can understand or appreciate my present without an autobiographical understanding of my past, the ol' Siddhartha syndrome of trials, tribulations, TRUTH. For now, suffice it to say that I have been down 18½ years on a life sentence, that began with three years on death row before the Supreme Court abolished the death penalty in June of 1972. I shot and killed a man during an armed robbery.

I had been to the joint twice before that, and reform schools five times before that, a classic case of the state-raised rebel without a cause. Hell, I've been locked up over two-thirds of my life. I'm forty-one. I first became involved with yoga when still on the row. Somebody gave me a little volume written by some woman, who designed it for business executives who could only devote 15 minutes a day to their practice. Actually, it was more or less intended to teach the fuckers how to relax and avoid ulcers. It wasn't at all spiritual in nature, and I had no warning about the closet doors meditating and snorting pran could open.

The next thing I knew my head had become Pandora's evil little box. There was a long dark night with my soul with much wringing of hands and gnashing of teeth as I had to face the dirty little coward that shot poor Mr. Howard, if you know what I mean. But you must understand that in my case there was nothing subtle, no gradual easing into the transition with even a hint of what was happening. One day I was a cold, callous, coldblooded sonofabitch with a colossal fuck-it-attitude, and the next morning I was scared shitless and sincerely wanting to meet the holy spirit! I needed the "ghost-busters" in a bad way. But that fabled instantaneous born-again-feeling didn't take on me.

The strange thing is I never did snap to what triggered all the guilty recriminations, and like all good things I ever stumbled onto, I sat like a real dummy overdosing on pran, I mean I literally knocked myself out frequently by hyperventilating. There for a while I was as wacky as a hoot owl living in a belfry.

Eventually things began to mellow out, and I started having some insights during meditation that put my life in a perspective I could accept and live with. There is a saying that "yoga teaches yoga," and I think you wrote something to that effect yourself. Well, I know what that means. I've been awed more than a few times by thoughts too big and beautiful to be my own.

I'll never forget the first real experience I had during meditation that was the pivot-point that began a turnabout in consciousness for me. I was absorbed in that special stillness I can reach maybe only once in every 50 meditations. I had two technicolor memories back-to-back followed by a question whispered by that small, still voice that resounded in my mind like a thunderclap.

It went like this: First I recalled a time when I was about eight. My folks were separated and me and an older brother was living with my mom in an apartment. We had a little yellow canary we called "Tweety." On the weekends my bro and I would go visit our dad and mom would go stay with relatives. One particular time we all stayed gone something like a week, and mom forgot to tell a neighbor to feed poor little tweety. So, when we returned we discovered its stiff little carcass in the bottom of the cage. The three of us sat at the kitchen table and bawled our eyes out at the loss of our little feathered friend, just like it was family.

Now, immediately following that sad recollection, I remembered the night of the crime that put me on death row. My fall-partner and I robbed a convenience store, and we were concealed on the blind side of the owner's panel truck when he closed up and came out to go home. Our cue to move around on him was the moment he put his key in the door. My partner had never robbed anyone so he came up behind the man and I from the front, and I was doing the the talking. He was well over six feet tall and had a menacing appearance in the dark. But we popped up like a couple of jacks-in-a-box and startled the guy. IIc madc a sound like, "Oh!" and made a sudden reach for his hip-pocket.

From my partner's position he thought he said, "No!" and looked like Matt Dillon going for the draw. So he shot him in the back. I reacted on impulse and reflexively pulled the trigger, hitting him in the chest. When he fell I frisked him down because I was afraid to turn my back thinking that he could still blow me away because he was still conscious at that time.

He didn't even have a pistol. He had just been reaching for a bank bag in his hip pocket. My fall-partner observed all this and when we were in the car he started copping deuces because I had told him not to shoot unless it was absolutely necessary. But I told him, "Fuck him. I hope the bastard dies." We had been drinking and eating black mollies, and at that time I meant it. I didn't feel a fucking thing for the man. Now, the question I mentioned earlier, asked by that small, still voice was simply: WHAT HAPPENED? HOW COULD THE CHILD WHO WEPT SO BITTERLY OVER THE DEATH OF A CANARY BECOME SO CALLOUS AS TO MURDER A FELLOW HUMAN BEING AND FEEL NOT A FUCKING THING???

I doubt that any of that would make much of an impression on many people. But it was presented to me in a scenario designed to set me on a quest for self-understanding. I've been trying to answer that question for almost all of this 18-1/2 years.

Some of the pieces are still missing and others are faded and frayed, but I've been privileged to see enough of the picture to solve the puzzle to my own satisfaction. I can't glue it to a board and hang it up for the world to admire, but I can drag it out once in a while and appreciate the time and effort spent on getting it together. The work wasn't one smooth, continuous chore, I've lost my cool more than a few times and slapped all the pieces off the table. But there's something about those fucking puzzles like that that just won't let you rest in peace until you get it all together, if you know what I mean.

Well, I'll be a sonofabitch if I didn't get a couple chapters of that autobiography in on you anyway! If you ever piss me off, I'll make you read a couple more. You guys take care.

In spirit, M

● ● ●

Dear Bo,

Life plods along here at its regular pace. I would like to ask for some advice. To put it kindly, I am not the most popular of fellows. I am pretty much a well-talented loner. I can draw and write (and organize, talk...), but still feel out of place. There are very few people I have been able to talk and share views with.

For me, there is only one set of rules, and they must apply to everyone, especially myself. The values I've found are humanistic: each as equal, each as brother. In a divided society, such as prison, it leaves people suspicious of my motives. Which the only motive I have is, treat no one as outcast. Oddly, in general, I've become the "outcast." It hasn't really bugged me; it seems I've been an outcast, an outsider, all my life.

God granted me a talented mind. The difficulty is finding a place which does not view that as threatening or otherwise hostile.

In me still roots a desire for normalcy. A wife, kids, the family dog... The whole American pie dream. Yet, each day, that fades more and more. The desire seems rooted from an unwillingness to take a chance with the unknown. I come to a point where I know the path has divided and I just stumbled on. Now I don't know where to turn. Poets are not among the highest paid professions.

I have read from Plato to Kant and more than a few stops in between. I am Catholic, but the views I have now differ far from the church's doctrine.

Bo, I am very much scared of the changes that are happening within me. I've had to throw off a lot of baggage. One of the greatest things I am wrestling with is the pain that has been carried within me. Bitterness, I gladly gave away. Anger and self-righteousness, then the hubris. But, the pain. It so much shaped the past. I am currently unable to put it in perspective.

Do I think I'm crazy? No, just extremely different. I question too much my sanity to really be crazy (or, at least, that's my logic). I honestly fear writing this letter. You talk about blind trust, writing this letter is something I would never even attempted a year ago, even though my heart wished it. It's difficult to reach out like this and expose my vulnerability. Hell, when my cousin B got out of this prison last year I could barely find the courage to hug him and wish him well. That realization hurt.

> *Whatever you can say, or direction you can give, I trust. I
> apologize for my longwindedness. I wish you peace.*
>
> *Agape, P*

Dear P,

Most of my life I've felt very different and a loner, very much
out of place. But I see it differently now. In the sense that I still
feel out of place, it's comical rather than dramatic. I feel like Mr.
Spock, the Vulcan on Star Trek, beaming down to this quaint
little planet to study its people who are pretty different from me.

Yet in a larger sense, I no longer feel different or out of place
at all. I may be unconventional, but essentially my life -- and
yours, whether you can see it or not -- is exactly the same as the
lives of all the people around us. We each wake up in the morning and try to make the best sense of what comes that day.

You've had a need to see yourself as "very different and well-
talented," and now that unhealthy need is no longer satisfactory to
you. You've grown past it, yet it's still a habit of the ego -- hence
the friction inside of you. It's a crock to blame it on your
"humanistic set of rules" or things like that. Who are you to set
rules? We're all just students, learning as we go.

When someone like myself talks about universal laws like
kindness, courage, self-honesty and humor, we don't hold them up
as a set of rules people have to follow in order to meet our
approval. You've missed the point. Those are natural laws, like
gravity. Learn about them and live by them, and your life flows
better. But people can't be required to adhere to them. They'll
cop to them as soon as they're able.

You think your perceptions are "far deeper" than the people
around you, but again, you're looking through old egoic eyes.
Even the shallowest people around you have their hidden thoughts
and secret hopes and innocence. You write them off too easily.
You're the one creating your separateness.

What it's really about is to *open*, not close. The more you
open, the easier it'll be to tolerate all sorts of people and to
speak many languages without feeling so threatened. We can talk
about bowling all night if we're with a bunch of bowlers. We don't
have to back away and spout spiritual platitudes or Kant or Plato.
What do we care what language we're using?

Our job is to *be* the truth, not incessantly repeat it. Our job is also to see the countless faces of the divine, not just the ones most secure for the ego. It's hard work until the resistance dies, but then it's easy, and even fun. I'm lighter today in my forties than I ever was when I was younger. I'm still me, I'm still different and talented, but also the same and equal. Lighten up. It's easier than waiting for the whole world around you to change.

Sorry to be so blunt with you, but it'll get a lot softer after about the tenth reading. I know you well; we're a lot alike.

Love, Bo

Dear Bo,

It's taken me a little while to realize more than just what your words had to say. A part of me is coming back to consciousness after a long and troubled sleep. I want to call it an innocence, but I know that is wrong. It's a realization. You said lighten up. I try.

There are a lot of things said and done over life which can never be fully appreciated until their proper time. I am lucky. I am getting the chance, or taking it for a change. I pray a lot for peace, personal peace. For now, I must give myself time to know what is buried. It causes pain and anguish, but I am looking now.

I never felt anger or betrayal from your letter. It was honest. Too often, that is missing. I won't say I am "happy," but I can live with myself again. No more sudden panics in the middle of the night. There is a lot more to do. I have the commitment for the effort/success. I haven't had that since high school.

You're right, being an outsider is no longer satisfying. I am using my abilities to help others and benefit not just myself but everyone here, staff and inmate. It's difficult, but it seems to be the only one the heart says is right. I'll follow my heart. Several people are accepting me for that. That is what I have sought, just acceptance. In short, I am finding the path meant for me.

There are a lot of things I don't know if I'll ever talk about. Some out of a fear of vulnerability. Some from an inability to fully understand. For now, I'll be satisfied with this. Peace go with you.

Agape, P

[in the same envelope:]

Dear Bo,

Pardon if this is difficult to read. I really can't see straight right now. It is nearly 4:00 in the morning, and pain, anger, and frustration are eating away at me. For the last five years, I have prayed and sought to extradite this pain from me. Sometimes I think I've succeeded, and then, I wake up wanting to scream out. For fear of judgement I have not said why I am incarcerated.

Feb. 20 '83, I attacked and raped another man. In part, I know the answers why: for all the pain and rage and injury I endured and held to, I struck out and humiliated another person in a way no one should suffer. I pray for forgiveness. But nights like this it gnaws at my being. I so trained myself for control and discipline, I forgot why. Letting that control fall away is hard. That's the reason Mr. Spock has been a sort of hero. I admired the rigidness and control.

As a kid, I didn't question the price of such control. Now, I have learned the price, 12-40 years of my life. If fortune is with me, I will be out in 1991 in time for my 30th birthday. Bo, by the time I hit thirty, I thought I'd have been married, be mortgaging my first house, and have a couple of kids.

You're right, I felt comfortable in my isolated intellect. I still have all this anger held inside. I never realized how much anger a person could hold. I bleed off what I can through writing, working, and meditating; but there is so much more. It is to the point where it often drives me to work harder than three men.

The reason Kant, Plato, and Socrates are comfortable to me, they feed my intellect. Only with pen and prayers do I feed my soul. I neglected "soul" too long. Now, I bear the pain of that reconciliation.

In short, I royally screwed myself. I care what happens to me. I am not passive. That got me here. I didn't want to admit my failings and do what was necessary. I do now. Peace go with you and your friends.

Agape, P

P.S. Bo, I know you don't judge others. I am sorry I didn't give you this trust sooner. P

Dear P,

I'm happy you took the leap of trusting me with your secrets. I'm also happy you expressed yourself in writing, because I think writing is a key for you. It's a way of using the mind, but reflecting inward as well when you read what you've written and try to see the truth under it more clearly. A lot of what we write is bullshit, and by re-reading ourselves, we gradually come to admit it.

You got straight with me, now gradually get straighter and straighter with yourself, and things will really begin to change.

Write something and then leave it alone for a few days. Then read it and be merciless in becoming aware of melodrama, self-pity, ego, self-hatred, and so forth. Then sit quietly, allowing yourself to let it really sink in that you don't want to just keep bullshitting yourself. Then write some new stuff and repeat the process all over again. You'll be surprised how quickly your writing gets more honest and humorous.

And very importantly, spend time each day looking around at everyone in the joint, forcing yourself to understand they're in the same process you are. Everybody has their secret stash of self-hatred, everybody has a secret innocent child inside of them who just wants to feel better. It's time for you to see that.

Keep going, Bo

[some months later:]

Dear Bo and Sita,

Peace be with you, my friends. How are things going? I am on a high. Well, as of 20 February 1990, I have been "locked up" seven years. It seems kind of funny, but I feel great! As you've always said, life is full of irony.

For all the newsletters, letters and books, I want to say thanks. I appreciate you being there, both you and Sita. Well, seven years passed by, but it hasn't been wasted. With the encouragement from people like you and a certain inborn stubbornness, the time has worked to make me better. I think you know the time hasn't been easy. It's definitely been tough!

If there is one lesson to be learned, it's twofold. One, life is ironic, as you have many times pointed out to me. Second, remember the first. I am still on occasion a short-fused hothead, but I am improving. Patience is still not one of my greatest virtues. Probably the single hardest thing I have had to to do is let people in. The ivory tower I was living in was getting pretty lonely.

Bo and Sita, I love and care for you as friends and family very much. You've shown me more about kindness and giving than most people I've ever met. I am still working on letting go of the pain. Thank you for walking along this journey with me. I know you're busy, so no need to reply. Again, Peace go with you.

Peace, love, and friendship, P

Dear P,

After reading your letter, a verse from a Bob Dylan song ran through my mind, so I thought maybe it's for you.

> I have gone from rags to riches
> in the sorrow of the night;
> in the violence of a summer stream,
> in the chill of a wintry light;
> in the bitter dance of loneliness
> fading into space,
> in the broken mirror of innocence
> on each forgotten face.
> I hear the ancient footsteps
> like the motion of the sea;
> sometimes I turn and there's someone there,
> other times it's only me.
>
> I am hanging in the balance
> of the reality of Man.
> Like every sparrow fallen,
> like every grain of sand.

Keep on keeping on, my brother, Bo

Dear Bo,

Thank you. I had all but forgotten the song. It ended up being a very special birthday present. My birthday is the day you wrote the letter. Peace go with you both.

Love, P

● ● ●

Dear Bo & Sita,

Greetings. I am writing to you in search of some help and advice. In your newsletter, you give answers from the heart and speak truthfully, pulling no punches, and the answers fit.

I have a very severe problem. As you might know or have heard, there was a riot here at (name withheld). *It was the worst riot in state history. Over half the prison was ruined, 15 or 20 million in damages, 145 injuries, no deaths though.*

You see, I came back to prison for a parole violation and was given 18 months back time to do. When the riots happened, I was waiting for my parole plan to come back. I had a so-called bro here who I thought was a pretty decent dude. He hooked me up with his sister, she wrote me, visited me and even got some pussy on the visit from her and head and hand jobs.

But you see, I turned my life over to Christ and that ended the smut on visits. We remained friends and she still came to visit me. I thought me and her brother were real tight.

Well when the riot kicked, I met up with her brother and we hung together during the riot. We didn't do anything but watch our backs in case of trouble. Things were set on fire, inmates were stabbed and beaten along with guards, living quarters were set on fire, the whole works. Well due to the unavailability of space, I was transferred to a new jail. I was brought back to this riot-torn prison in January because someone was saying I did something.

After 57 days in lockup, I was arraigned on four new charges: Arson Endangering Property, Arson Endangering Persons, Riot and Criminal Conspiracy to Commit Arson. I am accused of telling two black inmates to set one of the Modular Housing Units on fire, and a small mobile trailer. Total loss estimate $472,000.

I now stand to face if convicted, 23½ to 47 years more in prison, a $40,000 fine and total restitution for the trailers. Not only that, the county this jail is in and my home county told me one more felony conviction, I'll be hit with the career criminal act that gets ya anywhere up to life in prison. I now face all this because the guy I spoke of in my letter earlier, made the statement against me. I am really pissed and hurt. I have a daughter who just turned 2 years old on March 25 who, if by some miracle I get convicted, I may never get to see grow up.

I am filled with so much anger and hostility that I'm losing my mind. I'm INNOCENT. I did nothing Bo and Sita. I became a Christian in 1988 and have lived a life of a Christian since then. This guy knows that and knows I wouldn't bring harm to anyone. But I am slipping. I have started letting anger control me deeply and in my heart. I've already started plotting revenge. I want to kill this guy, his family, everything associated with him.

I done sent him a letter through the prison grapevine, in someone else's handwriting letting him know, if I get convicted, I will either escape and make it out and kill him, all his sisters, mom, dad, cat, dog, anyone including his daughter and wife. If I don't make it out I will die trying.

I know it's wrong to think and talk like this but I can't help it. I don't know what to do. I just want to kill him and all his family instead of forgive him and pray for the best.

Bo and Sita, I just got my ex-old lady to give me another chance because she thought or thinks I changed and I did, but now this is giving her different thoughts. I love my ol' lady and kids, I have 2 daughters to her, one's 2 and the other is 11. I can't stand to lose her because some dude I thought was cool with me is trying to hang me. Do you have any advice?

Love, your brother, R

Dear R,

I'm really sorry to hear how hard things are for you right now and all the shit that's coming your way. I hope you're hanging on, even if only by a thread. If you allow yourself to go over the edge, then you lose no matter how it turns out -- whether you're in prison or on the streets, you're back at square one, being an angry, bitter guy with a very clouded mind.

Obviously I can't say much about why your friend has fingered you or whether the charges are going to stick or not. So the best way I can help is to focus on your state of mind no matter which way things go. For example, are you better able to combat these charges with a calm, clear mind, or an angry, confused mind? You'd better decide what your highest priority is: Is it clearing yourself of the charges, or is it vengeance on your old friend?

If it's clearing yourself, then you'd better get your mind back on track so you can prepare your defense without being a raving lunatic. If your higher priority is to be a righteous vengeful convict, then go ahead and wallow in all those feelings, but you may as well stop bitching about doing more time, because you're going to do more time.

So which is a more important picture in your mind -- your wife and children's sweet faces around the dinner table, or your ex-friend's dead face at your feet?

Those convict games will be going on forever, they never stop. Somebody's always fucking up somebody else. You just have to decide when you're going to grow up and step out of the game. There's such a bigger world than that! That scene only seems big and important while you're in it. Once you step out, you'll look back and think, "My God, how was I so stupid for so long?"

And for you, there's even a bigger issue to consider. You say you turned your life over to Christ. Well, did He just blow it this time? Is your ex-friend more powerful than Christ? It's very easy to go to a revival and say "I turn my life over to Christ," but then when He sends you something heavy to deal with, you freak out and say, "No, no, I didn't mean this!"

How do you think Christ helps you become stronger -- by making things easy? It's easy to say "I want to give up anger and hatred" while you feel cool; but you can't really give it up until you're feeling it. Christ is here, ready to take it from you, but you're saying "I have a right to be angry! I have a right to hate that dude!"

But the spiritual journey ain't about rights; it's about ripping off all the layers of hatred, fear, and fury that keep us from our God-nature. Was Christ guilty of the crimes which got Him crucified? Was that fair and just and right?

Turning your life over to Christ means accepting the struggles and trials He sends your way, R. In fact, as bad as your situation is, 90% of your pain is from your resistance to reality. So have you turned your life over to Christ or not?

If you stop resisting what's happened, then what you're left with is simply to prepare a vigorous defense to prove your innocence (remember the line, *God helps those who help themselves*?).

But that's not the pain and suffering you wrote about in your letter, was it? Your letter was about resistance, bitterness, hatred, anger, violence, self-pity. Your letter was "THIS SHOULDN'T BE HAPPENING TO ME!!!!!!!" So have you turned your life over to Christ or not? Is life supposed to be easy or smooth, always fair and just? Have you turned your life over to Christ or not?

That's the question which holds the key to your mental state right now. I'll be pulling for you, my friend.

In His Name, Bo

Dear Bo and Sita,

Greetings, friends. I come to you in peace, love and guidance in my life again through God. I did receive your letter and it kicked me where I needed it. I must say, it helped me get my act back together. I am no longer holding on by a thread, I've gotten the whole spool back. I may still be in prison awaiting trial for my new charges, but I'm doing what I need to do to be a better man.

For the last 2 months since your letter, I've done my soul searching, asking God for forgiveness and getting the hatred and anger out of me towards the non-believer who has me still here. Christ says, "When you are weak, I am most strong." I believe it.

Your letter is so strong and full of truth. I really dig it. I have it framed in cardboard and hanging on my wall as a reminder. My lady and kids are more important to me than some ass____ who is trying to save his own a__. At least I still have my lady and kids, what does he have, about 9 convicts wanting his neck in a wringer. This guy has told on at least 11 people so far.

So, I can turn back to Christ, give him my anger and prayer for his will and guidance and that the truth shine through at trial. There are enough cons who want him and I don't need to waste my time. My hands are washed of him. I pray for his (snitch) deliverance and that he comes clean in life, but I don't foresee it. Someday, he'll answer for his mistakes and misdeeds.

I have a defense of 8 convicts for trial. Being this took place in prison, I can only use cons, but it's whether the jury will believe me and 8 other cons or 1 guy. I'm not gonna worry. I leave it in God's hands. I'll win. I have a very strong case and defense.

I wish I had the statement that the inmate made against me. You'd laugh. At the beginning of his statement, he says me and these 2 guys came through Modular Unit 5 into Mod 6, then in another paragraph, he said he met me outside of Mod 6. This is where me, a white guy, was supposed to tell 2 black guys I don't even know, to set a fire. What a joke. This guy is telling on so many people it's pitiful. I pray justice prevails and I win as I am wrongly accused.

This does hurt inside because I'm missing my summer with the lady and kids and by rights, I should be out there. But now I will probably miss the summer and Christmas. Since I came back to this destroyed jail, I have received 4 misconducts for snapping verbally on the guards. They taunt ya till you snap, then write ya up. A person sitting locked in a cell can only put up with so much before he lets loose.

Take Care, keep in touch and brother, your letters are strong and helpful, keep it up.

Love, R

[two months later:]

Dear Bo & Sita,

I have been on a writing campaign trying to get justice. My charges were "noll prossed" due to lack of evidence. But now the jail refuses to take back the misconducts and insists on leaving me with a misconduct and hole time 'til '92. Because of this, I can't get my parole back. So, I've been writing to a senator, the commissioner of corrections, the governor, and also filed a Habeas Corpus in federal court. Somewhere I'll get justice, but I will probably max out which is 16¾ months away.

Christ is here with me and still in my heart. He always will be. I may get down, but he's still there. I'll never turn my back on him again. He has brought me so much peace and love in my life, and blessings. He is there now and always will be here with me.

Peace & Love, R

● ● ●

We turn to God for help when our foundations are shaking, only to learn that it is God who is shaking them.

-- Charles C. West

Dear Bo,

When I first got your books and newsletter, I read them. The "Lineage" book really blew my mind, brother, let me tell you. It took me out of here and into sanity and peace with myself.

Well, that was about a month ago. Now, I'm back in the hole for fighting. Some dudes were pressuring people on the yard, and when they got to me, they found a whole different breed of cat. I would not submit to giving up my money at canteen, or my ass, so they told me they were going to send me on "a mission." They sent me after this dude on the yard they said was a snitch, and if I didn't take care of him, they'd roll me off the yard.

Well Bo, I had about four months left at the time, so I jacked the dude in the library figuring on at least getting away from the instigators for a couple of weeks. Well, they slapped me with 30 days and put us both back on the yard a week later.

So then, I had shaved my head, beard and moustache, disguising myself. Well, about 1½ months later, right when things were going along good, and I got myself a good job as vocational clerk, these guys recognize me and start in with their bullshit again. Again, I didn't go for it and they told me if I didn't do what they asked, they would "stick" me. Well, at this point I only had five weeks left to parole, so I figured I could put them off or bluff them.

It didn't work. I got punched in the mouth and knocked to the floor while at work. I don't remember the rest, as I am under psychiatric medication. The guards said that I flipped out and now I'm looking at more time. But, at the psychiatrist's suggestion, I gave up the dudes that were doing the pressuring, and the investigator got six other guys to back up my story.

The dudes are in the hole, with me, but haven't seen me yet. Did I do right? Please let me know, as I think of you as a friend and value your opinion. I'm confused and want to go home.

> your friend, J

Dear J,

You asked whether I think you did the right thing by giving up the guys who attacked you. Well, you're the only one who knows that, but I don't think it's an important question right now anyway. You did what you had to do. The only important thing right now is to keep you safe and out of trouble for the rest of your bid. Then you can go home and leave it all behind you.

You didn't mention how much added time you got for this thing. But if it's not too much, I think you should ask for p.c. or stay in the hole. You'll have plenty of time to socialize out on the street. Spend your time alone for now -- meditating, praying, breathing, studying, exercising, making plans, etc. Get serious about cleaning up mind and body before you hit the street. Since you've already been honest with the staff about what happened, be honest also about telling them why you don't want to be in population and that you don't want any "mistakes" to be made where those guys may be able to get to you.

Good luck, brother, and keep me posted.

Your Brother, Bo

Dear Bo,

Well, I gotta kind of admit though, I'm one step ahead of you on the protective custody shot. I've been here in pc for sixteen days already, and you know what? It ain't that bad! I've been doing my breathing and stretching exercises and I feel great!

As for me catching more time, I didn't. They found me not guilty. So, I get out on December 9, 1989. I already signed my parole papers. It's just a wait away now! Well, gotta go for now. I love you guys. Thanks for being my friends.

Love and respect, J

● ● ●

Dearest Bo and Sita,

I hope you're all well. I need you now, I need for you to shine some light on me, as my world lately has been very dark.

Bo, you wrote me a beautiful letter, oh, it's been about 2 years ago now, I guess. I can't even describe how good you made me feel. When times are trying, I just get out that letter to read, and it helps tremendously. And I read We're All Doing Time *on a regular basis, just to remind myself of my own spiritual journey, so I never lose sight of it.*

But the teachings, meditation, spiritual awareness -- none of this seems to comfort me now. There's an ache in my heart that consumes me every moment, and it's become steadily worse. I don't know what to do to help myself. Meditation only leaves me curled up on the floor, sobbing hysterically, feeling as if I'll self-destruct any day now.

The love and compassion that was once the essence of my being is now being suffocated by this other emotion: hatred? I'm not sure -- I never felt I was capable of hatred. But it's ugly -- whatever it is. And it's not me.

As you know, I'm married to my soulmate, who's in prison serving life. For the duration of our marriage I've been an activist for prisoners' rights. I'm sure you're aware prison officials don't like people like me, and will do whatever necessary to discourage us. Last December, after threatening my husband's life, they took away our visiting privileges for an indefinite period of time.

Well, that wasn't the first time that's happened, but it definitely did discourage me! All the stress took its toll; I became sick of the inhumanity, harassment, degradation. I ended up separating from my husband, figuring "What's the use?" I love R with all my heart, it's the prison I can't take. Even now, the thought of going back puts me in a panic. I miss my R so much, but apparently not enough to weather the storm I must endure to find my way back to him.

So, since I left him in December, I've gone a little "off." I'd been attending school, trying to get my personal life in order, and it seems everything I'd planned has fallen to pieces. I'm so messed up now I can't even function in my daily life.

The only thing that kept me from completely losing it was my pen-pal, S. We shared a lovely friendship and I became dependent on him, which was a serious mistake on my part. It turns out he wasn't as sincere as he claimed. And that hurts.

But the biggest loss I've experienced was of the child I carried inside me for 2 months. The father of this child was someone I'd considered a friend; again, a serious mistake. When he found out about the baby, he left me alone to deal with the pain.

I was very sick -- couldn't eat or sleep. The pain at being abandoned didn't help. But no matter how sick I became, no matter how hurt, I was very aware of the tiny soul developing inside me -- a soul separate from mine, but inside me nonetheless.

I spent 2 months agonizing over what to do. Should I have this child and raise it on my own, knowing what a mess my life is, knowing I'd be completely alone, with no one to help? It was an agonizing time for me.

It seems now, the decision had been made from the very start. My doctor recommended an abortion because he was concerned about my health. What a nightmare it was! My doctor was kind enough to put me under for the surgery, but God, waking up was dreadful. No one there to hold my hand...

I feel I've become a child again -- I ache for comfort, for someone to hold my hand. I feel empty inside, I miss that special presence that had become so precious to me. I cry for the baby, I cry for me. I've become bitter and alienated almost everyone around me. I have been betrayed by people I trusted. And I'm afraid to trust anyone, now.

I can't even go outside without feeling alienated myself. I don't feel comfortable around people any more, I'm very self-conscious. And I'm sure everyone senses my hatefulness. It's not like me to be this way, but how can I be rid of this pain? Before I completely disassociate myself from the world that I must live in?

I have read your book again, searching for answers. I can't meditate because I just ended up crying. I keep thinking I'll run out of tears, but so far I haven't. There's no peace in my heart, only sorrow. I've lost three people that meant so much to me, plus one more person I never even had the chance to know.

I understand this is karma; there is a purpose behind this all. I hold onto that as my lifeline. And I prepared myself for an emotional upheaval, but God, this is so much more than I'd planned on. When will it stop? Or will it?

I'm supposed to begin a new job soon, but it's all I can do to get out of bed each morning. Life doesn't stop to allow us to deal with our troubles; the bills are piling up and I can no longer ignore them.

This is why I'm writing -- I'm desperate. I need help. I simply can't go on this way any more. I'm not giving up on my meditation, and I'm making a conscious effort to grasp the love that I know still exists, but I know the two of you have some insight to help me through this hard time.

I know the love still exists within me -- I feel it so much for you both. And the book helps too, it really does. It helps me realize there are beautiful people in this world. I have much spiritual work ahead of me, and I just need a hand -- two hands actually -- to help pick me up out of this rut and give me a gentle push into the light.

I love you both! Thank you. J

Dear J,

I'm sorry you're going through such a bad time, dear friend. I'm enclosing our recent newsletter which deals quite a bit with experiencing negative stuff, and also a copy of my book, *Lineage and Other Stories*, which focuses on things you could apply to your own life.

But I feel so puny offering words. All the words in the world aren't going to do your work for you; they can only point you in the right direction. It's up to you to go through the eye of your needle yourself. It's up to you to figure out how to simplify your life down to the basics: Living with self-honesty, courage, kindness, humor and wonder. You have to take a very honest look at how you're living and what you're doing and with whom, and make whatever changes you need to make in order to simplify your life.

I hope the enclosed writings help, J. I don't know how else to say the things I've said in there. Life is hard, it really is. I know that. But you do have the same range of choices to make that everyone else has. They're hard choices, for sure; that's why Jesus called it the "Narrow Way." But you have to become willing to do what is necessary to bring balance back into your life, to become a simple, focused person who doesn't let things get out of hand.

Bo

Dearest Bo,

Once again, you've touched my life with a seemingly clairvoyant sense of knowing what I truly needed! Yesterday was spent reading your new book of lovely stories -- how can I express my deep appreciation for what you have given me?

What a way you have with words! I find all your writings <u>so</u> inspirational, because I could relate to them in so many different, magical ways. The irony of it all is overwhelming, and I cried tears of joy and relief at least a dozen times yesterday.

Okay, Bo, I've gotten myself back together. Physically, sometimes I feel like I've been hit by a Mack Truck, but I'm not complaining about that! My spiritual progress more than makes up for my physical shortcomings.

I wrote to you because I was in so much pain, it was freaking me out. My emotional trauma manifested itself in so many intense ways; no matter where I might be, what time of day or night; I could be strolling through the grocery store and suddenly collapse from grief and anguish. I became horrified of going outdoors, and cut myself off from all people, so I wouldn't be scrutinized or analyzed. I see now it was an exaggerated head trip, played by me, but at the time, <u>all</u> I could feel was excruciating, emotional pain. I couldn't seem to get through it.

I've always prided myself of the fact that no matter how negative an experience was, some good always came out of it. In most cases, for me, it's been a spiritual awakening or enhancement, but this recent experience seemed to be pulling me further and further away from my spirituality. It frightened me. All of a sudden, I became forgetful, paranoid, self-conscious, and bitter. Definitely not usual characteristics for me.

After writing you that desperate letter, I began to settle down a bit, knowing that help would soon be on the way. That knowledge alone was an incredible comfort, and after that things seemed to pick up. I began forcing myself to go out -- if even just for a short walk. I began paying attention to the world around me

-- the birds, the clouds, a friendly hello from a passerby. Once it was hard for me to greet a stranger; now it's a pleasure!

I still feel loss -- but my world doesn't have to end over it. I know because of your experience with Josh, you understand. I've finally put my loss in perspective; just another necessary step on my path. And I feel <u>LOVE</u>, Bo -- so much love! It's beautiful, and yes, it hurts, but now I see <u>that's</u> beautiful too. Thank you!

I lived a carefree, innocent childhood, but there was a deeper side to me, one that I kept to myself. It was my secret, but one person I did share a part of it with was my best friend, Janelle. And then, the end of my safe, secure childhood arrived with a traumatic blow: Janelle was brutally murdered one night as she walked home alone from a neighborhood convenience store.

Had it been any other night, I would have been with her. But an extraordinary set of circumstances kept us apart that evening. I could never view that as coincidence. I see now it was karma. It was the Great Mystery you speak of. It took me ten years to realize this, fifteen to pinpoint it. And I did that with your help.

In 1984, <u>I</u> was the victim of a brutal crime. Unlike Janelle, my physical being survived, but my mental being died. I suffered through depression, a nervous breakdown, and then attempted suicide. I had a great fear of being brutally murdered, and saw this as premonition -- therefore, rather than die at the hands of an angry stranger, I wanted to end my life myself, my own way.

How ironic that one year later, I would find myself in California's toughest prison, facing the very men I had come to fear! But what I felt wasn't fear at all; I felt love, trust and compassion. I had finally reached my spiritual turning point!

Once again I thank you from the bottom of my heart for sending Lineage and Other Stories. It blew me away to read about Hector's "anxiety attack" in the main story -- the same thing happened to me a couple weeks ago and I thought I was dying!

My love to you both, and my deepest thanks. I didn't mean to get so carried away in this letter, but you've touched me, and I had to share it with you. Thank you so much!

All my love, J

● ● ●

Hello my friends,

I'm studying your book, We're All Doing Time. *A friend dropped it on me. To be honest, it sat in my own cell for quite some time, and even wound up in the garbage can once, before for some unknown reason, I dug it out and decided to pass the time by reading a few pages. Eureka! (smile). How happy I am I made that decision! Your book has given life to some of the best feelings I've ever experienced in twenty-nine years on this earth.*

Bo, I should parole in seven months, so being in prison (second time) is the least of my problems. I have a high-school sweetheart who's graced me with a beautiful son and daughter. We're still very much in love & supportive of one another, which in turn makes for change toward the "light" that much sweeter.

Bo, my problems stem from the ghosts of my past. On nearly a daily basis, I'm confronted with confusion and the haunting knowledge of some dirty deeds of my past. Because of lack of evidence, I was never brought up on charges in two separate murders. I still feel strong about the reason which led up to both acts, and what remorse I feel is more for the loved ones rather than the victims themselves. However, I feel a great need for understanding and growing past these ugly chapters in my life.

Bo please, any advice you could offer would very much be appreciated. I hope to become your friend. Please keep in touch.

Please keep in touch, D

Dear D,

You definitely have some opening to do about the pain you've caused. And that opening will be a very personal experience. But I don't think you have to confess to old crimes in order to deal with it. Our justice system is a whole other set of crimes. If you've rehabilitated yourself and are getting back to your family, go for it. A good and moral life, being of value to society, doing volunteer work to help others, etc., would be a far better way of paying for your crimes than going back to court and to prison.

If you've brought pain into the world, then live in a way that helps reduce pain. Let your guilt lead you to become a humble, compassionate person. My very best to you, brother.

Keep working, Bo

● ● ●

Dear Bo and Sita,

I am a year and a half into my journey, but still have my ups and downs like everybody else in the joint. But I'm keeping the faith, and growing stronger every day! <u>Smile</u>!

I've been locked down two years this June, at which time I see the Parole Board. I've got good chances of making it, but I still have this "<u>fear</u>," of <u>not</u> making it, when I reach the outside (<u>streets</u>). Just writing that word "<u>fear</u>" makes me feel bad!

I'm 22 years (young) old, stand 7 feet tall, and weigh 200 lbs. I've been through a lot of rough shit in my life, and have hurt a lot of people in the process.

The fact that I'm tall has always given people the impression that I'm a "bad ass," and well, for years, that's the impression I've given people. I mean, I can be one rotten son of a bitch at times! But that was then you guys, and this is now, and I've overcome that feeling of wanting to hurt people. I want to follow my heart, and God's will, and help people, not hurt them.

I've raised a lot of hell in the town that I'm going to be paroled to. I've made enemies with every "cop" within a 50 mile radius of the town. It's gonna be hard for me, I know that, but I don't want to turn back to crime the minute I think things are going bad! If you can dig that!

Light on your journey, Tree

Dear Tree,

Listen, nearly every convict has a lot of fear about whether or not he can make it on the street. If you've really changed -- you know, if your mind has really gone through the BIG change -- then you're gonna make it fine. You'll have your ups and downs like everyone else, but you'll ride them out and learn lots of lessons along the way.

If it's a small town you're going back to, you might consider taking the bull by the horns, and walking right into the police station to say "Listen y'all, I just want you to know that I'm out of the joint, I'm a changed man, and I'd appreciate it if you guys just keep an open mind about me, 'cause I ain't gonna cause any more trouble. I just want to get on with my life."

If it's a bigger town or city, hell, most of the police officers have changed or transferred anyway in a couple of years, and you won't have such a big problem. And if you do occasionally catch some shit you don't deserve, you have to be prepared and patient about it. Don't let it freak you out so badly that you do something stupid and violate your parole. The old saying "The Truth will set you free" is what applies.

In the meantime, show what a good guy you are not just by staying out of trouble, but by doing good stuff also. Volunteer down at a boy's club or the salvation army, or the soup kitchen or something like that. Pay some dues into the community you live in. You don't have to be all gung-ho in a phony way; just quietly making it clear that you care.

The other thing is, as hard as it may be, you're going to have to steer clear of some of your old friends whose minds haven't yet changed. One drowning man can't save another. If some of your buddies are still doing a lot of shit, you're going to have to have the courage to stay away, and make new friends. I know that can be hard as hell, but who ever said life was supposed to be easy?

The bottom line is, you can do fine if you want to. Think positive, bro. You may feel like a weirdo or a freak because of your size, but hell, I've always felt like one too, because of my ideas. I catch shit all the time. I know the story. Meanwhile, my life is as happy and as full as I make it, because we're all just doing our time here on Earth the best we know how.

Love, Bo

["Tree" next wrote nearly five years later.
    He didn't make it on the streets:]

Dear Bo, Sita, and Josh,

Greetings from the "Hole."

"Rings and knots of Joy and Grief, all interlaced and locking." Beautiful! This is the first time I've ever wrote to the three of you. Before, it was always "Dear Bo," but that was years ago, and usually asking for help of some sort.

Yeah, I'm in the hole; but damn do I feel good! And that's why I'm writing. To share my good health, and happiness with the three of you; pass it on. "Tree" is back in the joint and feeling better than ever! I read We're All Doing Time *daily; mostly "Dear Bo...," but the rest as well. Reading the letters helps me to "remember..." here is where I am, and I feel pretty good.*

And I'm not just talking about awareness of "self." I'm talking about "life," man! My life, your life, their lives! All interlaced and locking! I heard a man imitating a "barking dog" one evening here in the hole, and I silently blessed him for reminding me of my youthfulness, and the "child" within each of us; and the sweet, sweet "madness."

Bo, Sita, Josh, I've discovered "the" purpose. And because you guys have been such a very "BIG" help in my awareness, over the past 4-6 years, I want you to have a copy of one of the songs I've written. One of the many that no one has ever heard me sing. Read these lines, and enjoy them as if I were right there singing them to you. After all, I really am, ya know. I love you guys with all that I am; all 7 feet of me! And your love, and spirit is alive in my heart, even today.

My journey is long, with many obstacles. But I'm moving into them head on and "loving every minute of it." My bag of karma ain't quite as heavy, though I still carry a load. With all these pushups I'm doing, I'll be able to handle it (Ha ha). Someday I want to write a one-page book and dedicate it to the whole world. I'll title it "One Million Ways to say... pg. 1 -- "I Love You!" Much love, and plenty of light to guide you on your journey!

Your friend and brother, Tree

Left Out in the Cold

By "Tree"

I saw a smile on a little face of a lonely boy, in a lonely place; when he looked at me I saw a tear in his eye. He tried to speak, but couldn't find the words, and when I touched his hand, a sigh was all I heard. Oh, oh, oh.

That little boy was the image of me, when I felt alone, and my eyes couldn't see, the friends that I had, and the people that cared for me. In the land of make-believe, was the only time we were happy. The lonely hearted. Oh, oh, oh.

I saw a young man wearing ragged blue jeans, a dirty t-shirt, his life had no means. His mind was lost, in some fantasy. Did he go to school? Did he have a home? Or did he live his life, walking all alone through the lonely world of his dreams?

That lonely young man was the image of me, when leather was cool, and drugs were free from the pushers; you and me. When everybody understood just one thing; it's the life ahead, and what will it bring, and who's gonna make it? Oh, oh, oh.

I saw an old man in the light of day. He walked with a cane, his hair was grey, and silently he wandered. Oh, oh, oh. Could he see the road that he was on? Could he find his way? Would it lead him home? Does he have a family? Oh, oh, oh.

Did he live a life of right and wrong? Did he say a prayer? Did he sing a song? Were people good to him? Oh, oh, oh.

That lonely old man was the image of me when my mind was lost, and my eyes couldn't see. and my life was wasted on the road. When time was old, and friends were few, and I found no peace between me and you; and my heart was left out in the cold. Yeah, my heart was left out in the cold.

Thank God, this song is about my past, and not my present. But also, thank God this is my past. How else would I be where I am today? I love you! I hope you enjoy this as much as I do when I sing it to my only audience, me.

Maybe our paths will cross someday when I could sing for you, so you can feel the power in this song. I love you!

Tree

● ● ●

Dear Bo,

I received your book a few months ago and I can certainly relate to some of the letters from prisoners like the hate and frustration that Maury was going through before his death.

I have nothing but murder on my brain! When I go to sleep at night I lie awake for a hour at least thinking up new and different ways to knock off my ex-old lady and my fall partner who are now together in a relationship. While I'm laying here in this prison cell they are probably having a go at it in the sack right now! They both deserve deer slugs in the fuckin' forehead! And if I don't get some help before I get out in 27 months, then there's gonna be two less people on this Earth to speak of.

I've been played like a real live fool and no matter how I try to get on with my life and put my past behind me I can't get these two snakes out of my brain. I shot dope in my jugular vein for the first two-and-a-half years that I was in here and it helped drown my hate but now I'm locked up 24 hours a day and haven't any way to run the dope trail so you see it's burning in my brain all day and night.

I need someone to get my head back like it used to be before I get out 'cause this prison cell isn't the place I'd like to make my home for life.

in a prison of hate, T

Dear T,

First of all, you obviously don't want to keep hating and planning to kill. If you did, you wouldn't have written to me at all. So instead of using me as an excuse to change directions, start with yourself. You don't want to do it. And you don't like these thoughts burning a hole in your brain and heart every day.

With that settled, now the only question is, how do you gradually make that change? You're going to need some patience, because real change usually takes time. But if you start working on it a little bit every day, you'll be surprised at how much you can learn to control the thoughts and memories until they just start losing their power over you.

You mentioned relating a lot to the letters section of my book, but what you most need right now in your life is to work with some of the techniques in the middle of the book instead. You need to spend a lot of time with the meditation chapter, the chapters on breathing & power ("Pranayam"), and even the chapter on prayer.

There's no better advice I could give you in personal letters. It doesn't matter how well somebody talks or writes or preaches --- the bottom line is, you have to start working faithfully with some actual methods every day. Words just won't cut it.

I know it may be very hard at first, and you may think "Man, I just ain't cut out for this stuff." But if you want to stop being played for a fool (not by your ex-wife and partner, but by yourself), you'll stick with it at least for a few months and see what happens.

And by the way, you don't have to lay there in bed with all those thoughts of how you could kill them. You can start being the master of your mind instead of the victim, and just keep changing your train of thought when those things come up. If you don't develop any control over your mind, you'll never be happy no matter whether your ex-wife and partner are dead or alive. Write me in a few months and let me know how it's going.

Love, Bo

Dear Bo,

I thank you for your advice and concern a few months ago. But I haven't changed my plans and I really doubt that I will in the next ten months before I'll be able to laugh and pull the trigger! After I do my crime and come back to prison I'll be able to sleep and dream and wake up with peace in my mind and body. I mean for the first time in five years I'll be at peace with myself. You know, the kind of peace you speak of in your book.

I know the only way I can stop hating the girl I gave my mind and heart to is to send him and her both on their way. They can be together there if they wish to be with each other that much. You see Bo, he just recently was released from a pre-release program this past week and they are living together now for the short time until I am released.

You probably won't hear from me again until I have found that morphine-like feeling of PEACE.

Respect, T

Dear T,

You say that after you waste your girlfriend and her new guy, you'll finally have peace with yourself. That's the biggest crock of shit you could sell yourself, brother. You're never going to have a peaceful day for the rest of your life if you don't use the next ten months to get over this thing and put it behind you. I know you've got a great deal of pain, but you don't have to let it destroy all three of you, and that's exactly what you're planning to do.

Being dumped isn't exactly the newest experience on Earth, you know. It's one of the oldest. And although there's a lot of pain and anger, millions of people have learned how to deal with that without grabbing a gun. There'd be few people left on this planet if everyone did what you're planning to do.

The biggest thing you're missing is: this is something you're supposed to learn from. Life is hard. We need to develop strength, self-honesty, courage, patience, and a huge sense of humor in order to be really happy. We fall in love with people and then sometimes things change; they change or we change; whatever. But killing isn't the answer. This is life; it may even happen again.

I'm not saying you got a fair deal. All sorts of "unfair" things happen to people, like a kid getting his arms caught in a silage machine, little babies dying of AIDS, or whatever. You're a fool if you don't take some time to learn from your bad times instead of picking up a gun. You'll never find the peace you hope for. The wound will never be healed. If you kill them, the next person you'll kill will probably be yourself. Think it over; don't let your pride destroy you. That's not real strength; that's just fear.

I love you, Bo

[several months later:]

Dear Bo,

Hello there once again! I hope this letter finds you in the best of spirits and health. I am glad to say I'm on a positive road and I hope that I keep this attitude once I am released next month.

A couple months ago I was in the hole for getting busted with a needle stuck off into my leg and off to the hole I went and it was while I was there I received your newsletter, and as I read the page where you printed our complete correspondence, I really got the chance to see all the hate and frustration that I have been letting rule my mind and thoughts so I told myself that I am gonna work on a whole attitude change and I am proud to say that I have been doing just that.

My first step to positive change was leaving the needle alone and my second step was to join the Jaycees here in the prison and it has turned out Bo that was the best move toward a change I could have made for myself.

I still think of the slut and backstabbing freak that drove me nearly insane but as long as I stay busy I have found that I can control them moods and thoughts instead of letting them years of hate control me. I guess I owe a big thanks to you for laying it all out in front of me so I could look at the rest of my life and stop worrying about how to revenge my past. I am forever grateful for your attention on my situation that surely could of turned out to be a nightmare.

a friend forever, T

● ● ●

[*editor's note:* Well, a start's a start!]

Knock and it shall be opened,
Seek and ye shall find.
Wisdom appears in the simplest of places
In the nick of time.

-- Bunny Wailer

RUSTED HEARTS AND HARLEYS

[Next time you see a 300-lb. biker glaring at you from his chopper, you might think back to these letters. Of course, that doesn't mean you should hug him at the next stoplight...]

Dear Bo,

I got your book I requested. I used my being a shut-in, lazy, non-functional most of the time on S.S.I, brother of a convict, me a former child of institutions and homes, to get a free book. I had the money. Truth is, poverty of not just money, but of love, has made me like this. I cried when I got your book and began to read it. The book also scares me as it deals with such a dark area of human nature, yet I applaud you for helping those who desperately need it, including myself. I also caught myself wondering if you were a scam artist. I do not believe you are.

As a youth I suffered greatly. Today as a man I am a cripple. I am an addict of 18 years to tranquilizers. I am a former abuser of drugs and alcohol (severe). Now my body can no longer tolerate this abuse, occasionally I need "relief" and have a relapse, but my health is fragile and any abuse is a slap in my own face.

I am also an overeater, over 300 pounds. My appearance is of a biker. I have used Harley Davidsons over the years as props. They have left me lonely and empty. People see an illusion in me. How lonely and frightened and empty I am out there. I've never held a steady job in my entire life. I will be 35 in September. I feel that I am no good. Yet I know that is not true!

I have emotional and psychological problems, lifelong. I've been told I have a problem between my head and my heart. I have difficulty making decisions. I have a wife and child. My wife and I are mismatched and our relationship is impoverished and sick. Our daughter is wonderful, brilliant, we are blessed but we may soon break up to save our own sanity. We do not communicate well -- we are not in harmony. We never were. I never was in love with her. She is from an abused upbringing and hostile and immature, so am I.

We both want love but are destitute with each other. We have suffered a lot in our 10 years. Humiliation, homelessness, severe abuse, stress, poverty, lack of love. We have been through a lot of deprivation and rejection.

Also there has been illness. I seem to be always sick. I've had all types of physical problems -- from gastrointestinal disease to heart arrhythmia (from stress). Being an addict I never feel well. Withdrawal attempts have failed. I develop severe anxiety and panic as well as nervousness, hallucinations, neurological problems -- it's Hell. So I remain an addict because I seem unable to cope with long term withdrawals. (18 years valium -- now since 10/86 -- xanax.)

I recently went to a mental hospital by choice. I would wake in the night and "freak out" much like a Viet Nam vet. Any time I leave home I improve somewhat. But I fear people, I've been called agoraphobic. I have a lot of anger in me and potential for violence, yet I also am full of love, and I'm alone. I have been mind-fucked many times. There have been many mistakes and failures. I want to be loved but I fear and don't trust most people.

My front is dark clothes, sunglasses, a beard, tranquilizers, and a "STIFFNESS" within myself -- underneath is a person dying to be accepted, to give and receive love. Past experiences have scared me inside. Nature seems to help me. I live in the shithole city -- I hate it! I am telling you all this wondering what advice you could give me?

My relationship with my wife of 10 years is void. Sex is a turnoff. We aren't compatible, never were. So for ten years in order to have "a female" I took the first one that would take me -- result a decade of misery and loneliness. It distorted both our lives. I supposed she once loved. But not I her. I tried. But she was/is hostile, aggressive, immature. There was no way for us. I used to be violent to women years ago. I used to beat women. I was vicious and brutal in earlier days. I've broken bones, I've kicked, whipped -- bitten. This was years ago. My own disgust and time cured it. I rarely do even a slap now. But I feel violent. I suppress thoughts. Ugly thoughts. My mind has been perverted and made unclean by my early years of abuse.

Where can I fit in? A scared frightened 300 pound emotionally disturbed, fearful, desperate for love old biker? I don't think I'm crazy. I have just gone hungry for human warmth, love, understanding. I've not been in harmony. I am confused, lazy. I need some place to fit in. Some place to belong.

Sincerely, L

Dear L,

I hear you loud and clear, brother. Of course, that's not as important as whether *you* hear you loud and clear. You're definitely a man who wants to change in major ways, and I'd surely like to help you do that any way I can. The thing is, the effort and patience all have to come from you. All that I or anyone else can do is to help point out new directions, old bad habits, wrong thinking, etc.

I think you should consider what your immediate plan is -- you know, the small steps that'll lead to the big changes. One thing is for sure: You're not going to change your life by going over and over your whole history, family problems, hardships, bad breaks etc. Most of the people I know had tough lives, including me. At 35 years old, it's time to drop all that baggage and take control of your own life. Otherwise you're going to be in this same shape when you're 45 and 55 and 65.....

I can't tell you what to do, exactly. We don't have any sort of group living scene or community thing for you to come to. You could look for one, but frankly that's a real crapshoot. If you're willing to leave all the drugs behind and really uproot yourself in a big way, I'd say you should join a major human relief organization like Oxfam or Plenty or Save the Children or something like that. A local librarian can help you find the names and addresses of human service organizations. Pure service has a wonderful power to heal all the wounds of heart, mind and body. If you could suddenly find yourself in the middle of Ethiopia feeding starving children, maybe all the dramas and hangups of your life would instantly be put in a whole different perspective forever.

I think major change like that would work the best. If not that, try whatever degree of change you're willing to do. Obviously you have to stop doing all drugs, period. None of this shit about not being able to, freaking out, etc. It's real hard, but people do it every day, and you're no weaker or less able than all of them. At the same time, take some weight off and get your body in better shape. These changes will start whittling away at your self-hatred and give you a lot more hope and confidence.

Talk is cheap. Change is real. Be humbled for a while about how far you've let yourself go, and let it quiet you down. Begin to see your life -- and life in general -- as a *student* instead of as a troubled, obese, addicted, abused, confused, angry, fearful...... and all the other ways you look at yourself. Just a student; someone who realizes he has so very much to learn about himself and the world around him.

Don't be so quick to judge what you love, what you hate, what this is about, what that's about, etc. Just quiet down, observe life with more openness and respect for what you don't understand.

These changes are accomplished not in any huge picture, but one moment at a time, and they are under your control. Don't let the day get away from you. Stay aware of the changes you want to make, and don't take any "time out."

I can't tell you what to do about a marriage which you described as so empty and loveless. Obviously you have to begin taking control of your life -- which includes your role in the marriage -- in a way that brings things into the new life you need to create for yourself. If you can't do that with your wife, then at some point you'll have to leave. On the other hand, maybe you could at least try letting your wife in on this letter and all your frustrations and self-hatred, and maybe she might be just as inter- ested as you are in creating a new and better life for both of you.

One thing I do know is this: Life is passing so quickly it's incredible. You have only two options: Begin right away to become the person you really would like to be, or else waste this whole beautiful world and die someday with self-hatred, depres- sion, and indescribable loneliness. Too many people let it all slip away by thinking that maybe they'll change next week or next month or next year.

Don't be a sucker, L. In your heart, you know better. And don't bullshit yourself about being too far gone or anything like that. If your life goes down the tubes, it won't be because of your entire life history; it'll be simply because you let this opportunity go by one more time. You have everything you need to turn the whole thing around. Get serious about it, bro.

Love, Bo

[I received an extremely long, rambling letter from L, repeating and expanding on everything he said in his first letter. We omit that letter here for your sake! My response follows:]

Dear L,

You wrote on your envelope, "your replies and time truly appreciated," yet then you went on to completely ignore every single word I had written to you. I've got to tell you, bro, I feel bad that you're in so much pain, but I'm not a connection for just endless bitching and complaining.

I'm in touch with thousands of people across the world who are in just as bad shape as you or worse, and they're using their time to make their lives work better. If you're not willing to take even a single step, what good can I or anyone else do you?

You talk a lot about fear. Well, that's what courage is all about. Courage doesn't apply to somebody without fears. Who needs courage if you have no fears in the first place? What courage is about is feeling exactly like you're feeling, and standing up straight to do something about it.

You don't have to change your entire life around in one moment. All you have to do is make a tiny little change for a start. Improvement comes from a bunch of tiny changes over a period of time. And there's nothing in your genetic makeup or your past history or your current disabilities, that makes you incapable of changing your whole life around.

You have to make the effort, bro. I assure you it's nowhere near as hard as the life you're living right now. And by the way -- as far as a job goes -- any job can be done with self-respect and dignity, whether that's factory work or a car wash or washing dishes or sweeping a floor. What are you holding out for? You're wallowing around in self-hatred and then refusing to take a single step to change that situation. If you want a shoulder to cry on, you picked the wrong one. I'm here to help people find their courage and strength to change their own lives around. Start using the resources in your own community to pull your life together. Then you can start becoming a resource as well. It works, I swear.

Always your brother, Bo

[four months later:]

Dear Bo,

Just a progress report: My wife and child left me after a violent argument. Now we are reunited as a family though we have our tough moments. We also now have more Love and understanding -- my wife and I. I finally realized I was full of self hate. We are both abused people who were repeating the same shit to our own family.

Even though you pointed this out I did not see it, nor believe it. I go` to a men's group for batterers, my wife goes to the group for abused women. My wife has a problem, too. We are both at fault. Our home has been full of mental and some physical abuse. I praise God now we are getting help. We are also getting help from the many referrals from the women's shelter. I have some mental problems (I have a lot of all types of problems) so I am going to talk with a psychiatrist and see if I can get help.

I am making the effort to do T.M. I try to do it at least once a day. I need to do it twice. I have been doing T.M. off and on for a while. It does seem to help. I just yesterday felt I needed "one success." Something to do and follow through so I could feel good about myself. The men's group says we need to nurture ourselves -- so I am putting together an old air compressor and it is good therapy to restore it as I am doing.

I bought a Bible. I seemed to need the "proverbs" after a close friend comforted me with a process where one takes the date and looks in the proverbs and reads it for that particular day. I have prayed more though I never feel I do everything I should do -- enough. I make an effort to help my wife now in the home. I'm finding I have a real gold mine in my own wife!! We almost lost each other. Now we realize we do love each other.

We had the pleasure of taking clothes and food to a thrift shop that helps needy and hungry people. We felt so good inside to finally be able to give back, for so many times we have taken when we were needy. I felt guilt for feeling so good inside.

I hear about the starving children in Ethiopia, something you mentioned in your letter the first time. I would like to help by sending some money, even if it's $10.00. So I am going to try to find out the address of "Save the Children" or whoever does the relief work in Ethiopia. I want my money to go there specifically. I will go to the library and ask for the address.

I want God to be "more" in my life. I am a good decent human being. It's a real blessing now to be receiving help and having our family grow more. I seem to be embarrassed to *become a Christian. I find a spiritual need, yet I resist for fear of getting in touch with my own emotions. I have not clearly understood "spiritual." A friend recently told me it is a "feeling" one has in their daily life. Is that correct?*

I just wanted to keep in touch. I have plans to start a small business either overhauling or buying and selling used tools, or welding. I'd like to say thank you for your feedback to me and say that I'm grateful. I know you're very busy with so many so you need not reply unless you desire. I will continue on the road to self improvement. With God's help -- I believe Life will be much better than it has been the last 35 years.

Love, L and Family

P.S. The road to Healing may be full of potholes but I'm finally on the road -- we as a Family and myself. I pray to God we can (I can) get it together and have Happiness and Love in our Lives.

[two years later:]

Dear Bo,

Hi, I thought I would drop you a line and let you know how I am doing, as well as share some thoughts with you. I think back to the time in my life (about 3-1/2 years ago) that I received your book We're All Doing Time. *I cried after receiving and reading the first part of the book because I felt someone cared about me after all.*

I had a few letters from you and at one point was quite upset with your response. However as difficult as it is for me to admit, I needed straightforward, hard-biting Honesty. It made me think. I enjoy receiving your articles or newsletters in the mail. (I've yet to donate, but will soon.)

I do not agree with a lot of your views, but I agree with your direction of travel -- assisting and helping others. I sometimes find your views a bit off the wall...too Hippyish, or too far East. Or just strange. I see the idea and end result is a freedom, peace, direction, hope, kindness and love for others. Interesting that as I wrote this, without realizing it until it happened, it came out kindness and love, and that's the name of your organization!

These days I get by doing hauling and salvaging what others throw away. Although I'm not entirely self-supporting I do better now than ever before. I manage to help support my family. I still have many problems. Problems I am not proud of. But as time goes by I have an increased awareness of them, how I might make positive changes. And the key is for me to "do." Yet easier said than done. But I've got more knowledge. The ball is in my court.

I am grateful for the response from you personally over the years. I am grateful for being on the mailing list. I am grateful for *We're All Doing Time. God Bless, take care.*

Thank you, L

Dear L,

Just wanted to say it's nice to get such a positive letter from you and to hear that you're doing okay. I know it's been a lot of hard work on your part, and I admire you for it.

Through thick and thin, Bo

• • •

[the following correspondent is also a 6'5", near-300 lb. biker
with a gold swastika emblazoned into his front tooth, whom Sita
and I have known in and out of prison for many years.]

Dear Bo and Sita,

*Greetings from the land of Oz. Got a few things to tell ya
about your book "Lineage," first off, it is a fantastic adventure...It
comes alive and talks to me....Shit Bo, I would have thought you
was a convict, due to the amount of passion and realism that the
words spoke....Even ignorant old me came away with a better
understanding of the way life goes, without having to try.....*

*If I had a favorite story, it would be the one about Doug
Swanson, entitled "The Slowest Way," It kinda spoke to me in a
language that I understood, I went with that dude through the
whole adventure....Thanks for the escape...Damn Bo, How do you
know what it's like to go through a trip like that????? Are you
sure you weren't in that joint a lifetime ago?*

*I'm hanging on by a thread, but Hell Bo, ain't no use tripping
on it, I kinda always knew deep in the inner recesses of my mind
that I'd end up doing my life's trip in one joint for ever and ever.
What it boils down to is, I don't know a motherfucking thing....*

*I guess what goes around comes around Huh? I'm too tired to
care, shit I'm so fucking lazy I don't even wanna think...My brain
just shuts down and goes on automatic pilot...This may sound like
a contradiction but, every now and then I try to figure out how a
person who has so much goodness within his heart can be such a
fuck-up, and get into tons of bullshit without trying?*

*Lots of times in the stillness I lay there and become someone
who wipes out disease, hunger, pain, suffering...How come it only
happens in my mind and doesn't become a reality? Maybe I just
talk a good game, shit man I don't know, it trips me out, when I
look at all the opportunity that has presented itself to me....It
confuses and depresses the hell out of me and I feel so fucking
lost and alone....I wonder what the other side of life. I once tried
to take myself out, and came within a hair's breadth in doing
so....But I didn't actually cross that fine line....I keep wondering
why I made it back when I know I was almost on the other
side....Is there something that I didn't do that I have to fulfill?
What's my mission Bo?*

I don't know exactly how long I have left, but I have a strange feeling it ain't going to be all that long....The music is about over and the dance steps are growing weary Bo....Don't get the impression that I'd try to take myself out again, I'm not in that frame of mind, but somewhere deep down inside I know what I know, ya dig?

I have no fear of death, I've been on the edge, so I guess it ain't going to be all that bad....I just want to know why I was born, what was my reason for existing? Did I fulfill my obligation, mission, calling, or whatever the term is? Or will I fulfill it before the final curtain comes down on the last act?

Questions, Bo, maybe they don't even mean anything, maybe we are just a part of a bigger thing's dream, maybe we ain't real at all. Fuck, I've been ranting and raving so much that I'm afraid you're gonna think I need some medication (smile). Anyway, just wanted you all to know that you're in my thoughts.. I love you folks.....Remain strong and keep the faith.

   Love & Stuff, Your friend and Fellow Time Traveler, G

Dear G,

I'm glad you related to *Lineage and Other Stories*. In fact, based on the rest of your letter, I think you should read the title story again several times, because it applies to how weary you are of all the shit. That's what happened to the character named "Monk," and eventually to Hector too. In fact, that's also what happened to Doug Swanson in *The Slowest Way*. Your weariness about life can turn out to be your greatest blessing, because maybe you're finally ready to give up and give in in a good way.

You talk about being close to death -- but maybe it's a different kind of death. Let this be the time you're finally ready to let the old G die. That doesn't mean you stop breathing, you know. But you can really give up that old ego-self which has played itself out. It's not even that it was bad or anything like that; it's just an identity you no longer require. It experienced what it had to experience and now it no longer serves a useful purpose.

G, if any of us had to make all our changes at once, nobody would ever change. But like I wrote another friend years ago, the only lie you have to stop telling is the one forming in your throat right now. The only scam you have to resist is the one entering your mind right now. The only kindness you need to find is the kindness required by the situation you're in right now. Big changes are just a bunch of little changes. You don't need a huge dose of energy; just enough to get you through this moment headed in the general direction you want to go.

You'll be getting this letter around Good Friday, which is when Jesus let His old self die. Then on Sunday is Easter, the day He let His new self rise. Let this be your own Good Friday and your own Easter this year. Take a profound leap instead of just waiting for it to happen on some other day. All it takes is being tired enough of your old life and asking God to take it from you.

And yes, you're damn right it's all a dream and not real. But what a dream! It ain't a nightmare.

I Love you, old buddy, Bo

Dear Bo,

Got your kite, glad you took the time to respond, it helped me out of my self-dug pit of depression somewhat.

Look Bo, I ain't one to bullshit you, or even try, cuz I don't think I could get it past you anyway, not that I would try, got respect for you, and all the things you've done for me directly and indirectly over the last two decades worth of time, more or less.

I really relate to the main people in Lineage, *I've been stuck in this personality and body for forty years. Shit man don't you think I'm bone tired? Like I said, if I could just lay on down and stop breathing I would....Life to me has become too much, I don't see any of those rainbows lingering ahead of me, I don't have no pot of gold waiting, nor delusions that tomorrow is going to be a brighter day.....Shit looks bleak brother...and that is the reality each day that I am forced to drag my ass out of bed.*

I am not looking to blame anyone for my situation brother, I created it through circumstances I was involved in...I've always been the one to not want to come live on the good side of the tracks, I'm an underdog of sorts, my fight is for the underdog.

I would just like to know how can a person have so much goodness, kindness, gentleness in his heart, and turn out to be a rotten son of a bitch? At one time in 1982 I got involved sincerely with a full gospel church, got saved, baptized in the Holy

Ghost...And all that that entails, met a family who had a seven year old autistic boy named Emery, well that kid was drawn to me....I spent a lot of time with him, cuz I wanted to, plus I thought that God was going to smile on me, and use me to heal this kid...to make him "quote" normal.

So, one day I placed my hand upon his head and prayed a sincere prayer, and I knew in my heart that this kid was going to march into the house and tell mom and dad "Look at me, I'm normal, I can play baseball now and be just like every other kid."

When I finished the prayer, I knew this kid was going to be normal in every way. After the prayer, he just looked up at me and smiled, and went right into being his old autistic self....I just couldn't figure out how I failed, I wondered if perhaps my prayer wasn't good enough, and how in the hell could God do this to a kid....Cuz I prayed out loud and told the kid before I prayed that he was gonna be fine and normal, and when I spoke to him it appeared that he understood, and that he believed me, but after the prayer, he just had a smile on his mug, like thanks G, but this is meant to be me.

I know that there is a message in there, don't know exactly what....Can speculate and assume a number of things, like, he was saying "Hey man ya tried but this is me..?" Or, "I'm O.K., G, I ain't got no hangups being me....It don't bother me, how come you're tripping on it?"

Maybe it's beyond my understanding, maybe that little dude is a monk in his own right, and that's the way it's supposed to be, cuz that is the way he wants or needs it to be? or maybe he ain't got the power to come out of himself?

Maybe he wants to be in there....? Shit man he looked and acted happy all the time. But, the question remains, how come I had that great big real feeling that when I took that step in faith that he was going to be healed, and then all I get was a smile and he is still autistic? Fucked up my whole faith....Began drinking again, and got right back into the only life I knew, being a biker....

Writing to you is helping, you don't know the glimmer of hope that passed through me when I found your address again....You and Sita have been a lifeline to me many times and many years....But I ain't ready to do anything Bo....I don't got the strength nor desire to take any steps, cuz if I said, hey bro I'm *going to follow what ya suggested, I'd be bullshitting you, I ain't going to do that brother....If you were someone I didn't give a fuck about, I'd do that. I hope you and Sita and Josh are all fine and hanging tuff. All my love...If I got any left... is sent to you.*

Love and insanity (smile), G

Dear G,

What can I say that you don't already know? I think you even know that you suckered yourself with that prayer for the autistic boy. It may have come from the kindest place in your ego, but it did come from ego, and set you up for a big fall, which you took.

Real prayer doesn't require God to do one particular thing. Real prayer asks for faith and strength to endure whatever God sends us. You're right -- you couldn't understand why the boy was sick or who he really was under that autism, or what he may be learning or teaching by being the way he is. So since you couldn't understand, what business did you have asking God to change it?

Wouldn't it be more relevant to ask God for strength and to shine His Light on this beautiful child? The Light may sometimes heal, like you asked, but sometimes it may simply shine, like the boy's smile. Let's not be too quick about manipulating the universe when we readily admit we don't understand what's going on.

You have the power to begin changing your life, and someday you'll do it, so I'm not worried about you at all. I only wish you'd do it now to give yourself a break, that's all. But if you don't, I know you're all right anyway. You're a good guy with a whole lot of games going on, and it's great that you're tired of playing them. Your despair is the very best thing you have going for yourself these days. Wake up, my friend. The alarm's ringing.

Your bro, Bo

Dear Bo,

You sure can be a pure asshole and a prick at times.

I wrote you some serious shit man, and you come back at me yelling that I was wrong to tell God to do something, or that I was already suppose to know all the answers... Fuck that shit, if I knew all the answers to everything, then I'd put in an application to be an assistant God, in case the real one wanted to go on vacation... This way, I'd take care of the mess he lets run wild across this world when he takes a break from being God. And if I get the job I'll shoot you in the ass with a lightning bolt for that fucked up letter you sent me.

Look Bo, I got into a full gospel type holy rolling church. The pastor taught us that we were to become like Jesus here on earth and to go around doing all sorts of shit, he even backed it up with scripture, so I got it in my mind that I was going to become a holy motherfucker, and wait on an important assignment...Fuck changing water into wine, I was gonna pray to make a retarded kid normal. So he could be happy and have a life like everyone else....I was brainwashed into thinking that God would direct me in a special type of ministry....So I thought that I heard the voice of God, and hey, I did what I was told that I could do.

Yet we know nothing happened....Then you get in my ass about who the fuck did I think I was trying to tell God "Yo man heal this dude cuz he slipped by your quality control booth, and he ain't right, so hold up on creation and all of the important shit ya do just sitting around being God, and fix this kid." What was I suppose to do Bo, yell at God and tell him "Hey man" you did a ass kicking job on this kid, right on, we all need a little entertainment and a good laugh, so fuck fixing the kid, why not send us a lot more just like him, so we can chuckle all day long?

How come in the Bible Jesus and the disciples went around healing the blind cripple and crazy....then we get into a church, and we are told we are to do this also, then nothing happens???? I mean give me a break Bo. Being an outlaw was my life's vocation, and I did pretty good at it. But it grew old man, I wanted to be a positive person, wanted to make up for the past bullshit that I created....You know, kinda balance it all out smooth things over, and begin again, but this shit just threw me, to the point that I said in my own heart and mind, "fuck it" life ain't shit, it ain't been fair to me and I'm tired, and I wanted to die.

Then I explain all that shit to you, and you tell me I know the answers already, hey, maybe you're right, but did you ever stop to think that you're at a certain stage in your spiritual development, and that I still got a long ways to go yet?

You tell me I got the power to change....What if I'm satisfied with the way shit is now and don't want to change? And what's so bad about me that I got to change anyway?

Oh well, I got that shit off my chest..... Have a nice day. Remain strong..My love to the family.

Love your bro, G

Dear G,

What happened? Did you get into a bad batch of Xerox fluid or something? I didn't "yell" at you about anything in my last letter; I wrote you as a brother like I always have. One of the problems with writing instead of face-to-face is that you can't hear the tone of voice. Maybe what you read ain't how I "said" it.

And then you ask what's the matter with the way you are now? G, *you're* the one who's been writing me saying you want to die, that you can't stand your worthless existence, etc. Make up your mind. You can be any way you like as far as I'm concerned.

Maybe you could read my last letter again and try to imagine I was saying it all gently, and see whether it makes any more sense to you. If not, that's cool too, brother. You and I are exactly who and what we are regardless of how we disagree. As far as I'm concerned, you're a good guy who suffers terribly from his own games, and I'm a friend just trying to help you kick those habits.

Still here, Bo

Dear Bo,

I would assume that you misunderstood the tone of my last letter, it may be that the point I was trying to make got lost in the slang. You must always remember that I got a sense of humor unmatched in this dimension, so to speak.

I was questioning you on a theological aspect that I was made to believe. Then my humor ran away on me, it ain't no big deal Bo, because I know more about the happenings inside of my space than people give me credit for. You know I'm not stupid, although I do dumb and stupid shit.

I'm just a bit player in all of this bro. Life's a stage and we all must play a part, I'm just doing my thing, no matter how confused I get at times. I don't think that anyone gets handed a script when they're born, telling them their lines, or giving them their direction, blocking, etc.

It's my experience that we walk out on stage at birth and mostly improvise until we think that we know we are ready to take the lead role. *Everyone is a star, there are no bit parts to life, every aspect is important where life is concerned, all that bullshit about my part is bigger than yours is just that, "bullshit."*

Shit man, since the beginning of time it's the same old song, same old movie, same old play, the beat changes, but if ya wait long enough it will revert to the old, the songs change from time to time, but it's all basically one beat. The majority of humans live scared of the unknown future, everyone is fed a pile of bullshit from the moment of birth, that at times ya just want to scream "what's it all about?"

Then some bright person comes up with the term "shit happens" well fuck Bo shit's always been happening, all that asshole did was put it on a T-shirt. He didn't tell us anything that we already didn't know.

I'm a bit player in the sense that I am in a controlled environment at this point in my quest...I got directors up the ass telling me when to eat, shit, bathe, change clothes and shower, that's my bit part for the time being, I'm in the process of helping the guards be stars, but the rotation will change and everyone will get his/her moment in the "son..." So no sweat bro, I'll get my chance to shine, although I hope it ain't nothing like Cagney where he stands on top of that gigantic gas can and shouts "Look at me, ma, I'm on top of the world!"

If I could have been anyone in history I guess I would like to have been in all honesty "me..." I guess that would sound kinda funny coming from someone facing the rest of their life in holes like this, but what the fuck Bo, I'm just me.

By the way, I guess my application for assistant God was rejected. And I want you to know that if it was accepted I would have made you the official patron saint of fuck ups (smile). Cause bro, I'm a classic fuck up, and I think you're a saint. Remain strong and keep the faith.

Very much love, Your bro, G

● ● ●

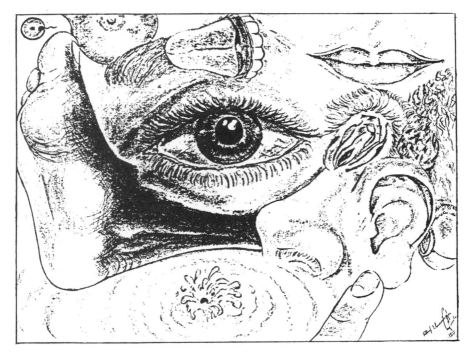

Chief E. Running Fox Goode

I just want you to hurt like I do;
Honest I do, honest I do,
Honest I do.
                    -- Randy Newman

I JUST WANT YOU TO HURT LIKE I DO

Dear Bo,

I've been helping the AIDS patients so well that they have me working in the hospital at nights, until they can hire some new nurses aides. Now I'm working from seven in the morning 'til ten at night, seven days a week, taking care of my brothers in need.

At night, I take care of the paralyzed patients and also brain-dead. Some of them have a lot of money. One of the guys I work with is robbing the patients of their commissary ($50 every two weeks). That same co-worker is in here for raping a 12-year-old. I caught him putting his fingers in one of the patient's ass. I wanted to kill him, but knew in my heart that wasn't the answer.

I confronted the guy, he tried to justify he was only helping the guy move his bowels. There was no reason for this, because the nurse just gave the patient a suppository. The patient can only mumble things, but he told me that my co-worker fondles his penis when changing his diaper. The guy also denies that.

I didn't beat him up. I went back to my cell in a rage and cried. I never cry, but my heart for some reason cried. If I tell the cops, I'll be labeled a snitch. If I kill the guy, I'll end up doing more time, go backwards in my spiritual growth, and never have inner peace. By not doing anything, the patients will remain getting robbed and sexually abused. I spoke to a few guys and they all tell me to mind my own business, because this happens in all prison hospitals.

Loving people is turning me into a real pussy and a piece of shit. I'm crying and feeling not only for the victims, but also for the attacker, because of the sickness he has, the pain he must have and is now taking out on defenseless victims, and for the karma he is creating for himself.

What the hell is happening to me? Am I the one who is turning sick? Here I am crying and feeling also for a rape-o and abuser, plus not wanting to resort to violence. I have no patience, but I've turned it over to God in prayer. Are you sure everything is perfect? What can I do, because snitching is out? How am I supposed to grow from this?

happy and hurt at the same time, J

Dear J,

I can't tell you what to do; this is your test of courage, and no one can take your place. But I can remind you that this whole ugly situation is indeed a spiritual lesson for you and everyone involved. It's still true that life isn't just a random bunch of events. That doesn't mean everything is beautiful, but it does mean everything is right on time. Horrible sometimes, but right on time.

I don't think you can ignore the whole thing like your friends have advised you to do. This is a test, a lesson. If you ignore it, you'll just keep getting it in other ways. It obviously has something to do with courage and compassion, and it has something to do with deciding who you are. I think you would lose a lot of respect for yourself if you allowed helpless patients to get robbed and fondled. If you won't help them, who will?

So the question is, what're your options? It seems to me you're painting yourself into a corner. On one hand, your new spiritual self wants to save the patients from the guy's abuses, without beating him up or killing him. Great. But the straight-up convict in you says "snitching is out," which means you won't discuss this with anyone who may have the power to stop it.

So the war is in yourself. If you were only the spiritual seeker, you might tell the authorities what's going on. If you were only a "righteous" con who doesn't believe in snitching, you'd probably use violence to stop the guy.

Maybe there are compromise solutions. You don't want to kill the guy, but does that mean you can't threaten to? The guy is a child molester. That means he wouldn't be too popular with the other cons, especially guys who are fathers and guys who don't yet know what he's in for. You might threaten to talk him up in population if he doesn't ask for a transfer out of the hospital job. These ideas could keep you within the bounds of the Convict Code and still do your spiritual duty for the patients.

I've got to admit, though, that after sixteen years of working with prisoners, I'm pretty sick of the "Convict Code." It's a set of bullshit ethics laid down by a bunch of old gangsters, and just because it has become sacred in prisons, that doesn't mean it's right. I mean, you're telling me that if, out of compassion for defenseless, ailing convicts, you told a doctor what this guy is doing, the other cons would hate you more than they hate a child molester who robs paralyzed people, plays with their jollies, and sticks his finger up their asses! Is that a code you want to live by?

Everywhere we go, we come across situations which require personal courage. How we respond determines a lot of our self-respect and spiritual development. If it were always easy, it wouldn't take much courage. What takes courage is to do what you feel is right, even if the whole world thinks you're wrong. It means to do what you think is right even if it puts you in danger.

Human progress has always been advanced by people who lay their freedom or their lives on the line for what they know is right. Edmund Burke once said, "The only thing necessary for the triumph of evil is for good people to do nothing."

I don't know exactly what you should do, but I know you're not a "real pussy and a piece of shit." You're a loving, honest spiritual brother who is encountering a tough test along his Great Adventure. Like all the ancient stories of the trials of Hercules, Jason and the Golden Fleece, David and Goliath and so forth, you and I have the opportunity to become genuine heroes by meeting our challenges with basic human virtues such as self-honesty, courage, kindness, humor and wonder.

Life may get dangerous and troublesome and tiring and confusing, but it's also a great mysterious adventure which has payoffs beyond description for the few people who live it as such.

Please let me know how you're doing and what you decide to do. Sita and I care very much.

Love, Bo

Dear Bo,

Hello! Thank you for your honest and caring letter concerning the abuse of my patients. I had already done what I felt was right to stop the abuse, but your letter sure gave me some well-needed peace. I let the nurses know what's been happening and they now have an investigation going on.

I guess you would think I'm happy, but I'm not happy. Their investigation consisted of buying the one patient a new combination lock for his locker, where only the cops have his combination. The nurses, doctors, and cops don't give two fucks about the sexual abuse.

The cops would be in all kinds of trouble if the guy was proven to be sexually abusing the patients. They could also be held for legal damages, so they just call the guy a "sick mother-fucker". The nurses don't want it proven because the guy would be fired, and he does all their work. Even work he's not qualified to do. He's also teaching the nurses to speak Spanish.

Nothing but fucking politics. I "care," so I didn't just give up. I threatened to kill the dude, and gave him a chance to fight me, but he punked out. I'm also telling everyone in population what he's doing and what he's in for. I'm trying to make his life hard.

My job always seems to be on the line, because I try to get what the patients need. A simple thing like taking the patients out to the yard for fresh air has the cops trying to jam me up, because it makes their job harder. They have to walk to the yard with us and open the gate. Real hard work, right?

I got a nurse who gives me a hard time just because I get a 77-year-old patient out of bed to shit in the toilet instead of his diaper. They tell me it's quicker, easier, and cleaner to let him continue shitting in his diaper. I'm trying to build the guy's spirit up so he will "live". The man has already stopped eating. No one else is even trying to build his spirit up. I'm just trying to grasp at anything that might work.

I got bawled out and threatened because I tried to reassure a patient's family that I was giving him the best care possible. I told the family also that he wasn't eating, and to please build his spirits up. The cop told me not to tell the family members anything, because the families need to remember that they are in a prison, not a regular hospital. They tell me this also every time I ask for something for one of the patients. I think that's bullshit.

Patients are human and deserve the same care any patient on the outside gets. The system talks about rehabilitating and helping inmates, yet when those inmates truly need help and rehabilitation, the system turns its back on them.

I had something else happen I want to share with you. It has to do with a lesson I learned in false judgements and caring or helping. A patient kept asking his counselor for help in getting certain legal work done. The counselor came to see the guy and became angry with the patient because he wasn't comprehending what he was saying. Turns out, the patient is a little slow and can't *read or write. I found this out by asking him if he needed help.*

The patient is serving time for child abuse. I put that aside for a second and sure got a surprise! He had a letter (certified) from the Child Welfare Services. This letter states that the agency found no wrongdoing on his part. The story was made up by his ex-girlfriend. Him being slow, and not able to read or write, he copped to five-fifteen years. He blew his chance for an appeal because he didn't understand that it had to be filed within 30 days. He didn't even know that the letter clears him. I'm writing the legal aid lawyer that represented him to see what can be done. A lesson in judgement.

You mentioned in your letter that my true struggle is between being a convict and just being myself (caring). I could hug you for that statement. You made me face the truth. First, I'm now ridding myself of my old convict morals, and just doing what I feel is right in my heart. I've discovered why so many of us choose to be convicts instead of true individuals. A "convict's" life is simple: Block out all feelings and emotions. Follow the majority of other tough guys. When decisions come, don't think, just strike out. Be dependent on the weak and naive to live comfortably in prison (robbing and extorting).

We never fail, because we never change. Never feel uncomfortable either, because of never changing. No real responsibilities, never seeing the truth, we just blame others for everything. If any pain comes along, just hide in drugs and booze.

Being ourselves is being a _real_ tough guy. It involves change, fear, possible rejection, planning, responsibility, honesty, caring, helping and a lot more. Learning only to be myself is not easy, though I need to. Every day a new change or emotion comes up.

Bloom like a flower, J

Dear J,

I admire you for the hard work you're doing on yourself, and I hope that you can go through all of this realizing that you may not make all the right moves, but you're doing as best you can.

Try to remember the old prayer that goes "Give me the peace to accept the things I cannot change, the courage to change the things I can, and the wisdom to know the difference." Some of your frustration has nothing to do with it being a prison hospital.

Patient care in this country is really terrible in many hospitals and nursing homes. *Thousands* of orderlies and aides are frustrated by nurses, and nurses by doctors, and doctors by hospital policies. Your complaints about the elderly patient and your conversations with patients' families -- no matter how heart-breaking -- are typical complaints from medical workers who find out the people around them don't care as much as they do.

I'm not saying you shouldn't try to change anything. But you need to have a special kind of patience to work in that field without burning out. You sound wired, tense, depressed, frustrated. You need to take a good, honest look at your own abilities and limitations like the prayer above talks about.

How do you think Sita and I feel about all the prisoners' problems and terrible conditions we can't do anything about? If we focused only on those, we'd have burned out long ago. Instead, we focus on what we *can* do, and many thousands of people, like yourself, are glad that we've stuck around.

It gets back down to the basics -- meditate, pray, try to clear your mind enough to move through these complicated challenges as compassionately as you can. And if you find yourself burned out, you may need to step back for awhile to regain your balance. No matter how terrible or wonderful the daily events seem to be, they are not the whole picture. If we keep forgetting that, we'll be suffering more and more instead of stumbling toward the Light.

I love you, Bo

Dear Bo and Sita,

Hello! I hope that all is going well with you. After seeing two of my letters published in your newsletter, I went through a lot of changes that I didn't know how to express to you.

At first, I felt like you broke my trust by publishing my letters without telling me that you were gonna do so. [editor's note: J has since given us specific permission to use all his letters]

You see, a lot of people instantly knew that they were my letters. What a lot of them told as we walked the yard was, "All the people who aren't close with you only see a tough guy but we who are close to you see right through that tough guy bullshit, and see a loving and caring guy who's trying to do easy time." I then had a close friend who told me that my time will never be easy because

I've seen a reflection of my true self and are that person when not in the Big Yard or Cell Block.

Bo, what I was really mad at was not you, but myself, for I realized that I was not a "tough guy" without feelings but a caring and loving dude doing time for my blindness. Oh, I tried to hide from this truth the whole summer by staying high and walking the easy and old prison routine. The Great Spirit being so loving allowed me to be locked down for 120 days (now) to force me to look within once again and get back on track.

There is some real great news though. As a result of my letters being published and people talking behind my back that they were my letters, the institution got wind that I spoke up to the outside world, and fired the rapist for sexually abusing the patient who has multiple sclerosis and is almost brain dead. The institution was taking too long to do anything so I went a step further and wrote the patient's family. The combination of everything caused the rapist firing and some eyes to be opened.

Oh, before my lockup I also had to pay a price. The rapist had been doing a lot of the nurses' jobs which we are not qualified to do. This was one of the reasons why the night nurses closed their eyes to what was going on. The nurses then started wanting me to do all their work which I'm not qualified to do.

They locked me up for refusing to do their work. I then got to see that I really had friends. All the other nurses aides and patients went to bat for me and were willing to be witnesses on my behalf. I was let off lockup and went back to work for 2 days then they fired me. No one has told me why I was fired and they won't tell the other nurses aides why either. I think it is because I immediately got in touch with Prisoners Legal Service.

Three days later I was locked up again for refusing to take a urine test. The cop tried to degrade me by standing 2 inches away from me while I tried to piss. I blew up and refused to go which caused me to be locked up now for 120 days. I would've got less time for having a dirty urine.

In all honesty, I'm now wondering if I didn't intentionally want a lockup to get away from the mainstream of population?

The rapist had some heavy karma to pay. First, from the inmates. Second, some old sex charges came up and he is in out-

side court now trying to fight being locked up for the rest of his life. I hope he gets life so no other children are ever hurt.

Some more good news. I have opened up communication between me and my family once again. My father even drove 600 miles to come see me so we could work out our differences.

I now have a beautiful woman named L. from Houston in my life. We are making plans for when I eventually get out.

My problem is the same repeated one. How just to be myself? I always try to take the easy way out by playing the part of a tough guy when a problem arises, or I'm faced with a new emotion or situation.

I may have some head problems to still work out but I feel real good that I stood and fought non-violently till the system put an end to the abuse of patients. I really thank you for your help and guidance in a time of need. May your week be filled with enough happiness to keep a smile flowing on your faces.

I love you, J.

Dear J,

Sorry about this whole thing over using your letter. I always assume that people who write me understand that their letters could wind up in a newsletter or book. Like Dear Abby, nobody should be shocked to see their letter in print, because that's a big part of what I do. That's how we share the teachings with others. Of course, when somebody says "don't print my letter," we don't.

You must admit that it turned out okay. You wanted to get this guy off the ward, and our newsletter helped do exactly that.

Yeah, you still have many things to work out, but you're doing okay. Just keep remembering who you want to be and who you don't want to be. It takes one moment at a time. And one decision at a time -- like lightening up on getting stoned. Maybe each Christmas you should give yourself a present of giving up one more bad habit. If you live enough Christmases, you'll be perfect!

Love, Bo

● ● ●

Dear Bo,

I've been in sort of a dilemma this week which stemmed from one of your letters in the Summer '89 newsletter (the inmate who worked in the hospital ward). I was disturbed that the inmate had laid his trip on you and as per usual, was blind to any part he played in his reality, and I wasn't in the least surprised that his decision to report the incident, or to threaten the other inmate physically, had no positive results. Even if that particular problem had been solved, I highly suspect that another similar one would have arisen in another form, and that the process will continue in his life until he goes inside to discover the part he is playing in those kinds of tragic dilemmas.

I personally don't solve any of my problems by going to the guards or officials. In my first few years of incarceration it was because I hated guards, cops, and "the system" with such intensity, and wanted a reputation as a bad ass (state-raised since I was a child). Then after I was introduced to the Spirit, I saw clearly that it had been only a reflection of myself that I'd hated all those years, and I found means of solving my personal problems through my "inner Source." I no longer consider guards or officials any less human than convicts, but I don't go to <u>any</u> outside source to solve my disputes or conflicts within the "Illusion."

I love you guys with all my heart and hope that by sticking my nose in this I haven't offended you. But now I'm going to stick my neck out even further and chance that I'll really piss you off with my opinion about the Texas censors.

For starters, I haven't written them a letter because my guidance tells me that such would contribute to even further polarization and "good guy / bad guy" vibrations, and that if we will all go inside and take it up with the <u>real</u> problem-solver, it will be a piece of cake to the source powerful enough to keep the universe running smoothly.

I know, without the slightest doubt, that going inside ourselves to find the answers is the <u>opposite</u> of doing "nothing," and that with <u>any</u> situation, no matter how perplexing, using the Energy in order to connect with the Source is the only way to fly.

Getting back to the guy in the hospital ward, it would be extremely difficult for me to believe that if he had truly gone inside and forgiven that part of himself which was being mirrored by the "child molester who robs paralyzed people, plays with their jollies and sticks his finger up their asses," and projected the resulting enormous power from that experience in terms of compassionate energy rather than threatening words, that the entire drama would have been transformed.

*I'm trying really hard to not come off like some sanctimonious jerk sidelining the plays, but man, we **have** to start using this stuff. **You know, Sita knows, I know,** and so do a lot of other folks, that IT WORKS!! When it's done clean, that kind of power just <u>cannot lose</u> for us.*

*When I was outside the Spirit and into the external hustle, I must have been a part of -- and witness to -- about as much violence and bloodletting as any con in the country on a daily basis for nearly thirty years, and a funny thing happened when I truly made the inner changes: Man, I haven't even **seen** a <u>fistfight</u> in over two years. It just hasn't been a part of my reality (and I'm not doing time with a bunch of pussies or pc's either, my friend; these guys are <u>hard cases</u> that the feds have farmed out to the state, most of them "known troublemakers.") But the energy in this reality just hasn't fed the violence trip.*

You are my brother, man, and Sita is my sister, and no matter how much it hurts we have to keep pulling each other's shirttails because there just aren't enough of us around who can truly "grok" all of this.

I love you both, I really do, F

Dear F,

Don't worry for a second about my being pissed off with you or anything like that. I know we're brothers, and to me the greatest respect we can have for each other is to be straight, like you were with me in your letter. You spoke your mind eloquently and I certainly appreciate it.

The points you made address some of the deepest issues about spiritual life and truth. You express a view that non-conflict is always right. My view is that even if it's right 99% of the time, there's always going to be a 1% wild card just to keep us on our toes. If there weren't, then spirituality wouldn't be such a moment-by-moment personal challenge and process of discovery. We could just learn "the rules" and abide by them.

I think you and I feel exactly the same about going within and opening to our higher guidance, but you seem to be sure that the guidance will always be to refrain from struggle or conflict. But life is filled with struggle, just as it's filled with joy and harmony too. You and I surely struggle with ourselves from time to time, so what's the big deal about struggling with others? Standing up for our beliefs is one of the greatest spiritual boosts in our lives, yet it usually means we're standing up *against* some other way, against a stronger or more popular force.

During the Nazi extermination of the Jews, when troops stormed into a house and asked whether any Jews were hiding there, should the German Christians have told the truth if Jews were in the attic? Some did, feeling that lying would only worsen the overall spiritual dilemma. Others lied, feeling that saving lives was more important than their allegiance to speaking the truth.

Which was right or wrong? Do you feel qualified to say? I surely don't. And they may all have gone inside themselves looking for their parts of the problem, asking for higher guidance and so forth, and still wound up doing opposite things. Like the Bible says, There is no form to the Spirit.

All of that said, you do make a strong point about the guy I wrote to in the last newsletter. I suspect you're right in saying "even if that particular problem had been solved...another similar one would have arisen..." And in fact, his next letter was indeed about another such problem. If you recall my response, I pointed out that he needed to change his inner attitudes in order to continue being in that line of work. You put it better than I did, but we're both saying the same thing.

So it seems where we're not saying the same thing, is simply whether conflict is ever the right choice. And that's okay; we can still be friends and brothers even if we don't agree on that. I honor and admire your way, it's just not what my inner guidance shows me. I have no doubt at all that your change of attitude is the reason you haven't seen so much as a fistfight in over two years. But that doesn't mean it always works that way. It means that for your nature, for your path, that's the way it is working -- I really believe that completely.

For others I've known, the same genuine inner changes seemed to result in *more* violence and challenges around them, because their lessons were different from yours. God indeed works in mysterious ways, that's all I'm trying to remind you.

Also, I think you may not realize that when I'm in conflict with, for example, the Texas Department of Corrections, to me it's still "us versus us," and not "us versus them." My Guru once said, "Do whatever you must with people, but don't shut anyone out of your heart, even for a moment."

I'm not forgetting that the Texas Department of Corrections is made up of people just like you and me, people who just want to feel good and safe and loved. But in this Grand Illusion of life, this Divine Comedy and Drama we find ourselves playing, there's a battle going on between my part and their part, and that's okay with me. I didn't write the play. I just try to play my part with grace, humor, and wisdom. And like anything else, this act of the play can help all of us to become freer or more hung up, depending on how we use it.

I'm not saying you're wrong about how you're doing things in your life. Maybe the world needs both reactions -- the purely internal, and the spiritual activist -- to serve as reminders to each other, and I hope we will, for many years to come. Sita and I appreciate your love and blessings, and you have ours as well.

Thanks for writing, Bo

● ● ●

Dear Bo,

If you would please take time out to listen to my problem I would like that. But first a little about myself. I am 19 years old and serving 7 years in prison and at times I want to agree with Maury about his feeling towards society and let everything else go to hell (excuse my rudeness). And if you could please give me a better way to deal with, I really would appreciate it a lot.

And one more thing, how to get over being gang-raped and then being harassed about it all the time.

Please write back, B

Dear B,

I know you've been hurt very deeply and nothing I can say will change what's already happened. But the main thing is, we can look at life as a never-ending source of hassles, or as a series of lessons bringing us to becoming enlightened.

For example, maybe being hassled is a lesson in humility: You learn how not to let it bother you. Or maybe it's a lesson in courage: Get up the nerve to lay it all out honestly to the chaplain or the shrink, and insist you get transferred someplace where you won't be hassled so much.

Or maybe it's a lesson in self-discipline: Insist on p.c., and do your whole time alone, using your whole bit for meditation and spiritual study. Or maybe it's a lesson in turning the other cheek: Keep your forgiveness and love so strong that eventually it overcomes the guys who hassle you and changes them spiritually.

These are just examples so you can see the basic attitude of being a spiritual seeker. A seeker tries to know at all times that whatever is going on, no matter how horrible or painful, it's some kind of teaching for him, and so he's always looking into it to learn something good. It's like turning horseshit into fertilizer.

If you spend as much time as possible practicing meditation, breathing, etc., and also find some way to serve humanity, I promise you you'll gradually heal all of the wounds inside your heart and you'll feel strong and great. It takes a lot of effort and a long time, but do you have anything more important to do?

I love you, Bo

● ● ●

Dear Bo,

Hello, there! I hope and pray, this letter finds you and Sita, in the best of health! I really liked your book, We're All Doing Time. *It was passed on to me by my ex-cellie, T.*

Well, for starters, I want to ask you your advice on some trouble I'm having. But, before that, let me tell you about my self. My name is C, I'm 24 years old, and this is my second time in prison. I had a very caring father and mother, but they are both dead. My mom died when I was eleven (suicide) and my dad, when I was seven.

I was never disciplined at all, just spoiled, rotten. I was never around violence, just Love from my parents.

Well, Bo, I have a problem, and I need some help dealing with it, before I do something real wrong, and ending up with a death sentence, when it is all over with.

I have a guy in here that is steadily trying to get me to fight him. He is doing a lot of time, and he won't care, one way or the other what happens. I even had to get moved out of the cell we were sharing, because of a bunch of Bullshit. I even let him slap me a couple of times. But, I turned the other cheek.

But, it is steadily getting worse every day. He is grabbing me on the butt and talking to me like I'm a girl or something!

Bo, I know, I have it in me to kill him and feel good about it, but I don't want to resort to that (if you know what I mean). How, can I overcome this urge? Yes, I have a lot of fear, too much, really, in me and I'm real shy, too. I only have 10 years and I can go home this year, if I keep my shit straight. I feel real low for not taking a stand at first, but this urge keeps building in me and I will eventually explode.

Sincerely, Love, C

Dear C,

I hope nothing bad has happened between you and this guy yet. There aren't any *easy* answers to one of these situations, so you just have to look honestly at what all your options are, and the consequences of each.

If you kill him, you'll get him off your back, but you'll have killed somebody, which is like the final failure of not being able to work things out. It's a pretty heavy weight on the heart and mind. Plus, his friends may be after you next, or you may pull more time, and louse up a bigger chunk of your life.

So what other options do you have? Can you possibly talk to the guy to change things between you? Can you get transferred by explaining the situation to a caseworker (without naming him)?

If neither of those options work, maybe you should consider going into pc for the rest of your bit. You said you're due for release this year. With the rest of your life ahead of you, maybe a few months in pc wouldn't be too much of a price to pay to stay out of bigger trouble with the guy.

It's not ideal, but the whole situation isn't ideal, so you just have to see what's the least bad way to go. It's even possible that standing up to the guy firmly but not aggressively would get him off your back. It's also possible that if you stay out of his way and put up with a little bullshit when you do see him, it'll never get worse and you'll be out of the joint soon enough.

Even so, you should try to remember that this whole situation isn't an accident. Everything comes to us to teach us something. So try to learn something helpful from this whole thing and do what you feel is most "right" -- which usually means the thing you won't regret for the rest of your life. Lessons may be easy or tough, but they are lessons all the same. They teach us about our fears, our self-honesty, our courage, our stupidity and pride, etc. Be a good student, brother. Let me know how it works out.

Love, Bo

● ● ●

*Honesty is to look and to see every living creature as yourself,
having your own will to live and your own fear of death.*

-- William Buck, *Mahabharata*

Dear Bo,

I have been in prison since 7/7/76 doing ten to life (murder 2), 2 years escape, 1 year attempt escape. I am 44 years old, and have been considered one of the old solid convicts. I never was a tough guy but never had any trouble. In short, I have always had a good name in the prison system. I am not claiming to be anything but all my life it seems like there are 2 people inside my body: One tender loving and caring, but the other one has caused me trouble all my life doing things that I didn't really want to do.

Now when I was on escape in 1981, to make a long story as short as possible, I was staying with some friends for a few days until the heat blew over. Along with the booze and drugs this woman showed up and we ended up in bed. She just happened to be another convict's wife. After a few days I went on my way, got caught and sent back to prison. Her husband found out that we were together, and she told him that she was afraid of what might happen to her if she didn't consent to my wishes and that was the only reason we were together.

Well it wasn't that way, it was a drunken drug sex party there all the time. Her husband is a stone killer in and out of prison, doing so much time he will never be out anyhow. After 4 years we both are at the same maximum prison and with escapes on both of us this is where we will stay for a long time.

When he approached me here he said I had raped his wife and he was going to kill me. I knew he might be pissed off if he knew I was with her, but raped, man I was shocked. I have done a lot of time and I also know this guy. He come to kill me, no doubt about it; just by a freak accident it didn't happen.

But I knew it was only a matter of time and he had already said to me what he had to say, so next time there wouldn't be any talk, just the feel of cold steel.

But I had some time, time enough to think. I could try to kill him first, which would be very hard, because of his size and experience. but if I did kill him, I signed my own death warrant, I couldn't live long enough to ever get out of prison with more time on top of what I have. I really didn't want to see him dead anyhow. But I do have a chance to get out of prison in a few more years so I didn't want to die either.

I know most of the time there is some other way, I have even been the go-between a couple of times and stopped a killing. But here there wasn't no way. I have said all that in order to say this:

I caught out! Went to protection! Rat row, punk row, etc. I didn't snitch on him, he didn't catch any heat behind the whole thing. But here I am, and man it is killing me. After 9 years in prison and me to end up on P.C.! I am trying to tell myself that I have finally wised up and this was the only way I could turn at the present time. That this is a chance for me to live the rest of my life the way I really always wanted to. But there is this other part of me that keeps saying, coward, it keeps saying I would have been better off dead.

We go across the rotunda for chow, everyone else is locked down, but almost every trip I see someone behind a locked door that I know. Man, there isn't any way to describe how it makes me feel. I was never friendly with the guards, but always showed them respect and them me. Even some of them has said, "T., never thought I would see you here," or "what happened to you?"

The strange thing is, I can't hardly look a guard in the face. I know that you know a lot about prison life, but I don't know if you can even relate to what it's like for a person like me to be on protection. I hope you can because I can't figure it out for myself.

Bo, I am trying to help myself, trying to get through this, but I need help. It's hard for me to ask, but I am asking. I don't know anyone on the outside except some ex-convicts, and now that I am on P.C. that friendship will be gone. I have never liked prison but I have always been socially accepted. Now I am an outcast from society as well as the other convicts, and it hurts. I think of the guys I have been friends with for years, but that's all gone.

Yes, I am feeling sorry for myself! I am wallowing in self-pity. And if there is anyone in the world that gives a damn it will have to be you! It just seems if I know anyone cares then I can start up. Because man this is the bottom of the pit.

Thanks for everything, T

Dear T,

I definitely understand the pain and frustration you're feeling from being a stand-up convict who suddenly finds himself in pc with all the punks & snitches. But at the same time, you didn't turn punk and you didn't snitch, so you shouldn't let yourself feel that kind of embarrassment. What you did was about the only thing you could do; it's a bum break, but consider a few things:

1) It's a lesson about the karma from messing with somebody's wife. It can help you make better decisions in the future.

2) It sounds like God may be sending you a blessing in disguise. Maybe this is what it takes for you to make a complete break with your whole life as a criminal and convict. As you said in your letter, now you're an outcast even in prison society! Maybe that's what it takes for you to really stay on the streets this time and do something better with your life than winding up in the joint. Think about it. Sometimes our very best breaks come disguised as terrible strokes of bad luck.

3) This might also be an opportunity to open up your understanding and compassion for all the people in pc. Now you know what it feels like. Maybe a lot of them are decent guys too, who only did what they thought they had to do.

If I were in your position, I'd do the rest of my time in pc, and create a whole new self from the ground up. You're getting older now; use this time to seek some real wisdom. You can do your pc time with dignity and self-respect if you really see that you have nothing to be ashamed of.

Let go of the whole convict social trip, let go of the whole idea of who you are or who you should be to the other cons. You can't control that; you never really could, you just *thought* you could. Now you have a chance to start a whole new life. Considering your other options, I think you should take that chance and do as much with it as you can. The results might be better than you could ever imagine, T! It's up to you.

Please keep in touch and let me know how you're doing; I definitely care what happens to you, bro.

Love, Bo

[this was 1985; never heard from T again]

● ● ●

Dear Bo,

I love your newsletters and the responses to the letters of others. I've read hundreds of "spiritual" books but none with the level of sincerity and wisdom as your talks and letters.

I would like to know your views on the death penalty. In your view, is it ever justified? And what about people out on parole such as the following: (a) the guy who raped that young woman and chopped off her arms, then left her for dead (Larry something or other). She lived (if you call that living). (b) The guy (Rosenthal, I think) who poured gasoline on his young son in a motel room and set the place ablaze (supposedly to get revenge on his ex-wife). The son lived and is horribly disfigured.

What kind of justice allows such people to go free while their victims suffer forever, and live in constant fear of their torturers? To me the death penalty seems too good for such perpetrators of evil (both of whom are Caucasian, by the way).

You are the one person I feel has the wisdom and experience to answer such questions. I'd sincerely like to know your views.

Sincerely, E

Dear E,

You might expect in all these years that I'd have received a lot of letters like yours, but actually this is the first time those questions have been put to me so clearly.

First, as you might expect, I'm not in favor of the death penalty. It has nothing to do with race or fairness of application or even a moral absoluteness about killing. I think some noble soul could've assassinated Hitler with a clear mind and compassionate heart, filled with regret that such a horrible deed had to be performed. But there's the key: Actions performed with clarity and compassion *reduce* the amount of suffering in the world. Actions performed without clarity and compassion *increase* the suffering in the world. It's as simple as that.

You can look around and easily see that the death penalty inflames hatred, vengeance, and downright evil. I don't use the word "evil" lightly. Now that there are mobs of people cheering "Fry him! Fry Him!" outside prisons where fellow human beings are executed, it seems to me we've crossed over that line.

Executions are not bringing out the best in us, nor are they adding to our hope for a better future. And statistics have repeatedly shown the death penalty has absolutely no deterrent effect; in fact, death penalty states have higher murder rates than non-death penalty states. So the death penalty makes neither moral nor practical sense. It would behoove us to learn how to deal with our problems rather than lashing out with murderous rage.

Which brings up your next questions, about the people who commit cruel, vicious crimes, and then get back on the streets while their victims continue to suffer. This is part of the same issue. An immature culture is going to make mistakes in *every* direction, hurting *everyone*. Our criminal justice system has nothing to do with truth, only with winning or losing.

The truth is, Larry Singleton is probably just as twisted now as he was when he hacked off the girl's arms, and may be a real danger to whatever community he's in. But we never called him "sick," we called him "guilty." We didn't remove him from society to help him work through those profound disturbances; we just sentenced him to prison for as long as the law allowed because we hated his guts. So when the time was up, we had to let him go.

But did anything at all get accomplished? The girl still has no arms; he still denies his depravity; and society still hates his guts. It never had to do with responsibility, with healing or renewal. It had to do with ugliness and blindness on both his part and ours. And the same holds true for Charles Rothenberg, who set fire to his son David.

Government has a responsibility to protect citizens from violent crime to the greatest degree possible without becoming a police-state. I share the public's outrage over the release of Singleton or Rothenberg, or a rapist or murderer or other violent felon who then commits the same kind of crime again. We're outraged that the government hasn't acted responsibly, and that's damn right.

But the lack of responsibility begins long before parole; it begins with *our* unwillingness to be a mature, compassionate society, our unwillingness to look at crime as a totality -- victim, criminal, the act itself, its lingering consequences -- and to strive toward the best total healing we can find.

Our irresponsibility continues all the way down the line -- as we ignore the wounds and vulnerability of the victim, often badgering and humiliating them during the trial; as we thoroughly crush any sane notion of justice under the weight of legal loopholes and strategies; and finally as we lock the offender up in a brutal system conceived in anger for the purpose of punishment. Our system manages to hurt everyone -- the abused victim, the banished offender, the amoral lawyers, the manipulated juries, the pressured judges, and the outraged, frightened public.

Once again, we can find no moral or practical benefit from the system we have created. Crime soars, violence increases, our prisons overflow, and instead of looking honestly at the heart of the problem, we elect politicians who shamelessly exploit our fears and anger by more "tough on crime" posturing. But things never get any better, because *we're* the ones making things worse.

I'm very much a realist, and that's why I question a criminal justice system which is more criminal than just, and a corrections system which not only fails to *actively* correct, but makes it almost *impossible* for correction to occur. Believe me, the thousands of prisoners I've known who've managed to turn their lives around in prison have battled uphill all the way. Not that there aren't good staff people around, because there are many. But they too have an uphill battle against a paranoid, violent system which rewards inertia instead of innovation, and submissiveness instead of rehabilitation.

People who defend the system, or who want to build even more prisons and sentence more people, are the idealists, not me. They're "negative idealists", because they have a punitive ideal which reality continues to disprove. It simply doesn't work. Hurting people who hurt us just perpetuates a lot of hurting.

I would say over 90% of prisoners would love to straighten their lives out if given a decent chance. Very few people are deadset on doing wrong. The vast majority of prisoners hate their lives, they feel like worthless losers, and they begin to shine when someone comes along and shows them they can be of value.

That's why I'm so passionate about prisoners doing some kind of "good works" instead of just getting an education and job skills. As somebody named Susie Gomez once said, "It is an honor to be asked to help." It's an amazing experience to introduce a prisoner to that honor, and watch the profound changes which take place!

I don't say to set everyone free. There may always be twisted people who need to be removed from society to protect the public. And sometimes somebody may even forfeit his right to *ever* again be trusted with his freedom -- perhaps like Singleton or Rothenberg, or David "Son of Sam" Berkowitz, or Charles Manson, or the crazy guy who swears that when he gets out he's going to kill the actress Theresa Saldana. Why should the public be guinea pigs?

But there are very few people like that, and we already have *more* than enough prisons to hold them. And even so, we can create optimum conditions for their redemption so that even if they're behind bars for the rest of their lives, they have an opportunity to become respected writers, inventors, thinkers, artists, or humanitarians, contributing to the world through their unique restrictions and the humility of their past.

But those are the few. The *many* are prisoners who would be better served through imaginative combinations of house arrest, community service, electronic monitoring, family counseling, restitution, drug and alcohol rehab and so forth. Prisons should be the last recourse. And prisons offer *no* solution to problems which are primarily social and medical, such as drug abuse. Our temporary insanity toward drugs and drug offenders exacts a terrible price on us all.

If we wish to live in a compassionate land, then we have to express compassion, even when we find it necessary to arrest someone, or restrict their freedom to harm others. We have to be able to look at both David Rothenberg *and* his father, the mutilated girl *and* her attacker, and feel terrible for all of them, and take the most responsible steps to begin the profound healing on all sides. Lock him up, yes. But don't feed the victim's hatred, nor the offender's sinfulness. Life always begins right now, wherever we are.

You said about the girl whose arms were chopped off, "She lived (if you call that living)..." Whoa! Of *course* I call that living! Don't you? Some people are *born* without arms, some lose their arms in farm accidents or car wrecks. Should they just chalk it up and die? That girl can experience joy and sorrow, marriage, motherhood, thrill and wonder. If she turns inward because of her suffering, she can make profound spiritual discoveries and contributions, as can little David Rothenberg.

Life at last is a mystery, not just a struggle. We can't understand why such horrible things happen, but we can choose our response. In a hundred years, the attackers and the victims, the judges and juries and you and I will all be gone. The most relevant question will not be "What happened?", but rather, "What happened next? What did the girl and David Rothenberg choose to do with their lives? What kind of future did we help to create by our response?"

Our society seems to be moving backward into more infantile reactions to our crime and justice problems. It would be a good idea to begin changing our attitudes as individuals. As John the Baptist said, "Before kingdoms can change, men must change."

Thanks for writing, Bo

● ● ●

If we could read the secret lives of those we want to punish,
we could find in each life enough grief and suffering
to make us stop wishing anything more on them.

-- Unknown

THANKS AND BLESSINGS...

This chapter was a last-minute idea. The following letters have been buried in a file, some of them for many years. Others come daily. The reason we keep them buried is that they're *so* grateful, *so* appreciative, *so* praising, we've always felt a little embarrassed at the idea of printing them.

Yet if we want to share personal, heartwarming letters with you, these are some of the most personal, heartwarming letters we've ever received. And anyway, they don't just gush gratitude, they also tell of profound transformations, insights, new beginnings, and include a lot of colorful perspectives on life.

These letters also remind us that although people can't change many of the toughest conditions of their lives, they can change themselves and their own lives even in the worst of places. Put more simply, this spiritual stuff really works!

We've tried to present a sampling of letters ranging from murderers to a ninety-year-old meditator. You may notice that most of the writers bless me and my family and pray for us. I haven't the slightest doubt that the enormous amount of "good luck" Sita, Josh and I enjoy in our lives is due to the continued blessings of so many people around the world.

We feel blessed, thanked, protected and loved, and we thank and bless you all right back.

Hi, Sita and Bo,

I love you.

Recent events have my physical future in a cloudy state. I've been placed back inside the fence from the Honor Farm. It seems my father is wanted for murder. Someone said he made threats to break me out. So for "my protection" and the good of everyone else, I was put inside.

At first it was unsettling. All the time I was trying to express love, and learn whatever lesson there was to learn, my social worker wanted to know why I wasn't mad. I can't really explain it, only that God is as much here as anywhere else. And there's just no one to be mad at.

I hurt terribly for two days in my heart chakra. My pain was for my father, for us, for me. He did 10 years, and got out, and I came in. We've never had a life together. He's on the run somewhere now. I'm praying for his safety, whatever is best for him. This is something only he knows and God.

You guys have been my family for so long. I still haven't developed a Hatha Yoga discipline nor learned Pranayam. But I know how to Love, how to relax, how to let go of all thoughts unlike Love & Peace. I'm a lot calmer, a whole lot happier, and freer than at any time in my life, since I was a little boy and telling the truth was easy.

I don't have the foggiest notion where my life's going. I don't reckon it really matters. I'll be where I'm supposed to be, doing what it is I'm supposed to be doing. I have a big sign written on a white formica top that is the bottom of a chessboard:

God is Love. Love everybody all of the time.
Love is All Spirit.

I wish the whole world could know you as I know you. You give so much in the craziest way. A man just wakes up and finds you by his side, holding a hand. I can't even remember you not being there; yet I don't know when you came.

I know words aren't ever going to say what I feel. Words feel phony as hell. But I think when I looked at that glorious sunset tonight and saw the smile of God, and returned to my cell and found goodies all over my bed, gifts from a gracious friend, and my crippled pardner laughed today, we shared something and I felt your Love and gratitude in these things.

Because once, I could not taste being alive. Now I am so happy it's sometimes unbearable not to jump and shout and sing. And I know (though not how) that you guys made all this possible, or God through you. And I'm so glad to be here, on the same planet, sharing this crazy world together.

Love, T

• • •

Randy Mills

Dear Bo and Sita,

I have been an ardent admirer of the work you do for many years. Of all the possible projects and good works to support, you have been my first choice for a long time. My financial contributions have been small and erratic as I am a medical student living on a marginal budget, but some day I hope to be able to offer you greater material support. In the meantime, I offer small donations but large numbers of blessings and spiritual well-wishing.

Some time ago, on a lark I suddenly decided to give a copy of We're All Doing Time *to my sister, H. H is a rather militant atheist and quite repulsed by so much as the* <u>word</u> *"spiritual." Yet she read your book from cover to cover and loved every word of it, as she told me repeatedly. I think your words touched a very deep place in her and may have awakened the seeds of a spiritual understanding for H.*

I have your family-photo Christmas card taped over my desk, the light and love that shines through the physical form is a reminder of the divinity which abides within us all.

Thanks for all the spiritual nourishment I've gained from the wonderful work you do!

I love you, C

● ● ●

Dear Bo and Sita,

We're All Doing Time *is a great help and a deep experience for me. I am 90 years old and an old meditator, having been exposed to many beautiful people from both East and West. Your complete simplicity, honesty and wisdom has led me back to being still and simple. Thank you.*

All my love and gratitude, L

● ● ●

Dear Bo,

I never knew where my life was going until I got run over by a train in December '84. When I'm not in jail I live on the streets. I've been all over California for two years, Canada, the Keys -- hitchhiking mostly. Both my legs are gone and I get out in my wheelchair and panhandle at shopping malls and go from town to town.

I enjoy this kind of life because I get to meet so many people of all sorts. And I think my purpose in life is to help other people. By just being myself I give hope and inspire other people to look at themselfs. I carry only a few clothes and books -- not much at all -- a blanket too; and I try to tell people that even though I have very little, I really have a lot, because everything I need is provided by God. People give me money and I buy food, a little beer and whatever.

But I never take more than I need and I stress that I'm a very rich man -- as long as I have a few clothes and a blanket and can panhandle enough for a big mac and a six-pak -- I'm very rich. I stress the fact that people in other countries would give anything for what the average bum on the street gets everyday. And people ask me how I can live this way and be happy, and I tell them "Because my nature is to be happy. I could be sad, but why?"

I'm very into what you teach but don't yet know all the facts. Some of the things you talk about I've known for years but didn't know it was connected to anything else. But I've always felt love and compassion for my brothers and sisters. I love to give.

Thanks a lot, E

PS: Love is not love 'til you give it away.

● ● ●

Dear Bo and Sita,

I received your book We're All Doing Time *two days ago and let me tell you that I'm elated. It is the most informative book I've ever run into. I really don't know what to say. I've never run into anything that has brought more effect into my life. I've laughed while checking out some of the cartoons and actually cried (something that hasn't happened in some time) when reading some of the letters.*

It's really strange but I already feel as if I know you, though I've never seen or heard of you in my life. I can't understand it.

Well, I guess I'll tell you a little about myself. I'm 22 years old. Was born and raised in Riverside, California until I was 13, when my folks moved to a small town in Missouri. I was always more or less a problem child but when we moved from big city to small town is when the big problems started.

I started using drugs, stealing and became very rebellious. I stole a car at age 14 and wrecked it just outside of town. For this I received probation. Then I stole a gun out of a store and that, along with my constant drug use, was too much and my folks told my P.O. that they couldn't handle me any more so I was placed in a group home.

The group home had a 2 month program but it took me 6 months to get out of it because I escaped once and raised a lot of hell while I was in it. I was out roughly 6 months when I conspired with this chick to bust her boyfriend out of jail. We stole a van, got a gun, and went outside of town where we "cocktailed" a gas station to act as a diversion. We never made it to the jailhouse, though. We were seen, pulled over and arrested. I was barely 16 at the time and still on probation, so I was sent to reform school where I spent about 3 months and then to another group home. I spent about 2 months in the group home and was sent home where I picked up where I left off until I was 17.

I finally got a job as a cook in a restaurant and soon had an apartment where I used to throw wild parties. After about 2 months though, I got bored so I sold all my furniture, packed what I could on my back and was off to California. On the way, I was picked up by a marine on his way to San Diego.

Well, I rode with him for a couple days until one night he got drunk and started running his mouth about how bad he was. We happened to be on a dark, deserted road outside of Las Vegas and when I got tired of listening to him I just got him to pull over (so we could leak) and I snuck up behind him and slit his throat. Then I jumped in the car, leaving him to die out in the desert.

When I got to California I ditched the car and went to my grandfather's house where I lived, working as a carpenter's apprentice. Everything was cool until my grandmother found a bunch of reefer and some "hot" items in the trailer out back where I was living and they kicked me out.

I went back to Missouri and lived with my folks again, doing drugs and ripping off anything that wasn't tied down until one night when I burglarized a building and set it on fire. I was arrested the next day because one of the neighbors saw me leaving the building when I was done.

I was jailed and was facing 14 years for my antics when I hung myself. I know that I didn't want to die because I let my cellmate know what was happening before I did it. He called the police downstairs and they cut me down. The next day the D.A. came with a deal of 5 years suspended sentence, 5 years probation and 6 months in a halfway house. I took it.

I ended up leaving the halfway house, and the state, a few months after that and bounced around the country. I finally ended up in Florida where I sold drugs and my ass for a living (*I got turned out by the Catholic priest who ran the halfway house*). I got in a gang down in Ft. Lauderdale and one night, after some trouble came up, 4 of us took a dude for a "ride" down to Miami. We beat, kicked, stabbed and caved in his head, then stripped him and threw him into Biscayne Bay.

The courts gave me 99 years for my involvement (I stabbed him). Two years later I jumped the gun squad (at D.C.I.) and after they tried to blow me away I was recaptured and taken to court to get 9 years for my escape. My 5-year Missouri sentence was mailed to me not long after that so that brings me where I am now. In Florida with 113 years.

I dislike being in prison but if I hadn't come I would probably be dead by now. The heavy drug use most of my life and the violent way I was living would've taken its toll. Plus I probably

357

never would've gotten into this spiritual stuff.

So you can see why I'm elated by your book. It's like an answer to a dream, only there is more to it than that and I can't quite place what it is. Maybe it's the love that is permeated into each and every page. You can actually <u>feel</u> it. It jumps out at you.

But anyway, I know pretty much what type of person I am. I'm not really hateful but I sometimes do hateful things. When I killed those two dudes I wasn't really trying to kill them. I was trying to kill the pain, guilt, and feelings of inferiority within myself. I was doing the same thing when I was using all those drugs. I was trying to numb the pain.

I'm in the process of straightening out my life. I made a big mistake when I came to prison at age 18. Right now I'm going through major changes with it. It will cause me a few fights but it will be for the good in the long run, I'm sure.

I'm not much on long letters (I can't believe I've written this much) so I'll close. Thanks again for the wonderful material.

Take care now, Love, F.

P.S. Last night after I finished the above, I sat down for some meditation and had the most wonderful experience. I was filled to the brim with the softest feeling of joy and peace I've ever known. I felt detached from the body to a certain extent and truly feel that I could have been completely swept away if I hadn't become somewhat frightened when taken into a sudden state of breathlessness. Ah well, that's just one more thing to work on with a beautiful reward at the end.

Much love, F

● ● ●

Dear Bo,

You may not believe how I got hold of your book We're All Doing Time *but I assure you I will be truthful and honest with you straight down the line.*

I got in a poker game one day and it lasted nearly eight hours. This guy ended up owing me a lot of money. He gave me twenty dollars and all his magazines, his radio and your book.

To be honest, before I won your book I didn't see too much of a reason to really give too much of a damn about anything.

Man, your (my) book really gave me a special high of warmth and security and hopefulness I haven't felt in years.

In the wind! K

P.S. The last time I cried is when my old man died of an overdose when I was thirteen. But when I read about Maury and at the end you said he was stabbed to death, I cried for a while. May Maury be happy and satisfied now!

• • •

My Brother Bo,

I want to thank you for sharing your time with us at F.C.I.B. I've traveled many paths, and for me they have led nowhere. After listening to you I see I may have moved much too quickly.

My point is, yesterday I received a letter from my stepmother. Just over a year ago my dear father passed away. She found a poem he wrote. It was sent to me. It was hard to read through the tears. I felt as I did when he had first left us. All of a sudden your words rang true. I felt the love, I smiled and enjoyed the pain.

I receive your newsletter already and I am grateful for it. At the end of the message I came forward to shake your hand. For but a brief moment our eyes met. For this lost soul, I ran into reality, for lack of better words. Love to all of you!

Love, R-J

• • •

Bo,

   Howdy   Bo; what   a   name. Well I've never written to some- one under these circumstances be- fore so excuse my reserve. Last year I asked for your book We're All Doing Time *and since I've received it I've attempted to let myself flow with the ways it teaches. Being in prison it's some- times impossible to let yourself go as I see is needed at times! Prison politics   dictate awareness at all times!*

   Still, this book has taught me so much more of life and its aspects than any prison program could ever hope to! For this I thank you very much! I used to be full of reasons for revenge and hate, now I feel a lot of inner peace and no longer want the pay- backs I had felt were called for. Yea, I was ratted on and got flopped 10 years but that's OK, the time I do will give me growth inside myself that was sorely needed! I've got 2 plus years in and 7 plus years to go, I only hope I won't stray from the way you so kindly passed on to me!

   I have never been a God's man and never had had any feel- ings for my fellow man, now I realize there is another way! Since I've been here I've lost all my worldly goods, i.e., car, ol' lady, etc., etc., but even that's OK, because anything lost can always be replaced, at least material goods. I still have problems handling loss of my ol' lady who I really loved and cared for, still I've realized past is past so onward I'll go.

Bo, even this writing paper reflects the change in me, I used to use swastikas, SWP, real stupid paper for letters, now I think back and know why so many of the people I wrote quit writing back, I was saturated with hate and tried to infect everyone around me!

Now I have hope, I'm more positive in attitude, more kind, caring and for the very first time in my life I have even begun to like myself! All of this is due to your kindness and your generosity! Thanks again Bo, I still think that's a strange name!

I want to add that lately my cell partner, a hardcore con, has been "caught" reading We're All Doing Time. *Each time I've been asked to put my stuff away, but Bo for some reason I know the book's place in our cell is within easy reach for all! With that I'll let you go, I send to you my best and my thanks to Sita and yourself for the help you've given me and all other prisoners!*

Love and respect, D

● ● ●

Dear Bo,

I am serving a 35 year sentence which belongs to someone else. I've been down 4 years and my lawyer has finally gotten statements from the investigating detective and prosecutor. They both felt the wrong man was on trial and since absolutely NO evidence was available except identification evidence from one victim who saw one half of the perpetrator's face, I am hopeful of proving ineffective assistance of counsel against my trial lawyer.

All of that aside, I was on a downward spiral on the streets. Alcohol and drugs were taking their toll. Several petty arrests for simple possession and other misdemeanor convictions put my picture in the mug book and the I.D. was made by picture, so in effect I brought this all on myself.

Recently I borrowed a copy of We're All Doing Time *from a friend. WOW! I've been so pissed off at the "system" I was slowly getting a <u>real</u> case of the "gotta kill them all"s. I read your book and am into meditation now. A remarkable change of attitude has taken place. A long ways to go yet.*

It occurs to me now that the life the system tried to destroy was actually saved by their attempt! My mind is open, I can be free in here!

Much thanks, M

• • •

Dear Bo,

Hi! It's me, another lost soul, seeking only the truth. I've been reading the best book ever printed, since the Bible: We're All Doing Time. *You are a man with a mission and I salute you and your cause.*

I'm not in prison, but my brother is, and I thank you for sending him a copy too. A friend of mine gave me a copy of your book at a point in my life where there wasn't enough left in life for me. The only thing I was living for was my 10-year-old daughter, the love of my life. I really believe that book saved my life.

Enough said, I really appreciate your time.

Always, S

• • •

Dear Bo and Sita,

Here is a long-overdue letter of appreciation. I was reading through We're All Doing Time *for the ten-thousandth time this morning, thinking especially loving thoughts about you wonderful folks. So, I figured the very least I could do would be to write and let you know what a positive influence you've had on my life.*

Last year, about this time, my case was coming before the State Court of Appeals and I wrote to ask for your prayers. You very promptly responded with a little card and supportive words, which I will always cherish dearly. I trust that I still had lessons to learn in prison, because my case was not overturned. And it is my strong belief that no snowflake ever falls in the wrong place.

Though it's sometimes real tough to admit, I am deeply thankful for this prison experience. Wow! It's unlikely, for example, that I'd ever have met you wonderful people and studied what you had to say about the Path with such sincere curiosity had I not been incarcerated (and desperate). It's a dead end to start second-guessing Life; I prefer to simply have the faith that everything is as it should be. Only my attitude needs the spiritual work.

At any rate, I sometimes can just lay We're All Doing Time *spread across my chest and pick up the beautiful vibes of your service. So I want you to have my most profound thanks for all that you're about.*

Your work has helped inspire me from feelings of vengeance and bitterness to the peaceful level of personal integrity, forgiveness and understanding, which is much closer to where we all belong: True Love.

Bless you all, D

• • •

Dear Bo,

Greetings and best wishes from death row. It has been many years since I was able to write to you. I received my last letter from you folks before you went down to NC. I lost your address during a shakedown and then spent five years in a strip cell in total 24-hr solitary confinement with no contact with anyone. No yard, no radio, no TV, no property, in a bare stone cell with a solid steel door. Your lessons in yoga and meditation worked like a charm and kept body and spirits healthy.

After that I got two death sentences for allegedly killing informers in Santa Cruz and I've been on San Quentin's death row ever since. I finally ran into a man who knew your address, and here I am back knocking on the school door looking for lessons and spiritual tools to work with before they snap me out of this incarnation.

I remember when Ram Dass and yoga instructors came in and worked with us in the yard. One of those pictures was published in your first book. Today lots of that class are dead as a result of stickings in Folsom and San Quentin and one was a suicide. I'm still hanging in strong (mid-50's) but all my family died during those years I was in "the hole", and lack of contact blew all outside friends to the four winds.

All this is just an historical update, not a problem or complaint. Every year I get more joy-filled, relaxed, calm inside and really free. I'm a happy man, content with life and its gifts. Total isolation has a way of forcing you to see yourself minus the deceptions, masks, lies and self-deceit and excuses. The "dark night of the soul" period is a real bummer but you come out into the Light a lot freer and absent any anxieties, fears, rage, resentments, and hostility. Plus, you don't judge or condemn as easily.

I'm happier now and saner than I've been in over fifty years. God keeps drawing you back to Him no matter how dumb you are or how much you resist.

Enough about me. I hope you both are happy and well. I'm very proud of you, you're still out there doing your best for people like us who the rest of society has completely written off. You are good people who live and practice your love and dreams for mankind. Your early teaching and courses in meditation, yoga and looking at reality with humor and patience gave me the path and tools to come through an experience I wouldn't even want to describe to sane folks. I care a lot and have kept you both in my prayers for 10 years.

with full respect and love, R

● ● ●

Leo Lozano

Dear Bo,

I've been getting it together some with meditation. I've come to realize that meditation is only a state of mind, and you're right, you can meditate walking around, laying down, doing whatever.

Still have a few problems, but don't we all? The main thing is that I am dealing with the problems. For a long time your advice to "just feel it and let it pass" didn't make sense to me. I thought is was like just drop all feelings and become a machine.

But now I'm getting a grasp on what you're saying. Emotions, good or bad, are all part of being human. When a bad thought or feeling comes along, let it flow through you. Feel the sadness, recognize it for what it is, and then go on with life, leave that sad feeling behind. It might come again, but just let it come, feel it, recognize it, and carry on, man. Don't let the feeling control you.

I've also realized, more than ever, <u>"It's all right here you know!"</u> and I thank you for pointing me in the right direction. At first I went at it with the expectation of total bliss, but now I realize there's going to be bad feelings, hurt, anger, despair, loneliness, etc., that's part of living, I mean, if your friend loses his life in a bike wreck, of course you're going to be sad, but you shouldn't let that sadness control you or your actions. You may always feel a sense of loss or sadness when you think of that friend, but you feel it, recognize it, and let it pass.

A reply is not necessary, I know there are people out there with a lot worse problems than mine -- but you know, three months ago I would have told you you're crazy if you told me I'd say that. I had been feeling so fucken sorry for myself Bo, I guess I hated myself for a while, the pain was enormous -- I thought no one gave a shit, I'm here for the rest of my life, no parole, nothing short of a large miracle would do for me. You made me realize not only that you care, but that I CARE, I LOVE MYSELF, which brought me around.

I wish they allowed us to write to other prisoners; if they did I might could help a few people.

See ya, M

● ● ●

Bo,

I love you. I just finished Lineage and Other Stories, *and I am filled with light for many reasons. In 1975 and 76, I was in prison for armed robbery. A friend turned me on to Ram Dass, and he in turn, turned me on to your project. You and I corresponded for two years while I was locked up. I made it back outside with a different outlook on life. I got a B.S. in math, and a masters in Education. I landed a job as an Adult Basic Ed. instructor in a prison of all places.*

I stayed there seven years, and was promoted to supervisor. I go to the prison weekly to check on my staff. Not long ago, one of my instructors, who is a close friend, told me of a rock & roll group that had been there recently, and he handed me your book. I was flabbergasted. Old Bo, my friend and teacher, our paths crossed again. Just as in Lineage, *the baton has been passed on. I walk in the light and my world is peace.*

I am now married and have 2 sons. The baton will pass again. I just wanted to tell you, that the path is still clear. We still walk together, after all these years. Time goes on and the world still turns, and the light shines eternal. All my energies are with you always. Drop me a line, send me some stuff to turn on to some inmates. It's all right here, you know.

Namaste, S

● ● ●

Dear Bo and Sita,

I just wanted to drop you a note to say that my prison experience is finally over. I should be home in a few weeks. Ten years has past and with you both those years have been easier. My path has been found!! My work will soon begin. There are others who need to find their path and I hope to guide some to their true nature.

Love always, B

● ● ●

Dear Bo and Sita,

At the last institution I was in (I've been in several!), I borrowed a copy of your book but was transferred here before I had a chance to finish it. Besides -- it's not the kind of book to just be read through, but the kind to be studied, pondered upon, kept and used. I have already begun to regularly meditate and also am employing pranayam on a daily basis (several times a day, actually).

Anyway...the Journey continues and wow!! there is no comparison between the way I feel and look at things now, and how I did before. I really do believe that I'm just where I should be at this point in time. I started on the path several months ago but am so pleased that your book came to me when it did. All IS going according to schedule, my life is beginning to come together and the beautiful part is that it's all GOD'S doing.

For the first time in my life I feel whole, complete, with a purpose and direction for my life, not just while I'm locked up, but for the long haul. No booze or dope for 11 months now, no sugar for 3 months. Still smoking cigs and drinking coffee, but have slimmed down from 208 lbs (I'm 5'8") to 152 lbs since January. GOD is so good to me, Bo! I know he loves me cause he shows it.

There are a lot of guys here with hard hearts and low energy trips, but there are also many here that are receptive and truly yearn to be free. Lots of work to be done here. Since I just got here I'll bide my time and ease into it, but I already know many as we've been in one place or another at the same time.

I want to share this little something that came through me recently via the celestial telegraph:

> There is no place in my life for fear.
> Change has come And will continue...
> My life is as the opening of a flower
> Lovingkindness Encompasses All

I've titled it "An Affirmation of Hope" and it came at just the right time. (Of course!) So...what started as a simple request for your book has developed into a letter. You know, Bo, I never ever felt OK before now, it was always me against everyone and everything. If something happened or I did something that turned out not to my liking, it was always somebody else's fault. I wasn't to blame. "They" were. "The Cops." "The System," my P.O., the Dept. of Corrections, ad infinitum, ad nauseum...I refused to accept responsibility for my behavior or consequences.

Now I understand that was all Bullshit! I'm here because I stabbed a man. It was needless and my fault and I'm sorry I hurt him.

I'm not trying to minimize but the injury was minor (I stabbed him in the arm) and he only missed 2 days work, but the bottom line is I let my fear and anger overpower me, control me, and I just as easily could have killed him. I harmed a fellow human being. Period. I'm working through this and am beginning to forgive myself just as GOD has forgiven me.

I've got a long way to go, I know, but the best part is I've already started. And it is beautiful indeed. Yeah Bo -- Love is the key. I get it. I got it! Thanks for helping me.

In love and with thanks, K

● ● ●

Keith Roach

Dear Bo and Sita,

I can't tell you how much I enjoyed Lineage and Other Stories *and* We're All Doing Time. *They both made me laugh, cry, shake my head in agreement and holler -- AMEN -- it's about time. I can't tell you how much I admire you for the work you're doing. Please don't ever stop.*

Bo, I work in a Texas prison mailroom, so I really sympathize with the problem you're having getting Lineage and Other Stories *to TDC inmates. When I was asked to read the books for unit approval, I recognized them for the beautiful spiritual tools they are, and approved them both. However, another unit denied them, and when one unit denies a publication, we all have to unless otherwise directed. So that's how it happened...they <u>almost</u> made it.*

There are other employees who feel as I do, that there is nothing wrong with the content. You know, we're not all ignorant redneck racists that work here. There are a lot of good people too, who really care about the inmates. And you know we have to battle some pretty bad stuff Bo, like the prison gangs, drugs, hits, rapes...sometimes it's just awful what the inmates do to each other. But those of us that really care are there every day trying to make it better.

I've been in metaphysics about 25 years now. When I went to work for TDC I got criticized a lot by others. "How can you do it?" they would ask, insinuating I had sold out spiritually. Little do they know I was very specifically guided there. That's where the "real" BOSS wants me. Learning and teaching and carrying my torch of love inside with me.

Knowing you and others like you reminds me we are not in this dimension alone although it can feel that way sometimes.

Take Care, F

PS: This photo is of my grandson, Jamie, who was born with open-cell spina bifida. The rocking-chair horse he is enjoying so much was done by an inmate, M, at the unit where I work. He was so excited to do this for

Jamie, and when I brought him a print of this picture, tears came to his eyes. The craft boss told me later that's all M talked about. Nobody ever did that for him before -- bring him a picture of something he had made.

Some of our artistic inmates delight in drawing pictures for Jamie of Mickey Mouse, Donald Duck, and dogs, dogs, dogs. Jamie loves dogs. I just wish sometimes that people knew that as bad as prisons are -- there's a lot of good stuff going on too.

● ● ●

Keith Roach

Tommy Moore

Dear Bo and Sita,

I had been looking forward to your newsletter and was really happy to hear from you again. Since I have been actively partici-pating in my own growing, in all areas of my life, I am amazed at the response, help, and encouragement I have received. From a sleazy, greasy, dope fiend to a creative, productive kid of the Creator. By serving as a friend and guide you have both added to my life.

In trying to walk my talk, by helping others, so much has been added to my own life. By attempting just one "nth" of energy towards practicing some of the "designs for living" that you cover in your books I am coming to know a life beyond my old ideas and lifestyle. You know, it hurts any way you do it, but at least today I see a purpose in life and the belief that "more will be revealed." Know that you are in my prayer and meditation.

"Peace," H

● ● ●

Dear Bo and Sita,

Hi! It's been a while since I last wrote, but it's not been time wasted. Meditation works REAL well. I was so scared of some of my own demons, I never thought about how other people might be worse off in their life, etc. (on death row, mental hospital, can't cope with their problems). I've set aside 15 minutes every day just to meditate for others' problems and my love to them.

I want to thank you for both of your love and understanding! I've controlled my terror, lust, pride, grief, guilt, greed and other problems I've had! I find peace of mind in my meditation every day. Also it's improved my outlook on life! I'm at a lesser security prison thanks to meditating my anger away! I've not been in any trouble since I last wrote. Thank you both so much!

In Loving Kindness, M

● ● ●

reading quite a few other books on the subject, Now I just need to keep at it. Thank You!

Hi Bo & Sita:
I just wanted to thank you for turning me on to Meditation practice and your newsletters. I have been

There isn't any money in this card, I already looked.

be happy & stay healthy

Respectfully
Randy Mills

Dear Bo and Sita,

How can I express how We're All Doing Time *has touched me? It's beyond words. How can one put a value on the love of a true friend, a kindred spirit on the same path, an instant family full of love and genuine concern for your well-being? Far beyond my limited abilities, and yet if we put all these thoughts and many more beautiful but un-expressed ones together, perhaps we come close to the feelings I have as it is possible for me to get.*

In a way I feel sad that your book arrived so near the end of my 3½-year stint here. I look back to the hardest times, shut in for long periods, when I began to doubt my sanity and despaired of surviving. What a Godsend your book would have been then.

Yet it was at that lowest point I made the most progress. As we proceed on the path, the means present themselves as they are needed. So this is the right time for the book to arrive. I can imagine you formulating your reply and thinking "So what the hell is so different to using the book outside as a manual?" Nothing, I grant you, and I fully intend to do just that. It is just that we have this magical opportunity in here with so much uninterrupted time to dedicate to the practice of meditation, etc.

I am in awe at the way you and Sita have centered your life around caring for others. It is awe-inspiring and inspirational to those of us teetering on the brink of dedicating our lives to serve others in whatever way we are guided. The theory is easy, but the courage required for that jump into the unknown is considerable.

For a quick thank you note this has turned into a letter of epic proportions. I hope you can grasp from my ramblings how very special and precious your love and support are to me/us.

No need to answer this letter, spare a thought for me at meditation time and wing some love and moral support to help me through this last hurdle and give me the courage not to get sidetracked by the material temptations I will inevitably encounter.

I wish I could salute you as a fellow Spiritual Warrior, but I don't deserve that title yet. I will get there eventually but there is a lot more learning and living to be done. I'm firmly on the path, headed in the right direction, with your help and inspiration.

A heartfelt thank you from a fledgling Warrior and brother, D

● ● ●

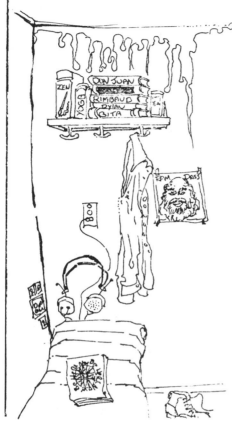

Dear Bo, Sita,

You may be interested to know that We're All Doing Time *is now more popular in our dorm than "Playboy!" Several inmates are now getting up at 4:45 a.m. and doing yoga exercises and meditation.*

You all have made possible many of the positive changes in some very negative lives. Thank you.

Thanks folks. Love ya all, R

● ● ●

Tommy Moore

"The whole world is good."

— Neem Karoli Baba

EPILOGUE: THE GOOD GUYS ALREADY WON

The greatest comfort, the best news of all, no matter how hard or frightening our journeys may be at times, is that the end has already been decided. The forces of Good and Evil have already had their final battle, and we know how it turned out. The Good Guys won.

Jesus said on the cross, "It is accomplished." The Buddha sat down under the Bodhi tree and vowed never to move again until that same victory had been achieved. Mohammed sat year after year in his cave, Moses spent forty days and nights alone and hungry on Mount Sinai; countless men and women have presented themselves point-blank before the Great Truth and actually touched it. They went through the looking glass, came back out and told us, "It is accomplished." Not just for them, but for us as well.

Light dispelled darkness. Love conquered hatred. Good triumphed over evil. Forgiveness reigned over anger. The Holy Ones have all assured us that these victories apply to our lives as well as theirs. There is only one set of rules, and they are absolute. We can count on them.

So our spiritual journey is like a war in reverse: The war has been won at the beginning, but to preserve the dignity of our individual free will, we each have to fight the same battles the masters fought, and make the same heroic choices they made. That may be a drag, but how discouraged can we become if we remember that the war has already been won? We just have to keep doing our part, aligning ourselves with the victorious forces — goodness, love, peace, forgiveness, longsuffering, humility, generosity, compassion. But we can already rejoice; the Kingdom is at hand.

Of course, we can surely lose battles, by aligning ourselves with the principles which lost the war: selfishness, cruelty, greed, delusion, hatred, fear. And yet, so great was the Final Victory, so total is the Great Mercy, that no matter how many such battles we lose, we'll still eventually make the right choices before it's all over. The most heinous killers will become the very embodiments of nonviolence. The biggest misers will give all their wealth to the poor. The most meanspirited politicians will be the sweetest, fairest people you ever met. It may take many lifetimes, but each one of us will eventually choose the Holy Path. The angels and masters and guides never give up on us. Like the great Rabbi, the Baal Shem Tov said, "I love the lowest of the low like you love your only child." Imagine.

Jesus said, "I am with you till the end of the world." The Buddha and all the Bodhisattvas have vowed to stay on Earth until every last one of us is fully liberated. The Jewish Messiah is guaranteed to come. The infinite mercy and compassion of Allah will never be exhausted. Hanuman, the Hindu Holy Spirit, is immortal and unconquerable, available everywhere at once to those who sincerely cry for help.

We human beings won't be able to uphold evil forever. It will wear us down until we just can't stand it anymore. We will tire of it and gradually choose to be kinder and humbler students of life. And when we do, all those spectacular forces of goodness will be on hand to help and comfort us through the long struggle of undoing the many nets of karma we have imprisoned ourselves in. We have no enemies other than ourselves, our own choices. But we have <u>lots</u> of friends in High Places.

After all the words, all the books, all the thinking and discussion, life once again presents to us this single next moment: What will we do with it? How will we exercise our free will? Will our choices bind us further or begin to free us? As we bind or free ourselves, we bind or free the whole world a little bit more. If we have had enough of holocausts, "ethnic cleansings," homelessness, racial divisiveness, pollution and destruction of nature, fear of our neighbors, then we need to get cracking on our spiritual journeys. We are responsible and we are powerful, even in a prison cell or hospital bed.

The buck always stops in this very moment, right at our feet. Everything will definitely turn out all right in the end, but we can drag out the misery or speed up the mercy and healing. I choose to do what I can to speed it up, and I pray you do too, because we're all in this together.

I hope you find some spiritual practices which suit your nature and do them faithfully. Spend a little time each day studying any source of classic wisdom. Take reasonable care of mind, body and spirit. Be kind to whomever life places in front of you at any moment. Don't do anything for a living which you feel contributes to what's wrong in the world. Discover what your basic values are and abide by them, even when there is a price to pay for it. Keep your life simple, uncluttered and modest so you won't be an object of anyone's materialistic envy. Don't add lies or hypocrisy to the world, as it can hardly bear any more.

The work has always been the same and always will be. Each and every one of us will make it to the Great Wonderfulness. Take comfort and help others to do the same. Breathe a sigh of relief. The good guys already won.

just another ending